1—Temperance

TEMPERANCE

*AS SET FORTH
IN THE WRITINGS
OF*
ELLEN G. WHITE

TEMPERANCE

*AS SET FORTH
IN THE WRITINGS OF*

ELLEN G. WHITE

"True temperance teaches us to abstain entirely from that which is injurious, and to use judiciously only healthful and nutritious articles of food."—*Health Reformer,* April, 1877.

PACIFIC PRESS® PUBLISHING ASSOCIATION
Nampa, Idaho
Oshawa, Ontario, Canada

Copyright, 1949, by
The Ellen G. White Publications

ISBN 0-8163-2037-3

Litho in U.S.A.

04 05 06 07

FOREWORD

Temperance was a favorite theme of Mrs. Ellen G. White, both in her writings and in public discourse. In many of her articles which appeared in denominational journals through the years, and in manuscripts and letters of counsel addressed to both workers and laity, she urged Seventh-day Adventists to practice temperance and to promote vigorously the temperance cause. In response to earnest requests that this wealth of material and instruction should be made available in a single volume, this handbook has been prepared by authorization of the Ellen G. White Publications, to whom Mrs. White committed the custody of her books and manuscripts.

These selections have been drawn from the whole range of Mrs. White's writings on this subject, including some now out of print, such as the following: *Health, or How to Live* (1865); *Christian Temperance and Bible Hygiene* (1890); *Special Testimonies* (1892-1912); and *Drunkenness and Crime* (1907).

Both in the outline and in the content of subject matter, the compilers have earnestly sought to reflect the emphasis which the author placed on the various phases of temperance.

The effort to gather such selections as would set forth her full contribution on this subject, and the desire to make quite complete the various sections on the different phases of the temperance question have naturally resulted in some repetition of thought. In the endeavor to present the subject matter in an orderly way so as to be of greatest service to the reader, and at the same time to avoid undue repetition, rather brief selections have sometimes been made. However, in omitting the context, great care has been exercised to alter in no way the thought or the emphasis of the author. In each case full source credit is given to the book, periodical, pamphlet, or manuscript from which the excerpt is taken.

The readers will recognize that Ellen G. White, having died in 1915, did her writing in a period when some terminology was quite different from that commonly employed today, and when detailed descriptions of conditions might vary from that with which we are now familiar. For instance, reference is made to the saloon. While the liquor dispensary of today may differ from the saloon of fifty years ago, everyone knows that the same types of beverages are dispensed that were used at the time in which Mrs. White wrote, and that their effects upon the body, mind, and soul are the same. The relationship between the use of alcohol and automobile accidents was not stressed as it should be today, for the simple reason that automobiles were not then in common use. However, the reader will find set forth in statements concerning the use of alcohol and accidents a description of causes and effects which are fully applicable to present-day conditions. The power of alcohol to undermine the home, to wreck the health, to ruin the morals, and to destroy the soul is as potent now as it was a half century ago.

The reader will quickly discern the significance of temperance as it was presented to Mrs. White through the long years of her rich ministry. In this respect this volume makes an invaluable contribution to temperance literature. The temperance sermons found in the Appendix typify Mrs. White's intense burden to save humanity from the soul-destroying curse of intemperance.

That this volume may, under God's blessings, accomplish a work of revitalizing the interests of Seventh-day Adventists in temperance and the temperance work and lead us to our heaven-assigned position in the forefront of temperance forces is the sincere wish of the publishers.

THE TRUSTEES OF THE
ELLEN G. WHITE PUBLICATIONS.

CONTENTS

Preface 5

Section I — The Philosophy of Intemperance

1. The Original Perfection of Man 11
2. The Inception of Intemperance 12
3. Impairment Through Indulged Appetite · . . . 15
4. Importance of Christ's Victory Over Appetite . . . 19

Section II — Alcohol and Society

1. An Incentive to Crime 23
2. An Economic Problem 27
3. Alcohol and the Home 30
4. A Cause of Accidents 34
5. A Public Health Problem 36
6. Alcohol and Men in Responsible Positions 43

Section III — Tobacco

1. Effects of Tobacco Use 55
2. Tobacco's Polluting, Demoralizing Influence . . . 58
3. Defiling the Temple of God 62
4. An Economic Waste 66
5. The Power of Example 68

Section IV — Other Stimulants and Narcotics

1. Abstain From Fleshly Lusts 73
2. Tea and Coffee 75
3. Drugs 82

Section V — Milder Intoxicants

1. Importance of Strictly Temperate Habits 90
2. Psychological Effects of Mild Intoxicants 92
3. The Intoxicating Effects of Wine and Cider . . . 94
4. Wine in the Bible 97
5. Christians and the Production of Liquor-Making Products 98
6. Temperance and Total Abstinence 101

Section VI—Activating Principles of a Changed Life
1. Only as the Life Is Changed 102
2. Conversion the Secret of Victory 104
3. The Will the Key to Success 110
4. Enduring Victory 115
5. Help for the Tempted 120

Section VII—Rehabilitating the Intemperate
1. Counsel on How to Work 126
2. The Temperance Worker 130

Section VIII—Our Broad Temperance Platform
1. What True Temperance Embodies 137
2. The Body the Temple 142
3. Temperance and Spirituality 146
4. Daniel's Example 151
5. The Food on Our Tables 156
6. Total Abstinence Our Position 163
7. Relation to Church Membership 165
8. Seventh-day Adventist Spiritual Leaders 166

Section IX—Laying the Foundation of Intemperance
1. Prenatal Influence 170
2. The Strength of Inherited Tendencies 173
3. Formation of Behavior Patterns 175
4. Parental Example and Guidance 180
5. Teaching Self-Denial and Self-Control 181
6. Youth and the Future 186

Section X—Preventive Measures
1. Education in Temperance 194
2. Signing the Pledge 197
3. Removing the Temptation 203
4. Diversion and Harmless Substitutes 209
5. A Sense of Moral Obligation 213

Section XI—Our Relationship to Other Temperance Groups
1. Working Together 217
2. Co-operating With the W.C.T.U. 222

Section XII — The Challenge of the Hour

1. The Present Situation 227
2. Called to the Battle 233
3. By Voice—A Part of Our Evangelistic Message . . 237
4. Temperance Education an Objective of Our
   Medical Work 245
5. The Influence of the Pen 248
6. The Power of the Vote 253
7. The Call to the Harvest 256

Appendices

A. Ellen G. White a Temperance Worker 259
B. Typical Temperance Addresses by Ellen G. White . 267
   1. At Christiania, Norway—1886 267
   2. A Talk on Temperance—1891 273
   3. At Sydney, Australia—1893 283

Subject Index 293

Section I

THE PHILOSOPHY OF INTEMPERANCE

1. The Original Perfection of Man

Created in Perfection and Beauty.—Man came from the hand of his Creator perfect in organization and beautiful in form.—*Christian Temperance and Bible Hygiene,* page 7.

Man was the crowning act of the creation of God, made in the image of God, and designed to be a counterpart of God.—*Review and Herald,* June 18, 1895.

Adam was a noble being, with a powerful mind, a will in harmony with the will of God, and affections that centered upon heaven. He possessed a body heir to no disease, and a soul bearing the impress of Deity.—*The Youth's Instructor,* March 5, 1903.

He stood before God in the strength of perfect manhood. All the organs and faculties of his being were equally developed, and harmoniously balanced.—*Redemption; or the Temptation of Christ,* page 30.

God's Pledge to Maintain the Body's Healthful Action.—The Creator of man has arranged the living machinery of our bodies. Every function is wonderfully and wisely made. And God pledged Himself to keep this human machinery in healthful action if the human agent will obey His laws and co-operate with God.—*Counsels on Diet and Foods,* page 17.

Responsibility to Heed Nature's Laws.—A healthy experience demands growth, and growth demands that careful attention be paid to the laws of nature, that the organs of the body may be kept in a sound state, untrammeled in their action.—Manuscript 47, 1896.

God Appointed the Inclinations and Appetites.—Our natural inclinations and appetites . . . were divinely appointed, and when given to man, were pure and holy. It was God's design that reason should rule the appetites, and that they should minister to our happiness. And when they are regulated and controlled by a sanctified reason, they are holiness unto the Lord.—Manuscript 47, 1896.

2. The Inception of Intemperance

Satan gathered the fallen angels together to devise some way of doing the most possible evil to the human family. One proposition after another was made, till finally Satan himself thought of a plan. He would take the fruit of the vine, also wheat, and other things given by God as food, and would convert them into poisons, which would ruin man's physical, mental, and moral powers, and so overcome the senses that Satan should have full control. Under the influence of liquor, men would be led to commit crimes of all kinds. Through perverted appetite the world would be made corrupt. By leading men to drink alcohol, Satan would cause them to descend lower and lower in the scale.

Satan has succeeded in turning the world from God. The blessings provided in God's love and mercy he has turned into a deadly curse. He has filled men with a craving for liquor and tobacco. This appetite, which has no foundation in nature, has destroyed its millions.—*Review and Herald,* April 16, 1901.

The Secret of the Enemy's Strategy.—Intemperance of any kind benumbs the perceptive organs and so weakens the brain-nerve power that eternal things are not appreciated, but placed upon a level with the common. The higher powers of the

The Philosophy of Intemperance

mind, designed for elevated purposes, are brought into slavery to the baser passions. If our physical habits are not right, our mental and moral powers cannot be strong; for great sympathy exists between the physical and the moral.—*Testimonies,* vol. 3, pp. 50, 51.

The brain nerves which communicate with the entire system are the only medium through which Heaven can communicate to man and affect his inmost life. Whatever disturbs the circulation of the electric currents in the nervous system lessens the strength of the vital powers, and the result is a deadening of the sensibilities of the mind.—*Testimonies,* vol. 2, p. 347.

Satan is constantly on the alert to bring the race fully under his control. His strongest hold on man is through the appetite, and this he seeks to stimulate in every possible way.—*Counsels on Diet and Foods,* page 150.

Satan's Scheme to Wreck the Plan of Salvation.—Satan had been at war with the government of God, since he first rebelled. His success in tempting Adam and Eve in Eden, and introducing sin into the world, had emboldened this arch foe; and he had proudly boasted to the heavenly angels that when Christ should appear, taking man's nature, He would be weaker than himself, and that he would overcome Him by his power.

He exulted that Adam and Eve in Eden could not resist his insinuations when he appealed to their appetite. The inhabitants of the old world he overcame in the same manner, through the indulgence of lustful appetite and corrupt passions. Through the gratification of appetite, he had overthrown the Israelites.

He boasted that the Son of God Himself, who was with Moses and Joshua, was not able to resist his power, and lead the favored people of His choice to Canaan; for nearly all who left Egypt died in the wilderness; also, that he had tempted the meek man, Moses, to take to himself glory which God claimed. David and Solomon, who had been especially favored of God, he had induced, through the indulgence of appetite and passion, to incur God's displeasure. And he boasted that he could yet succeed in thwarting the purpose of God in the salvation of man through Jesus Christ.—*Redemption; or the Temptation of Christ,* page 32.

His Most Effective Temptation Today.—Satan comes to man, as he came to Christ, with his overpowering temptations to indulge appetite. He well knows his power to overcome man upon this point. He overcame Adam and Eve in Eden upon appetite, and they lost their blissful home. What accumulated misery and crime have filled our world in consequence of the fall of Adam. Entire cities have been blotted from the face of the earth because of the debasing crimes and revolting iniquity that made them a blot upon the universe. Indulgence of appetite was the foundation of all their sins.

Through appetite, Satan controlled the mind and being. Thousands who might have lived, have prematurely passed into their graves, physical, mental, and moral wrecks. They had good powers, but they sacrificed all to indulgence of appetite, which led them to lay the reins upon the neck of lust.—*Testimonies,* vol. 3, pp. 561, 562.

Satan Triumphs at His Ruinous Work.—Satan exults to see the human family plunging themselves deeper, and deeper, into suffering and misery. He knows that persons who have wrong habits, and unsound bodies, cannot serve God so earnestly, perseveringly, and purely as though sound. A diseased body affects the brain. With the mind we serve the Lord. The head is the capital of the body. . . . Satan triumphs in the ruinous work he causes by leading the human family to indulge in habits which destroy themselves, and one another; for by this means he is robbing God of the service due Him. —*Spiritual Gifts,* vol. 4, p. 146.

3. Impairment Through Indulged Appetite

The Food We Eat and the Lives We Live.—Indulgence of appetite is the greatest cause of physical and mental debility, and lies at the foundation of the feebleness which is apparent everywhere.—*Testimonies,* vol. 3, p. 487.

Our physical health is maintained by that which we eat; if our appetites are not under the control of a sanctified mind, if we are not temperate in all our eating and drinking, we shall not be in a state of mental and physical soundness to study the word with a purpose to learn what saith the Scripture—what shall I do to inherit eternal life? Any unhealthful habit will produce an unhealthful condition in the system, and the delicate, living machinery of the stomach will be injured, and will not be able to do its work properly. The diet has much to do with the disposition to enter into temptation and commit sin.—*Counsels on Diet and Foods,* page 52.

Adam and Eve Failed Here.—Through the temptation to indulge appetite, Adam and Eve first fell from their high, holy, and happy estate. And it is through the same temptation that the race have become enfeebled. They have permitted appetite and passion to take the throne, and to bring into subjection reason and intellect.—*Testimonies,* vol. 3, p. 139.

Their Children Have Followed On.—Eve was intemperate in her desires when she put forth the hand to take of the fruit-forbidden tree. Self-gratification has reigned almost supreme in the hearts of men and women since the Fall. Especially has the appetite been indulged, and they have been controlled by it, instead of reason. For the sake of gratifying the taste, Eve transgressed the command of God. He had given her everything her wants required, yet she was not satisfied.

Ever since, her fallen sons and daughters have followed the desires of their eyes, and of their taste. They have, like Eve, disregarded the prohibitions God has made, and have followed in a course of disobedience, and, like Eve, have flattered themselves that the consequence would not be as fearful as had been apprehended.—*How to Live,* page 51.

Sin Made Attractive.—Sin is made attractive by the covering of light which Satan throws over it, and he is well pleased when he can hold the Christian world in their daily habits under the tyranny of custom, like the heathen, and allow appetite to govern them.—*Signs of the Times,* Aug. 13, 1874.

Satan Gains Control of the Will.—Satan knows that he cannot overcome man unless he can control his will. He can do this by deceiving man so that he will co-operate with him in transgressing the laws of nature in eating and drinking, which is transgression of the law of God.—Manuscript 3, 1897.

Every Function Enfeebled.—Many groan under a burden of infirmities because of wrong habits of eating and drinking, which do violence to the laws of life and health. They are enfeebling their digestive organs by indulging perverted appetite. The power of the human constitution to resist the abuses put upon it is wonderful; but persistent wrong habits in excessive eating and drinking will enfeeble every function of the body. In the gratification of perverted appetite and passion, even professed Christians cripple nature in her work, and lessen physical, mental, and moral power.—*The Sanctified Life,* page 20.

Failure to Perfect Character.—The controlling power of appetite will prove the ruin of thousands, when, if they had conquered on this point, they would have moral power to gain victory over every other temptation of Satan. But slaves to appetite will fail in perfecting Christian character. The continual transgression of man for six thousand years has brought sickness, pain, and death, as its fruits.—*Health Reformer,* August, 1875.

Death Preferred to Reform.—Many are so devoted to intemperance that they will not change their course of indulging in gluttony under any considerations. They would sooner sacrifice health, and die prematurely, than to restrain their intemperate appetite.—*Spiritual Gifts,* vol. 4, p. 130.

A Vicious Circle of Degradation.—The lower estimate men place upon their body, the less they desire to keep it pure and holy, the more reckless will they be in the indulgence of perverted appetite.—Manuscript 150, 1898.

The World Taken Captive.—Satan is taking the world captive through the use of liquor and tobacco, tea and coffee. The God-given mind, which should be kept clear, is perverted by the use of narcotics. The brain is no longer able to distinguish correctly. The enemy has control. Man has sold his reason for that which makes him mad. He has no sense of what is right.—*Evangelism,* page 529.

The Results of Natural Law Violated.—Many marvel that the human race have so degenerated, physically, mentally, and morally. They do not understand that it is the violation of God's constitution and laws, and the violation of the laws of health, that has produced this sad degeneracy. The transgression of God's commandments has caused His prospering hand to be removed.

Intemperance in eating and in drinking, and the indulgence of base passions have benumbed the fine sensibilities. . . .

Those who permit themselves to become slaves to a gluttonous appetite, often go still further, and debase themselves by indulging their corrupt passions, which have become excited by intemperance in eating and in drinking. They give loose rein to their debasing passions, until health and intellect greatly suffer. The reasoning faculties are, in a great measure, destroyed by evil habits.—*Spiritual Gifts,* vol. 4, pp. 124-131.

Let none who profess godliness regard with indifference the health of the body, and flatter themselves that intemperance is no sin, and will not affect their spirituality. A close sympathy exists between the physical and the moral nature. The standard of virtue is elevated or degraded by the physical habits. . . . Any habit which does not promote healthful action in the human system degrades the higher and nobler faculties. Wrong habits of eating and drinking lead to errors in thought and action. Indulgence of appetite strengthens the animal propensities, giving them the ascendancy over the mental and spiritual powers.—*Review and Herald,* Jan. 25, 1881.

Life Record Closed in Dissipation.—Many close their last precious hours of probationary time, in scenes of gaiety, feasting and amusement, where serious thoughts are not allowed to enter, where the spirit of Jesus would be unwelcome! Their last precious hours are passing while their minds are benumbed with tobacco and alcoholic liquors. There are not a few who pass directly from the dens of infamy to the sleep of death; they close their life record among the associations of dissipation and vice. What will the awakening be at the resurrection of the unjust!

The eye of the Lord is open upon every scene of debasing amusement and profane dissipation. The words and deeds of the pleasure lovers pass directly from these halls of vice to the book of final records. What is the life of this class worth to the world, except as a beacon of warning to those who will be warned, not to live like these men, and die as the fool dieth.—*Signs of the Times,* Jan. 6, 1876.

The Christian Controls His Appetite.—No Christian will take into his system food or drink that will cloud his senses, or that will so act upon the nervous system as to cause him to degrade himself, or to unfit him for usefulness. The temple of God must not be defiled. The faculties of mind and body should be preserved in health, that they may be used to glorify God.—*Manuscript 126, 1903.*

With Ceaseless Vigilance.—Men's natural appetites have been perverted by indulgence. Through unholy gratification they have become "fleshly lusts, which war against the soul." Unless the Christian watches unto prayer, he gives loose reign to habits which should be overcome. Unless he feels the need of constant watching, ceaseless vigilance, his inclinations, abused and misguided, will be the means of his backsliding from God.—*Manuscript 47, 1896.*

Indulged Appetite Inimical to Christian Perfection.—It is impossible for those who indulge the appetite to attain to Christian perfection.—*Testimonies, vol. 2, p. 400.*

The Spirit of God cannot come to our help, and assist us in perfecting Christian characters, while we are indulging our appetites to the injury of health, and while the pride of life controls.—*Health Reformer, September, 1871.*

True Sanctification.—It [sanctification] is not merely a theory, an emotion, or a form of words, but a living, active principle, entering into the everyday life. It requires that our habits of eating, drinking, and dressing be such as to secure the preservation of physical, mental, and moral health, that we may present to the Lord our bodies—not an offering corrupted by wrong habits, but—"a living sacrifice, holy, acceptable unto God."—*Review and Herald, Jan. 25, 1881.*

Fitted for Immortality.—If man will cherish the light that God in mercy gives him upon health reform, he may be sanctified through the truth and fitted for immortality. But if he disregards that light and lives in violation of natural law he must pay the penalty.—*Testimonies, vol. 3, p. 162.*

4. Importance of Christ's Victory Over Appetite

Christ's First Victory.—Christ knew that in order to successfully carry forward the plan of salvation He must commence the work of redeeming man just where the ruin began. Adam fell on the point of appetite.—*Health Reformer, August, 1875.*

His first test was on the same point where Adam failed. It was through temptations addressed to the appetite that Satan had overcome a large proportion of the human race, and his success had made him feel that the control of this fallen planet was in his hands. But in Christ he found one who was able to resist him, and he left the field of battle a conquered foe.—*Christian Temperance and Bible Hygiene, page 16.*

Cause of His Anguish.—Many who profess godliness do not inquire into the reason of Christ's long period of fasting and suffering in the wilderness. His anguish was not so much from the pangs of hunger as from His sense of the fearful result of the indulgence of appetite and passion upon the race. He knew that appetite would be man's idol, and would lead him to forget God, and would stand directly in the way of his salvation.—*Redemption; or the Temptation of Christ, page 50.*

Victory in Behalf of the Race.—Satan was defeated in his object to overcome Christ upon the point of appetite. And here in the wilderness Christ achieved a victory in behalf of the race upon the point of appetite, making it possible for man, in all future time in His name to overcome the strength of appetite on his own behalf.—*Redemption; or the Temptation of Christ, page 46.*

We, Too, May Overcome.—Our only hope of regaining Eden is through firm self-control. If the power of indulged appetite was so strong upon the race, that, in order to break its hold, the divine Son of God, in man's behalf, had to endure a fast of nearly six weeks, what a work is before the Christian! Yet, however great the struggle, he may overcome. By the help of that divine power which withstood the fiercest temptations that Satan could invent, he, too, may be entirely successful in his warfare with evil, and at last may wear the victor's crown in the kingdom of God.—*Counsels on Diet and Foods,* page 167.

Victory Through Obedience and Continued Effort.—Those who overcome as Christ overcame will need to constantly guard themselves against the temptations of Satan. The appetite and passions should be restricted and under the control of enlightened conscience, that the intellect may be unimpaired, the perceptive powers clear, so that the workings of Satan and his snares may not be interpreted to be the providence of God. Many desire the final reward and victory which are to be given to overcomers, but are not willing to endure toil, privation, and denial of self, as did their Redeemer. It is only through obedience and continual effort that we shall overcome as Christ overcame.

The controlling power of appetite will prove the ruin of thousands, when, if they had conquered on this point, they would have had moral power to gain the victory over every other temptation of Satan. But those who are slaves to appetite will fail in perfecting Christian character. The continual transgression of man for six thousand years has brought sickness, pain, and death as its fruits. And as we near the close of time, Satan's temptation to indulge appetite will be more powerful and more difficult to overcome.—*Testimonies,* vol. 3, pp. 491, 492.

Claim Christ's Overcoming Power.—Christ has power from His Father to give His divine grace and strength to man—making it possible for him through His name, to overcome. There are but few professed followers of Christ who choose to engage with Him in the work of resisting Satan's temptation as He resisted, and overcome. . . .

All are personally exposed to the temptations that Christ overcame, but strength is provided for them in the all-powerful name of the great Conqueror. And all must, for themselves, individually overcome.—*Signs of the Times,* Aug. 13, 1874.

What Will We Do?—Shall we not draw near to the Lord, that He may save us from all intemperance in eating and drinking, from all unholy, lustful passion, all wickedness? Shall we not humble ourselves before God, putting away everything that corrupts the flesh and the spirit, that in His fear we may perfect holiness of character?—*Testimonies,* vol. 7, p. 258.

Section II

ALCOHOL AND SOCIETY

1. An Incentive to Crime

Crime Is in the Land.—In these days when vice and crime of every form are rapidly increasing, there is a tendency to become so familiar with existing conditions that we lose sight of their cause and of their significance. More intoxicating liquors are used today than have ever been used heretofore. In the horrible details of revolting drunkenness and terrible crime, the newspapers give but a partial report of the story of the resultant lawlessness. Violence is in the land.—*Drunkenness and Crime,* page 3.

The Testimony of the Judiciary.—The relation of crime to intemperance is well understood by men who have to deal with those who transgress the laws of the land. In the words of a Philadelphia judge: "We can trace four fifths of the crimes that are committed to the influence of rum. There is not one case in twenty where a man is tried for his life, in which rum is not the direct or indirect cause of the murder. Rum and blood, I mean the shedding of blood, go hand in hand."—*Drunkenness and Crime,* page 7.

High Percentage of Crime Attributable to Liquor.—Nine tenths of those who are taken to prison are those who have learned to drink.—*Review and Herald,* May 8, 1894.

Sequence of Drinking and Crime.—When the appetite for spirituous liquor is indulged, the man voluntarily places to his lips the draft which debases below the level of the brute him who was made in the image of God. Reason is paralyzed, the

(23)

intellect is benumbed, the animal passions are excited, and then follow crimes of the most debasing character.—*Testimonies,* vol. 3, p. 561.

Why Alcohol and Crime Are Related.—Those who frequent the saloons that are open to all who are foolish enough to tamper with the deadly evil they contain, are following the path that leads to eternal death. They are selling themselves, body, soul, and spirit, to Satan. Under the influence of the drink they take, they are led to do things from which, if they had not tasted the maddening drug, they would have shrunk in horror. When they are under the influence of the liquid poison, they are in Satan's control. He rules them, and they co-operate with him.—Letter 166, 1903.

Nature of Crimes Committed Under Alcohol.—The result of liquor drinking is demonstrated by the awful murders that take place. How often it is found that theft, incendiarism, murder, were committed under the influence of liquor. Yet the liquor curse is legalized, and works untold ruin in the hands of those who love to tamper with that which ruins not only the poor victim, but his whole family.—*Review and Herald,* May 1, 1900.

Houses of prostitution, dens of vice, criminal courts, prisons, almshouses, insane asylums, hospitals, all are, to a great degree, filled as a result of the liquor seller's work. Like the mystic Babylon of the Apocalypse, he is dealing in "slaves, and souls of men." Behind the liquor seller stands the mighty destroyer of souls, and every act which earth or hell can devise is employed to draw human beings under his power.

In the city and the country, on the railway trains, on the great steamers, in places of business, in the halls of pleasure, in the medical dispensary, even in the church on the sacred Communion table, his traps are set. Nothing is left undone to create and to foster the desire for intoxicants. On almost every corner stands the public house with its brilliant lights, its welcome and good cheer, inviting the workingman, the wealthy idler, and the unsuspecting youth. Day by day, month by month, year by year, the work goes on.—*Drunkenness and Crime,* page 8.

The Drinker Not Excusable.—While intoxicated, every degree of crime has been committed, and yet the perpetrators have been excused in many instances, because they knew not what they were doing. This does not lessen the guilt of the criminal. If by his own hand he puts the glass to his lips, and deliberately takes that which he knows will destroy his reasoning faculties, he becomes responsible for all the injury he does while intoxicated, at the very moment he lets his appetite control him, and he barters away his reasoning faculties for intoxicating drinks. It was his own act which brought him even below the brutes, and crimes committed when he is in a state of intoxication should be punished as severely as though the person had all the power of his reasoning faculties.—*Spiritual Gifts,* vol. 4, p. 125.

Drunkenness and Crime Before the Flood and Now.—The evils that are so apparent at the present time, are the same that brought destruction to the antediluvian world. "In the days that were before the Flood" one of the prevailing sins was drunkenness. From the record in Genesis we learn that "the earth also was corrupt before God, and the earth was filled with violence." Crime reigned supreme; life itself was unsafe. Men whose reason was dethroned by intoxicating drink, thought little of taking the life of a human being.

"As the days of Noah were, so shall also the coming of the Son of man be." The drunkenness and the crime that now prevail, have been foretold by the Saviour Himself. We are living in the closing days of this earth's history. It is a most solemn time. Everything betokens the soon return of our Lord.—*Review and Herald,* Oct. 25, 1906.

God's Judgments in Our Day.—Because of the wickedness that follows largely as the result of the use of liquor, the judgments of God are falling upon our earth today.—*Counsels on Health,* page 432.

San Francisco's Object Lesson.—For a time after the great earthquake along the coast of California, the authorities in San Francisco and in some of the smaller cities and towns ordered the closing of all liquor saloons. So marked were the effects of this strictly enforced ordinance, that the attention of thinking men throughout America, and notably on the Pacific Coast, was directed to the advantages that would result from a permanent closing of all saloons. During many weeks following the earthquake in San Francisco, very little drunkenness was seen. No intoxicating drinks were sold. The disorganized and unsettled state of affairs gave the city officials reason to expect an abnormal increase of disorder and crime, and they were greatly surprised to find the opposite true. Those from whom was expected much trouble, gave but little. This remarkable freedom from violence and crime was traceable largely to the disuse of intoxicants.

The editors of some of the leading dailies took the position that it would be for the permanent betterment of society and for the upbuilding of the best interests of the city, were the saloons to remain closed forever. But wise counsel was swept aside, and within a few short weeks permission was given the liquor dealers to reopen their places of business, upon the payment of a considerably higher license than had formerly been paid into the city treasury.

In the calamity that befell San Francisco, the Lord designed to wipe out the liquor saloons that have been the cause of so much evil, so much misery and crime; and yet the guardians of the public welfare have proved unfaithful to their trust, by legalizing the sale of liquor. . . . They know that in doing this, they are virtually licensing the commission of crime; and yet their knowledge of this sure result deters them not. . . . The people of San Francisco must answer at the judgment bar of God for the reopening of the liquor saloons in that city.—*Review and Herald,* Oct. 25, 1906.

Significance of Present-Day Conditions.—Notwithstanding the many evidences of the increase of crime and lawlessness, men seldom stop to think seriously of the meaning of these things. Almost without exception, men boast of the enlightenment and progress of the present age.

Upon those to whom God has given great light, rests the solemn responsibility of calling the attention of others to the significance of the increase of drunkenness and crime. They should also bring before the minds of others the Scriptures that plainly portray the conditions which will exist just prior to the second coming of Christ. Faithfully should they uplift the divine standard, and raise their voices in protest against the sanctioning of the liquor traffic by legal enactment.—*Drunkenness and Crime,* page 3.

2. An Economic Problem

Liquor Traffic Breeds Dishonesty and Violence.—In every phase of the liquor-selling business, there is dishonesty and violence. The houses of liquor dealers are built with the wages of unrighteousness, and upheld by violence and oppression.—*Review and Herald,* May 1, 1894.

Millions Spent to Buy Wretchedness and Death.—"Woe unto him that buildeth his house by unrighteousness, and his chambers by wrong; . . . that saith, I will build me a wide house and large chambers, and cutteth him out windows; and it is ceiled with cedar, and painted with vermilion. Shalt thou reign, because thou closest thyself in cedar? . . . Thine eyes and thine heart are not but for thy covetousness, and for to shed innocent blood, and for oppression, and for violence, to do it."

This Scripture pictures the work of those who manufacture and who sell intoxicating liquor. Their business means robbery. For the money they receive no useful equivalent is returned. Every dollar they add to their gains has brought a curse to the spender.

Every year millions upon millions of gallons of intoxicating liquors are consumed. Millions upon millions of dollars are spent in buying wretchedness, poverty, disease, degradation, lust, crime, and death. For the sake of gain, the liquor dealer deals out to his victims that which corrupts and destroys mind and body. He entails on the drunkard's family poverty and wretchedness.—*Drunkenness and Crime,* pages 7, 8.

A Contrasting Economic Status.—The drunkard is capable of better things. God has entrusted to him talents with which to glorify God; but his fellow men have laid a snare for his soul, and built themselves up out of his property. They have lived in luxury while their poor brethren whom they have robbed, lived in poverty and degradation. But God will require for all this at the hand of him who has helped to speed the drunkard on the way to ruin.—Undated Manuscript 54.

Lawmakers and Liquor Dealers Held Financially Responsible.—Lawmakers and liquor dealers may wash their hands as did Pilate, but they will not be clean from the blood of souls. The ceremony of washing their hands will not cleanse them when by their influence or agency, they have helped to make men drunkards. They will be held accountable for the millions of dollars that have been wasted in consuming the consumers. No one can blind himself to the terrible results of the drink traffic. The daily papers show that the wretchedness, the poverty, the crime, that result from this traffic, are not cunningly devised fables, and that hundreds of men are growing rich off the pittances of the men they are sending to perdition by their dreadful drink business. O that a public sentiment might be created that would put an end to the drink traffic, close the saloons, and give these maddened men a chance to think on eternal realities!—*Review and Herald,* May 29, 1894.

Schools Could Have Been Established.—Think of the money wasted in saloons, where men sell their reason for that which places them wholly under Satan's control. What a change there would be in society if this money were used to establish schools where children and youth would be given instruction in Bible lines, taught how to help their fellow beings, how to seek and save the lost!

There is a work to be done for all classes of society. . . . We are not to forget the ministers, lawyers, senators, judges, many of whom use strong drink and tobacco. . . . Ask them to give the money they would otherwise spend for the harmful indulgences of liquor and tobacco, to the establishment of institutions where children and youth can be prepared to fill positions of usefulness in the world.—Letter 25, 1902.

The Starving Might Be Fed.—The cries of the starving millions in our world would soon be hushed if the money put into the tills of the liquor sellers were spent in alleviating the sufferings of humanity. But the evil is constantly increasing. The youth are being educated to love the vile stuff, and this is ruining them, soul and body. The work they might do in God's vineyard they refuse to do.—Manuscript 139, 1899.

Missions Might Have Been Established.—Think of the thousands and millions of dollars that are invested in drink that will make a man like a brute, and destroy his reason. . . . All this money could accomplish untold good if it were used in the support of missions in the dark places of our world. God is being robbed of that which is rightfully His. —Manuscript 38½, 1905.

Publications Could Have Been Increased.—When we obey the injunction of the apostle, "Whether therefore ye eat, or drink, or whatsoever ye do, do all to the glory of God," thousands of dollars which are now sacrificed upon the altar of hurtful lust will flow into the Lord's treasury, multiplying publications in different languages to be scattered like the leaves of autumn. Missions will be established in other nations, and then will the followers of Christ be indeed the light of the world.—*Signs of the Times,* Aug. 13, 1874.

Intemperance Increased by Holidays.—Drunkenness, rioting, violence, crime, murder, come as the result of man selling his reason. The numerous holidays increase the evils of intemperance. These holidays are no help to morality or to religion. On them men spend in drink the money that should be used to supply the necessities of their families; and the liquor sellers reap their harvest.

When drink is in, reason is out. This is the hour and power of darkness, when all crime becomes possible, and the whole human machinery is controlled by a power from beneath, when soul and body are brought under the control of passion. And what can stay this passion? What can hinder it? These souls have no certain anchorage. Holidays are leading them on to temptation; for on a holiday many think that it is their privilege, because it is a holiday, to do as they please.—*Manuscript 17, 1898.*

Millions for the Devil's Treasury.—Look at those that drink wine and beer and strong drink. Let them reckon up how much money they spend in this. How many thousands and millions of dollars have gone into the devil's treasury to perpetuate wickedness, and to carry on dissolution, corruption, and crime.—*Manuscript 20, 1894.*

3. Alcohol and the Home

Moderate Drinking.—Moderate drinking is the school in which men are receiving an education for the drunkard's career.—*Review and Herald,* March 25, 1884.

God's Blessings Changed to a Curse.—Our Creator has bestowed His bounties upon man with a liberal hand. Were all these gifts of Providence wisely and temperately employed, poverty, sickness, and distress would be well-nigh banished from the earth. But alas, we see on every hand the blessings of God changed to a curse by the wickedness of men.

There is no class guilty of greater perversion and abuse of His precious gifts than are those who employ the products of the soil in the manufacture of intoxicating liquors. The nutritive grains, the healthful, delicious fruits, are converted into beverages that pervert the senses and madden the brain. As a result of the use of these poisons, thousands of families are deprived of the comforts and even the necessaries of life, acts of violence and crime are multiplied, and disease and death hurry myriads of victims to a drunkard's grave.—*Gospel Workers,* pages 385, 386.

Marriage Vows Melted in the Fiery Liquid.—Look upon the drunkard's home. Mark the squalid poverty, the wretchedness, the unutterable woe that are reigning there. See the once happy wife fleeing before her maniac husband. Hear her plead for mercy as the cruel blows fall on her shrinking form. Where are the sacred vows made at the marriage altar? where is the love to cherish, the strength to protect her now? Alas, these have been melted like precious pearls in the fiery liquid, the cup of abominations! Look upon those half-naked children. Once they were cherished tenderly. No wintry storm, nor the cold breath of the world's contempt and scorn, was permitted to approach them. A father's care, a mother's love, made their home a paradise. Now all is changed. Day by day the cries of agony wrenched from the lips of the drunkard's wife and children go up to heaven.—*Review and Herald,* Nov. 8, 1881.

His Manhood Is Gone.—Look at the drunkard. See what liquor has done for him. His eyes are bleared and bloodshot.

His countenance is bloated and besotted. His gait is staggering. The sign of Satan's working is written all over him. Nature herself protests that she knows him not; for he has perverted his God-given powers, and prostituted his manhood by indulgence in drink.—*Review and Herald,* May 8, 1894.

An Expression of Satan's Violence.—Thus he [Satan] works when he entices men to sell the soul for liquor. He takes possession of body, mind, and soul, and it is no longer the man, but Satan, who acts. And the cruelty of Satan is expressed as the drunkard lifts his hand to strike down the wife he has promised to love and cherish as long as life shall last. The deeds of the drunkard are an expression of Satan's violence.—*Medical Ministry,* page 114.

Indulgence in intoxicating liquor places a man wholly under the control of the demon who devised this stimulant in order to deface and destroy the moral image of God.—Manuscript 1, 1899.

Calmness and Patience Lost.—It is not possible for the intemperate man to possess a calm, well-balanced character, and if he handles dumb animals, the extra cut of the whip which he gives God's creatures, reveals the disturbed condition of his digestive organs. In the home circle the same spirit is seen.—Letter 17, 1895.

The Shame and Curse of Every Land.—The bleared, besotted wrecks of humanity—souls for whom Christ died, and over whom angels weep—are everywhere. They are a blot on our boasted civilization. They are the shame and curse and peril of every land.—*The Ministry of Healing,* page 330.

The Wife Robbed, the Children Starved.—The drunkard has no knowledge of what he is doing when under the influence of the maddening draft, and yet he who sells him that which makes him irresponsible, is protected by the law in his work of destruction. It is legal for him to rob the widow of the food she requires to sustain life. It is legal for him to entail starvation upon the family of his victim, to send helpless children into the streets to beg for a penny or to beseech for a morsel of bread. Day by day, month by month, year by year, these shameful scenes are re-enacted, until the conscience of the liquor dealer is seared as with a red-hot iron. The tears of suffering children, the agonized cry of the mother, only serve to exasperate the rum seller. . . .

The liquor dealer will not hesitate to collect the debts of the drunkard from his suffering family, and will take the very necessaries from the home to pay the drink bill of the deceased husband and father. What is it to him if the children of the dead starve? He looks upon them as debased and ignorant creatures, who have been abused, kicked about, and degraded; and he has no care for their welfare. But the God that rules in the heavens has not lost sight of the first cause or the last effect of the inexpressible misery and debasement that have come upon the drunkard and his family. The ledger of heaven contains every item of the history.—*Review and Herald,* May 15, 1894.

The Drinker Responsible for His Guilt.—Let not the man who indulges in drink think that he will be able to cover his defilement by casting the blame upon the liquor dealer; for he will have to answer for his sin and for the degradation of his wife and children. "They that forsake the Lord shall be consumed."—*Review and Herald,* May 8, 1894.

In the Shadow of Liquor.—Day by day, month by month, year by year, the work goes on. Fathers and husbands and brothers, the stay and hope and pride of the nation, are steadily passing into the liquor dealer's haunts, to be sent back wrecked and ruined.

More terrible still, the curse is striking the very heart of the home. More and more, women are forming the liquor habit. In many a household, little children, even in the innocence and helplessness of babyhood, are in daily peril through the neglect, the abuse, the vileness of drunken mothers. Sons and daughters are growing up under the shadow of this terrible evil. What outlook for their future but that they will sink even lower than their parents?—*The Ministry of Healing,* page 339.

4. A Cause of Accidents

The Drinker Under Satan's Control.—Men who use liquor make themselves the slaves of Satan. Satan tempts those who occupy positions of trust on railways, on steamships, those who have charge of the boats or cars laden with people flocking to idolatrous amusement, to indulge perverted appetite, and thus forget God and His laws. He offers tempting bribes to allure them, that by indulging wrong habits and appetites, they may place themselves where he can control their reason, as a workman handles an instrument. Then he works to destroy the pleasure lovers.

Thus men co-operate with Satan, as his agents, his instruments. They cannot see what they are about. Signals are made incorrectly, and cars collide with each other. Then comes horror, mutilation, and death. This condition of things will become more and more marked. The daily papers will relate many terrible accidents. Yet the saloons will be made just as enticing. Liquor will still be sold to the poor tempted soul who has lost the power to stand up and say, I am a man, but who says by his actions, I have no self-control. I cannot resist temptation. All such have severed their connection with God, and are the dupes of Satan's deception.—Manuscript 17, 1898.

Judgment Impaired Through Liquor.—Liquor drinkers are under Satan's destroying influence. He presents to them his false ideas, and no confidence can be placed in their judgment.—*Review and Herald,* May 1, 1900.

Some official on a railway train neglects to heed a signal, or misinterprets an order. On goes the train; there is a collision, and many lives are lost. Or a steamer is run aground, and passengers and crew find a watery grave. When the matter is investigated, it is found that someone at an important post was under the influence of drink.—*The Ministry of Healing,* page 331.

God Holds the Drinker Responsible.—Are the men who command the great ocean steamers, who have the control of railways, strict temperance men? Are their brains free from the influence of intoxicants? If not, the accidents occurring under their management will be charged to them by the God of heaven, whose property men and women are.—*Review and Herald,* May 1, 1900.

Men on whom devolve grave responsibilities in safeguarding their fellow men from accident and harm, are often untrue to their trust. Because of indulgence in tobacco and liquor, they do not keep the mind clear and composed as did Daniel in the courts of Babylon. They becloud the brain by using stimulating narcotics, and temporarily lose their reasoning faculties. Many a shipwreck upon the high seas can be traced to liquor drinking.

Time and again have unseen angels protected vessels on the broad ocean because on board there were some praying passengers who had faith in God's keeping power. The Lord has power to hold in abeyance the angry waves so impatient to destroy and engulf His children.—*Manuscript* 153, 1902.

To Rebuke Liquor Drinking.—We have need of men who, under the inspiration of the Holy Spirit, will rebuke gambling and liquor drinking, which are such prevalent evils in these last days.—*Manuscript* 117, 1907.

The Only Safe Course.—How many frightful accidents occur through the influence of drink. . . . What is the portion of this terrible intoxicant that any man can take, and be safe with the lives of human beings? He can be safe only as he abstains from drink. He should not have his mind confused with drink. No intoxicant should pass his lips; then if disaster comes, men in responsible places can do their best, and meet their record with satisfaction, whatever may be the issue.—*Review and Herald,* May 29, 1894.

5. A Public-Health Problem

They Have Sold Their Will Power.—There is in the world a multitude of degraded human beings, who have, by yielding in their youth to the temptation to use tobacco and alcohol, poisoned the tissues of the human structure, and perverted their reasoning powers, until the result is just as Satan meant it to be. The faculties of thought are clouded. The victims yield to the temptation for alcohol, and they sell what reason they have for a glass of liquor.

See that man bereft of reason. What is he? He is a slave to the will of Satan. The arch apostate imbues him with his own attributes. He is a slave to licentiousness and violence. There is no crime that he will not commit; for he has put into his mouth that which has intoxicated him, and made him, while under its influence, a demon.

Look at our young men. And I write now what causes my heart to ache. They have lost their will power. Their nerves are enfeebled, because their power is exhausted. The ruddy glow of health is not upon their countenances. The healthy sparkle of the eye is gone. Its luster is lost. The wine they have drunk has enfeebled the memory. They are like persons aged in years. The brain is no longer able to produce its rich treasures when required.—Manuscript 17, 1898.

A Moral Sin and a Physical Disease.—Among the victims

of intemperance are men of all classes and all professions. Men of high station, of eminent talents, of great attainments, have yielded to the indulgence of appetite, until they are helpless to resist temptation. Some of them who were once in the possession of wealth are without home, without friends, in suffering, misery, disease, and degradation. They have lost their self-control. Unless a helping hand is held out to them, they will sink lower and lower. With these self-indulgence is not only a moral sin, but a physical disease.—*The Ministry of Healing,* page 172.

In a Desperate Situation.—The man who has formed the habit of using intoxicants is in a desperate situation. His brain is diseased, his will power is weakened. So far as any power in himself is concerned, his appetite is uncontrollable. He cannot be reasoned with or persuaded to deny himself.—*The Ministry of Healing,* page 344.

Body and Soul in Slavery.—Drinking houses are scattered all over the cities and towns. . . . The traveler enters the public house with his reason, with ability to walk in an upright manner; but look at him as he leaves. The luster is gone from his eye. The power to walk uprightly is gone; he reels to and fro like a ship at sea. His reasoning power is paralyzed, the image of God is destroyed. The poisoning, maddening draft has left a brand upon him. . . . Body and soul he is in slavery, and he cannot distinguish between right and wrong. The liquor dealer has put his bottle to his neighbor's lips, and under its influence he is full of cruelty and murder, and in his madness actually commits murder.

He is brought before an earthly tribunal, and those who legalized the traffic are forced to deal with the results of their own work. They authorized by law the giving to this man a draft that would turn him from a sane man into a madman, and yet now it is necessary for them to send him to prison and to the gallows for his crime. His wife and children are left in destitution and poverty, to become the charge of the community in which they live. Soul and body the man is lost,—cut off from earth, and with no hope of heaven. . . .

No Strength to Resist Temptation.—The victims of the drink habit become so maddened under the influence of liquor that they are willing to sell their reason for a glass of whisky. They do not keep the commandment, "Thou shalt have no other gods before Me." Their moral power is so weakened that they have no strength to resist temptation, and their desire for drink is so strong that it eclipses all other desires, and they have no realization of the fact that God requires them to love Him with all their hearts. They are practical idolaters; for whatever alienates the affections from the Creator, whatever weakens and deadens moral power, usurps His throne, and receives the service that is due to Him alone. In all these vile idolatries Satan is worshiped.

He who tarries at the wine is playing the game of life with Satan. He it is who made evil men his agents, so that those who begin the drink habit may be made into drunkards. He has his plans laid that when the brain is confused with liquor, he will drive the drunkard to desperation, and cause him to commit some atrocious crime. In the idol he has set up for the man to worship is all pollution and crime, and the worship of the idol will ruin both soul and body, and extend its evil influence to the wife and children of the drunkard. The drunkard's corrupt tendencies are transmitted to his posterity, and through them to the coming generations.

A Demon Power at Work.—But are not the rulers of the land largely responsible for the aggravated crimes, the current of deadly evil, that is the result of the liquor traffic? Is it not their duty and in their power to remove this deadly evil? Satan has formed his plans, and he counsels with legislators, and they receive his advice, and thus keep in activity, through legislative enactments, a multiplicity of evil, which results in much misery and crime of so terrible a character that human pen cannot portray it. A demon power is at work through human instruments, and men are tempted to indulge appetite until they lose all control of themselves. The sight of a drunken man, were the sight not so common, would arouse public indignation, and cause the drink traffic to be swept away; but the power of Satan has so hardened human hearts, so perverted human judgment, that men can look upon the woe, the crime, the poverty, which floods the world through the drink traffic, and remain indifferent. . . .

Day after day, month after month, year after year, Satan's death traps are set in our communities, at our doors, at the street corners, wherever it is possible to catch souls, that their moral power may be destroyed, and the image of God obliterated, and they be sunken in degradation far below the level of the brute. Souls are imperiled and perishing, and where is the active energy, the determined effort on the part of Christians, to raise a warning signal, to enlighten their fellow men, to save their perishing brothers? We are not to talk of devising methods to save those who are dead and lost, but to move upon those who are not yet beyond the reach of sympathy and help. . . .

By legalizing the liquor traffic, the law gives its sanction to the downfall of the soul, and refuses to stop the traffic that floods the world with evil. Let lawmakers consider whether or not all this imperiling of human life, of physical power and mental vision, is unavoidable. Is all this destruction of human life necessary?—*Review and Herald,* May 29, 1894.

The Responsibility of the Liquor Dealer.—Those who sell intoxicating liquor to their fellow men . . . receive the earnings of the drunkard, and give him no equivalent for his money. Instead of this, they give him that which maddens him, which makes him act the fool, and turns him into a demon of evil and cruelty. . . .

But angels of God have witnessed every step in the downward path, and have traced every consequence that resulted from a man's placing the bottle to his neighbor's lips. The liquor dealer is written in the records among those whose hands are full of blood. He is condemned for keeping on hand the poisonous draft by which his neighbor is tempted to ruin, and by which homes are filled with wretchedness and degradation. The Lord holds the liquor dealer responsible for every penny that comes to his till out of the earnings of the poor drunkard, who has lost all moral power, who has sunk his manhood in drink.—*Review and Herald,* May 8, 1894.

He Must Answer to God.—No matter what may be the wealth, power, or position of a man in the sight of the world, no matter whether or not he has been permitted by the law of the land to sell poisonous drinks to his neighbor, he will be held accountable in the sight of heaven for degrading the soul that has been redeemed by Christ, and will be arraigned before the judgment for lowering a character that ought to have reflected the image of God, to reflect the image of that which is below the brute creation.

In enticing men to educate themselves in the liquor habit, the rum seller is effectually taking away the righteousness of the soul, and leading men to become the abject slaves of Satan. The Lord Jesus, the Prince of Life, is in controversy with Satan, the prince of darkness. Christ declares that His mission is to lift men up. . . .

Jesus left the royal courts of heaven, and laid aside His own glory, and clothed His divinity with humanity, that He might come into close connection with humanity, and by precept and example uplift and ennoble humanity, and restore in the human soul the lost image of God. This is the work of Christ; but what is the influence of those who legalize the liquor traffic? What is the influence of those who put the bottle to their neighbor's lips? Contrast the work of the rum seller with the work of Jesus Christ, and you will be forced to admit that those who deal in liquor, and those who sustain the traffic, are working in co-partnership with Satan. Through this business they are doing a greater work to perpetuate human woe than are men through any other business in the world. . . .

The rum seller takes the same position as did Cain, and says, "Am I my brother's keeper?" and God says to him as He said to Cain, "The voice of thy brother's blood crieth unto Me from the ground." Rum sellers will be held accountable for the wretchedness that has been brought into the homes of those who were weak in moral power, and who fall through temptation to drink. They will be charged with the misery, the suffering, the hopelessness, brought into the world through the liquor traffic. They will have to answer for the woe and want of the mothers and children who have suffered for food and clothing and shelter, who have buried all hope and joy. He that has a care for the sparrow, and notes its fall to the ground, who clothes the grass of the field, which today is, and tomorrow is cast into the oven, will not pass by those who have been formed in His own image, purchased with His own blood, and pay no heed to their suffering cries. God cares for all this wickedness that perpetuates misery and crime. He charges it all up to those whose influence helps to open the door of temptation to the soul.—Undated Manuscript 54.

God's Sentence on the Liquor Seller.—He knows not, nor cares, that the Lord has an account to settle with him. And when his victim is dead, his heart of stone is unmoved.

He has not heeded the instruction, "Ye shall not afflict any widow, or fatherless child. If thou afflict them in any wise, and they cry at all unto Me, I will surely hear their cry; and My wrath shall wax hot, and I will kill you with the sword; and your wives shall be widows, and your children fatherless."—*Review and Herald,* May 15, 1894.

There will be no excuse for the liquor dealers in that day

when every man shall receive according to his works. Those who have destroyed life, will by their own life have to pay the penalty. God's law is holy and just and good.—Letter 90, 1908.

Encourage Not the Desire for Stimulants.—Let every soul remember that he is under sacred obligations to God to do his best for his fellow creatures. How careful should everyone be not to create a desire for stimulants. By advising friends and neighbors to take brandy for the sake of their health, they are in danger of becoming agents for the destruction of their friends. Many incidents have come to my attention in which through some simple advice, men and women have become the slaves of the drink habit.

Physicians are responsible for making many drunkards. Knowing what drink will do for its lovers, they have taken upon themselves the responsibility of prescribing it for their patients. Did they reason from cause to effect, they would know that stimulants would have the same effect on every organ of the body as they have on the whole man. What excuse can doctors render for the influence they have exerted in making fathers and mothers drunkards?—*Review and Herald,* May 29, 1894.

Warned That They May Escape the Evil Results.—With the awful results of indulgence in intoxicating drink before us, how is it that any man or woman who claims to believe in the word of God, can venture to touch, taste, or handle wine or strong drink? Such a practice is certainly out of harmony with their professed faith. . . .

The Lord has given special directions in His word in reference to the use of wine and strong drink. He has forbidden their use, and enforced His prohibitions with strong warnings and threatenings. But His warning against the use of intoxicating beverages is not the result of the exercise of arbitrary authority. He has warned men, in order that they may escape from the evil that results from indulgence in wine and strong drink. . . .

The liquor traffic is a terrible scourge to our land, and is sustained and legalized by those who profess to be Christians. In thus doing, the churches make themselves responsible for all the results of this death-dealing traffic. The liquor traffic has its root in hell itself, and it leads to perdition. These are solemn considerations.—*Review and Herald,* May 1, 1894.

6. Alcohol and Men in Responsible Positions

Lessons from the Experience of Nadab and Abihu.—Nadab and Abihu, the sons of Aaron, who ministered in the holy office of priesthood, partook freely of wine, and, as was their usual custom, went in to minister before the Lord. The priests who burned incense before the Lord were required to use the fire of God's kindling, which burned day and night, and was never extinguished. God gave explicit directions how every part of His service should be conducted, that all connected with His sacred worship might be in accordance with His holy character. And any deviation from the express directions of God in connection with His holy service was punishable with death. No sacrifice would be acceptable to God which was not salted nor seasoned with divine fire, which represented the communication between God and man that was opened through Jesus Christ alone. The holy fire which was to be put upon the censer was kept burning perpetually. And while the people of God were without, earnestly praying, the incense kindled by the holy fire was to arise before God mingled with their prayers. This incense was an emblem of the mediation of Christ.

Aaron's sons took the common fire which God did not accept, and they offered insult to the infinite God by presenting this strange fire before Him. God consumed them by fire for their positive disregard of His express directions. All their works were as the offering of Cain. There was no divine Saviour represented. Had these sons of Aaron been in full command of their reasoning faculties they would have discerned the difference between the common and sacred fire. The gratification of appetite debased their faculties and so beclouded their intellect that their power of discernment was gone. They fully understood the holy character of the typical service, and the awful solemnity and responsibility assumed of presenting themselves before God to minister in sacred service.

They Were Responsible.—Some may inquire, How could the sons of Aaron have been accountable when their intellects were so far paralyzed by intoxication that they were not able to discern the difference between sacred and common fire? It was when they put the cup to their lips that they made themselves responsible for all their acts committed while under the influence of wine. The indulgence of appetite cost those priests their lives. God expressly forbade the use of wine that would have an influence to becloud the intellect.

"And the Lord spake unto Aaron, saying, Do not drink wine nor strong drink, thou, nor thy sons with thee, when ye go into the tabernacle of the congregation, lest ye die: it shall be a statute forever throughout your generations: and that ye may put difference between holy and unholy, and between unclean and clean; and that ye may teach the children of Israel all the statutes which the Lord hath spoken unto them by the hand of Moses." . . .

Here we have the most plain directions of God, and his reasons for prohibiting the use of wine; that their power of discrimination and discernment might be clear, and in no way confused; that their judgment might be correct, and they be ever able to discern between the clean and unclean. Another reason of weighty importance why they should abstain from anything which would intoxicate, is also given. It would require the full use of unclouded reason to present to the children of Israel all the statutes which God had spoken to them.

Qualifications for Spiritual Leaders.—Anything in eating or drinking which disqualifies the mental powers for healthful and active exercise is an aggravating sin in the sight of God. Especially is this the case with those who minister in holy things, who should at all times be examples to the people, and be in a condition to properly instruct them. . . .

Ministers in the sacred desk, with mouth and lips defiled, dare to take the sacred word of God in their polluted lips. They think God does not notice their sinful indulgence. "Because sentence against an evil work is not executed speedily, therefore the heart of the sons of men is fully set in them to do evil." God will no more receive a sacrifice from the hands of those who thus pollute themselves, and offer with their service the incense of tobacco and liquor, than He would receive the offering of the sons of Aaron, who offered incense with strange fire.

God has not changed. He is as particular and exact in His requirements now as He was in the days of Moses. But in the sanctuaries of worship in our day, with the songs of praise, the prayers, and the teaching from the pulpit, there is not merely strange fire, but positive defilement. Instead of truth being preached with holy unction from God, it is sometimes spoken under the influence of tobacco and brandy. Strange fire indeed! Bible truth and Bible holiness are presented to the people, and prayers are offered to God, mingled with the stench of tobacco! Such incense is most acceptable to Satan! A terrible deception is this! What an offense in the sight of God! What an insult to Him who is holy, dwelling in light unapproachable!

If the faculties of the mind were in healthful vigor, professed Christians would discern the inconsistency of such worship. Like Nadab and Abihu, their sensibilities are so blunted that they make no difference between the sacred and common. Holy and sacred things are brought down upon a level with their tobacconized breaths, benumbed brains, and their polluted souls, defiled through indulgence of appetite and passion. Professed Christians eat and drink, smoke and chew tobacco, and become gluttons and drunkards, to gratify appetite, and still talk of overcoming as Christ overcame!—*Redemption; or the Temptation of Christ,* pages 82-86.

A Call for Clear-Minded Officials.—How is it with our lawmakers, and the men in our courts of justice? If it was necessary that those who minister in holy office should have clear minds and full control of their reason, is it not also important that those who make and execute the laws of our great nation should have their faculties unclouded? What about the judges and jurors, in whose hands rests the disposing of human life, and whose decisions may condemn the innocent, or turn the criminal loose upon society? Do they not need to have full control of their mental powers? Are they temperate in their habits? If not, they are not fit for such responsible positions. When the appetites are perverted, the mental powers are weakened, and there is danger that men will not rule justly. Is indulgence in that which beclouds the mind less dangerous today than when God placed restrictions upon those who ministered in holy office?—*Christian Temperance and Bible Hygiene,* page 19.

When Government Men Betray Their Trust.—Men who make laws to control the people should above all others be obedient to the higher laws which are the foundation of all rule in nations and in families. How important that men who have a controlling power should themselves feel they are under a higher control. They will never feel thus while their minds are weakened by indulgence in narcotics, and strong drink. Those to whom it is entrusted to make and execute laws should have all their powers in vigorous action. They may, by practicing temperance in all things, preserve the clear discrimination between the sacred and common, and have wisdom to deal with that justice and integrity which God enjoined upon ancient Israel. . . .

Many who are elevated to the highest positions of trust in serving the public are the opposite of this. They are self-serving, and generally indulge in the use of narcotics, and wine and strong drink. Lawyers, jurors, senators, judges, and representative men have forgotten that they cannot dream themselves into a character. They are deteriorating their powers through sinful indulgences. They stoop from their high position to defile themselves with intemperance, licentiousness, and every form of evil. Their powers prostituted by vice open their path for every evil. . . .

Intemperate men should not by vote of the people be placed in positions of trust. Their influence corrupts others, and grave responsibilities are involved. With brain and nerve narcotized by tobacco and stimulus they make a law of their nature, and when the immediate influence is gone there is a collapse. Frequently human life is hanging in the balance; on the decision of men in these positions of trust depends life and liberty, or bondage and despair. How necessary that all who take part in these transactions should be men proved, men of self-culture, men of honesty and truth, of stanch integrity, who will spurn a bribe, who will not allow their judgment or convictions of right to be swerved by partiality or prejudice. Thus saith the Lord, "Thou shalt not wrest the judgment of thy poor in his cause. Keep thee far from a false matter; and the innocent and righteous slay thou not: for I will not justify the wicked. And thou shalt take no gift: for the gift blindeth the wise, and perverteth the words of the righteous."—*Signs of the Times,* July 8, 1880.

Only men of strict temperance and integrity should be admitted to our legislative halls and chosen to preside in our courts of justice. Property, reputation, and even life itself, are insecure when left to the judgment of men who are intemperate and immoral. How many innocent persons have been condemned to death, how many more have been robbed of all their earthly possessions, by the injustice of drinking jurors, lawyers, witnesses, and even judges!—*Signs of the Times,* Feb. 11, 1886.

If All Responsible Men Were Temperate.—Should representative men keep the way of the Lord, they would point men to a high and holy standard. Those in positions of trust would be strictly temperate. Magistrates, senators, and judges would have a clear understanding, and their judgment would be sound and unperverted. The fear of the Lord would ever be before them, and they would depend upon a higher wisdom than their own. The heavenly Teacher would make them wise in counsel, and strong to work steadfastly in opposition to all wrong, and to advance that which is right and just and true. The word of God would be their guide, and all oppression would be discarded. Lawmakers and administrators would abide by every good and just law, ever teaching the way of the Lord to do justice and judgment. God is the head of all good and just governments and laws. Those who are entrusted with the responsibility of administering any part of the law, are accountable to God as stewards of His goods. —*Review and Herald,* Oct. 1, 1895.

Reason Dethroned at Belshazzar's Feast.—In his pride and arrogancy, with a reckless feeling of security, Belshazzar "made a great feast to a thousand of his lords, and drank wine before the thousand." All the attractions that wealth and power could command, added splendor to the scene. Beautiful women with their enchantments were among the guests in attendance at the royal banquet. Men of genius and education were there. Princes and statesmen drank wine like water, and reveled under its maddening influence. With reason dethroned through shameless intoxication, and with lower impulses and passions now in the ascendancy, the king himself took the lead in the riotous orgy.—*Prophets and Kings,* page 523.

At the very moment when the feasting was at its height, a bloodless hand came forth, and traced on the wall of the banqueting room the doom of the king and his kingdom. "Mene, Mene, Tekel, Upharsin," were the words written, and they were interpreted by Daniel to mean, "Thou art weighed in the balances, and art found wanting. . . . Thy kingdom is divided, and given to the Medes and Persians." And the record tells us, "In that night was Belshazzar the king of the Chaldeans slain. And Darius the Median took the kingdom."

Little did Belshazzar think that an unseen Watcher beheld his idolatrous revelry. But there is nothing said or done that is not recorded on the books of heaven. The mystic characters traced by the bloodless hand testify that God is a witness to all we do, and that He is dishonored by feasting and reveling. We cannot hide anything from God. We cannot escape from our accountability to Him. Wherever we are and whatever we do, we are responsible to Him whose we are by creation and by redemption.—Manuscript 50, 1893.

Awful Result of Herod's Dissipation.—In many things Herod had reformed his dissolute life. But the use of luxurious food and stimulating drinks was constantly enervating and deadening the moral as well as the physical powers, and warring against the earnest appeals of the Spirit of God, which had struck conviction to the heart of Herod, arousing his conscience to put away his sins. Herodias was acquainted with the weak points in the character of Herod. She knew that under ordinary circumstances, while his intelligence controlled him, she could not obtain the death of John. . . .

She covered her hatred as best she could, looking forward to the birthday of Herod, which she knew would be an occasion of gluttony and intoxication. Herod's love of luxurious food and wine would give her an opportunity to throw him off his guard. She would entice him to indulge his appetite, which would arouse passion and lower the tone of the mental and moral character, making it impossible for his deadened sensibilities to see facts and evidences clearly, and make right decisions. She had the most costly preparations made for feasting, and voluptuous dissipation. She was acquainted with the influence of these intemperate feasts upon the intellect and morals. She knew that Herod's indulgence of appetite, pleasure, and amusement would excite the lower passions, and make him spiritless to the nobler demands of effort and duty.

The unnatural exhilaration which intemperance gives to the mind and spirits, lowers the sensibilities to moral improvement, making it impossible for holy impulses to affect the heart, and hold government over the passions, when public opinion and fashion sustain them. Festivities and amusements, dances, and free use of wine, becloud the senses, and remove the fear of God. . . .

As Herod and his lords were feasting and drinking in the pleasure saloon or banqueting hall, Herodias, debased with crime and passion, sent her daughter, dressed in a most enchanting manner, into the presence of Herod and his royal guests. Salome was decorated with costly garlands and flowers. She was adorned with sparkling jewels and flashing bracelets. With little covering and less modesty she danced for the amusement of the royal guests. To their perverted senses, the enchanting appearance of this, to them, vision of beauty and loveliness charmed them. Instead of being governed by enlightened reason, refined taste, or sensitive consciences, the lower qualities of the mind held the guiding reins. Virtue and principle had no controlling power.

The false enchantment of the dizzy scene seemed to take away reason and dignity from Herod and his guests, who were flushed with wine. The music and wine and dancing had removed the fear and reverence of God from them. Nothing seemed sacred to Herod's perverted senses. He was desirous to make some display which would exalt him still higher before the great men of his kingdom. And he rashly promised, and confirmed his promise with an oath, to give the daughter of Herodias whatever she might ask. . . .

Having obtained so wonderful a promise, she ran to her mother, desiring to know what she should ask. The mother's answer was ready, The head of John the Baptist in a charger. Salome at first was shocked. She did not understand the hidden revenge in her mother's heart. She refused to present such an inhuman request; but the determination of that wicked mother prevailed. Moreover, she bade her daughter make no delay, but hasten to prefer her request before Herod would have time for reflection, and to change his mind. Accordingly, Salome returned to Herod with her terrible petition, "I will that thou give me by and by in a charger the head of John the Baptist. And the king was exceeding sorry; yet for his oath's sake, and for their sakes which sat with him, he would not reject her."

Herod was astonished and confounded. His riotous mirth ceased, and his guests were thrilled with horror at this inhuman request. The frivolities and dissipation of that night cost the life of one of the most eminent prophets that ever bore a message from God to men. The intoxicating cup prepared the way for this terrible crime.—*Review and Herald,* March 11, 1873.

No Voice to Save John.—Why was there no voice to be heard in that company to keep Herod from fulfilling his mad vow? They were intoxicated with wine, and to their benumbed senses there was nothing to be reverenced.

Although the royal guests virtually had an invitation to release him from his oath, their tongues seemed paralyzed. Herod himself was under the delusion that he must, in order to save his own reputation, keep an oath made under the influence of intoxication. Moral principle, the only safeguard of the soul, was paralyzed. Herod and his guests were slaves, held in the lowest bondage to brute appetite. . . .

The mental powers were enervated by the pleasure of sense, which perverted their ideas of justice and mercy. Satan seized upon this opportunity, in the person of Herodias, to lead them to rush into decisions which cost the precious life of one of God's prophets.—*Review and Herald,* April 8, 1873.

Divine Warnings.—The Lord cannot bear much longer with an intemperate and perverse generation. There are many solemn warnings in the Scriptures against the use of intoxicating liquors. In days of old, when Moses was rehearsing the desire of Jehovah concerning His people, there were uttered against the drunkard the following words:

"And it come to pass, when he heareth the words of this curse, that he bless himself in his heart, saying, I shall have peace, though I walk in the imagination of mine heart, to add drunkenness to thirst: the Lord will not spare him, but then the anger of the Lord and His jealousy shall smoke against that man, and all the curses that are written in this book shall lie upon him, and the Lord shall blot out his name from under heaven."

Solomon says: "Wine is a mocker, strong drink is raging: and whosoever is deceived thereby is not wise." "Who hath woe? who hath sorrow? who hath contentions? who hath babbling? who hath wounds without cause? who hath redness of eyes? They that tarry long at the wine; they that go to seek mixed wine. Look not thou upon the wine when it is red, when it giveth his color in the cup, when it moveth itself aright. At the last it biteth like a serpent, and stingeth like an adder."

The use of wine among the Israelites was one of the causes

that finally resulted in their captivity. Through the prophet Amos the Lord said to them:

"Woe to them that are at ease in Zion. . . . Ye that put far away the evil day, and cause the seat of violence to come near; that lie upon beds of ivory, and stretch themselves upon their couches, and eat the lambs out of the flock, and the calves out of the midst of the stall; that chant to the sound of the viol, and invent to themselves instruments of music, like David; that drink wine in bowls, and anoint themselves with the chief ointments; but they are not grieved for the affliction of Joseph. Therefore now shall they go captive with the first that go captive, and the banquet of them that stretched themselves shall be removed."

"Woe to thee, O land, when thy king is a child, and thy princes eat in the morning! Blessed art thou, O land, when thy king is the son of nobles, and thy princes eat in due season, for strength, and not for drunkenness!" "It is not for kings, O Lemuel, it is not for kings to drink wine; nor for princes strong drink: lest they drink, and forget the law, and pervert the judgment of any of the afflicted."

These words of warning and command are pointed and decided. Let those in positions of public trust take heed lest through wine and strong drink they forget the law, and pervert judgment. Rulers and judges should ever be in a condition to fulfill the instruction of the Lord: "Ye shall not afflict any widow, or fatherless child. If thou afflict them in any wise, and they cry at all unto Me, I will surely hear their cry; and My wrath shall wax hot, and I will kill you with the sword; and your wives shall be widows, and your children fatherless."

The Lord God of heaven ruleth. He alone is above all authority, over all kings and rulers. The Lord has given special directions in His word in reference to the use of wine and strong drink. He has forbidden their use, and enforced

His prohibitions with strong warnings and threatenings. But His forbidding the use of intoxicating beverages is not an exercise of arbitrary authority. He seeks to restrain men, in order that they may escape from the evil results of indulgence in wine and strong drink. Degradation, cruelty, wretchedness, and strife follow as the natural results of intemperance. God has pointed out the consequences of following this course of evil. This He has done that there may not be a perversion of His laws, and that men may be spared the widespread misery resulting from the course of evil men who, for the sake of gain, sell maddening intoxicants.—*Drunkenness and Crime,* pages 4-6.

Section III

TOBACCO

1. Effects of Tobacco Use

What It Does to the Body.—Tobacco is a slow, insidious poison, and its effects are more difficult to cleanse from the system than those of liquor.—*Testimonies,* vol. 3, p. 569.

Tobacco using is a habit which frequently affects the nervous system in a more powerful manner than does the use of alcohol. It binds the victim in stronger bands of slavery than does the intoxicating cup; the habit is more difficult to overcome. Body and mind are, in many cases, more thoroughly intoxicated with the use of tobacco than with spirituous liquors, for it is a more subtle poison.—*Testimonies,* vol. 3, p. 562.

Tobacco Users Guilty Before God.—Tobacco, in whatever form it is used, tells upon the constitution. It is a slow poison. It affects the brain and benumbs the sensibilities, so that the mind cannot clearly discern spiritual things, especially those truths which would have a tendency to correct this filthy indulgence. Those who use tobacco in any form are not clear before God. In such a filthy practice it is impossible for them to glorify God in their bodies and spirits which are His. And while they are using slow and sure poisons, which are ruining their health, and debasing the faculties of the mind, God cannot approbate them. He may be merciful to them while they indulge in this pernicious habit in ignorance of the injury it is doing them, but when the matter is set before them in its true light, then they are guilty before God if they continue to indulge this gross appetite.—*Counsels on Health,* page 81.

Resistance Lowered and Restorative Powers Weakened.—God's healing power runs all through nature. If a human being cuts his flesh or breaks a bone, nature at once begins to heal the injury, and thus preserve the man's life. But man can place himself in a position where nature is trammeled so that she cannot do her work. . . . If tobacco is used, . . . the healing power of nature is weakened to a greater or less extent.—*Medical Ministry,* page 11.

Sowing and Reaping.—Let old and young remember that for every violation of the laws of life, nature will utter her protest. The penalty will fall upon the mental as well as the physical powers. And it does not end with the guilty trifler. The effects of his misdemeanors are seen in his offspring, and thus hereditary evils are passed down, even to the third or fourth generation. Think of this, fathers, when you indulge in the use of the soul-and-brain benumbing narcotic, tobacco. Where will this practice leave you? Whom will it affect besides yourselves?—*Signs of the Times,* Dec. 6, 1910.

Among children and youth the use of tobacco is working untold harm. The unhealthful practices of past generations affect the children and youth of today. Mental inability, physical weakness, disordered nerves, and unnatural cravings are transmitted as a legacy from parents to children. And the same practices, continued by the children, are increasing and perpetuating the evil results. To this cause in no small degree is owing the physical, mental, and moral deterioration, which is becoming such a cause of alarm.

Boys begin the use of tobacco at a very early age. The habit thus formed, when body and mind are especially susceptible to its effects, undermines the physical strength, dwarfs the body, stupefies the mind, and corrupts the morals.—*The Ministry of Healing,* pages 328, 329.

Beginnings of Tobacco Intemperance.—There is no natural appetite for tobacco in nature unless inherited.—Manuscript 9, 1893.

By the use of tea and coffee an appetite is formed for tobacco.—*Testimonies,* vol. 3, p. 563.

The highly seasoned flesh meats and the tea and coffee, which some mothers encourage their children to use, prepare the way for them to crave stronger stimulants, as tobacco. The use of tobacco encourages the appetite for liquor.—*Testimonies,* vol. 3, p. 488.

Food prepared with condiments and spices inflames the stomach, corrupts the blood, and paves the way to stronger stimulants. It induces nervous debility, impatience, and lack of self-control. Tobacco and the wine cup follow.—*Signs of the Times,* Oct. 27, 1887.

Lives Are Sacrificed.—Alcohol and tobacco pollute the blood of men, and thousands of lives are yearly sacrificed to these poisons.—*Health Reformer,* November, 1871.

Nature does her best to expel the poisonous drug, tobacco; but frequently she is overborne. She gives up her struggle to expel the intruder, and the life is sacrificed in the conflict.—Manuscript 3, 1897.

Tobacco Use Is Suicide.—God requires purity of heart, and personal cleanliness, now, as when He gave the special directions to the children of Israel. If God was so particular to enjoin cleanliness upon those journeying in the wilderness who were in the open air nearly all the time, He requires no less of us who live in ceiled houses, where impurities are more observable, and have a more unhealthful influence. Tobacco is a poison of the most deceitful and malignant kind, having an exciting, then a paralyzing influence upon the nerves of the body. It is all the more dangerous because its effects upon the system are so slow, and at first scarcely perceivable. Multitudes have fallen victims to its poisonous influence. They have surely murdered themselves by this slow poison. And we ask, What will be their waking in the resurrection morning? — *Spiritual Gifts,* vol.4, p.128.

There Is No Defense.—Intemperance of every kind is holding human beings as in a vise. Tobacco inebriates are multiplying. What shall we say of this evil? It is unclean; it is a narcotic; it stupefies the senses; it chains the will; it holds its victims in the slavery of habits difficult to overcome; it has Satan for its advocate. It destroys the clear perceptions of the mind that sin and corruption may not be distinguished from truth and holiness. This appetite for tobacco is self-destructive. It leads to a craving for something stronger,—fermented wines and liquors, all of which are intoxicating.—Letter 102a, 1897.

2. Tobacco's Polluting, Demoralizing Influence

We Meet It Everywhere.—Wherever we go, we encounter the tobacco devotee, enfeebling both mind and body by his darling indulgence. Have men a right to deprive their Maker and the world of the service which is their due? . . .

It is a disgusting habit, defiling to the user, and very annoying to others. We rarely pass through a crowd but men will puff their poisoned breath in our faces. It is unpleasant, if not dangerous, to remain in a railway car or in a room where the atmosphere is impregnated with the fumes of liquor and tobacco.—*Christian Temperance and Bible Hygiene,* pages 33, 34.

It Curses and Kills.—Women and children suffer from having to breathe the atmosphere that has been polluted by the pipe, the cigar, or the foul breath of the tobacco user. Those who live in this atmosphere will always be ailing.—*Testimonies,* vol. 5, p. 440.

The infant lungs suffer, and become diseased by inhaling the atmosphere of a room poisoned by the tobacco user's tainted breath. Many infants are poisoned beyond remedy by sleeping in beds with their tobacco-using fathers. By inhaling the poisonous tobacco effluvia, which is thrown from the lungs and pores of the skin, the system of the infant is filled with poison. While it acts upon some infants as a slow poison, and affects the brain, heart, liver, and lungs, and they waste away and fade gradually, upon others, it has a more direct influence, causing spasms, fits, paralysis, and sudden death.

The bereaved parents mourn the loss of their loved ones, and wonder at the mysterious providence of God which has so cruelly afflicted them, when Providence designed not the death of these infants. They died martyrs to filthy lust for tobacco. Every exhalation of the lungs of the tobacco slave, poisons the air about him.—*Health Reformer,* January, 1872.

A Factor in Increasing Crime.—The use of tobacco and strong drink has a great deal to do with the increase of disease and crime.—Manuscript 29, 1886.

The use of liquor or tobacco destroys the sensitive nerves of the brain, and benumbs the sensibilities. Under their influence crimes are committed that would have been left undone had the mind been clear and free from the influence of stimulants or narcotics.—Manuscript 38½, 1905.

Satan Controls the Paralyzed Mind.—Thousands are continually selling physical, mental, and moral vigor for the pleasure of taste. Each of the faculties has its distinctive office, and yet they all have a mutual dependence upon each other. And if the balance is carefully preserved, they will be kept in harmonious action. Not one of these faculties can be valued by dollars and cents. And yet, for a good dinner, for alcohol, or tobacco, they are sold. And while paralyzed by the indulgence of appetite, Satan controls the mind, and leads to every species of crime and wickedness.—*Review and Herald,* March 18, 1875.

Will the Women Smoke?—God forbid that woman should degrade herself to the use of a filthy and besotting narcotic. How disgusting is the picture which one may draw in the mind, of a woman whose breath is poisoned by tobacco. One shudders to think of little children twining their arms about her neck, and pressing their fresh, pure lips to that mother's lips, stained and polluted by the offensive fluid and odor of tobacco. Yet the picture is only more revolting because the reality is more rare than that of the father, the lord of the household, defiling himself with the disgusting weed. No wonder we see children turn from the kiss of the father whom they love, and if they kiss him seek not his lips, but his cheek or forehead, where their pure lips will not be contaminated. —*Health Reformer,* September, 1877.

The Only Safe Path.—Many are the temptations and besetments on every side to ruin the prospects of young men, both for this world and the next. But the only path of safety is for young and old to live in strict conformity to the principles of physical and moral law. The path of obedience is the only path that leads to heaven. Alcohol and tobacco inebriates would, at times, give any amount of money if they could by so doing overcome their appetite for these body-and-soul-destroying indulgences. And they who will not subject the appetites and passions to the control of reason, will indulge them at the expense of physical and moral obligation.—*Review and Herald,* March 18, 1875.

Tobacco's Enslaving Power.—In fastening upon men the terrible habit of tobacco using, it is Satan's purpose to palsy the brain and confuse the judgment, so that sacred things shall not be discerned. When once an appetite for this narcotic has been formed, it takes firm hold of the mind and the will of man, and he is in bondage under its power. Satan has the control of the will, and eternal realities are eclipsed. Man cannot stand forth in his God-given manhood; he is a slave to perverted appetite.—Letter 8, 1893.

Those who claim that tobacco does not injure them, can

be convinced of their mistake by depriving themselves of it for a few days; the trembling nerves, the giddy head, the irritability they feel, will prove to them that this sinful indulgence has bound them in slavery. It has overcome will power. They are in bondage to a vice that is fearful in its results.—*Signs of the Times,* Oct. 27, 1887.

The Witness of Those Who Overcame.—While speaking, we asked those to arise who had been addicted to the use of tobacco, but had entirely discontinued its use because of the light they had received through the truth. In response, between thirty-five and forty arose to their feet, ten or twelve of whom were women. We then invited those to arise who had been told by physicians that it would be fatal for them to stop the use of tobacco, because they had become so accustomed to its false stimulus that they would not be able to live without it. In reply, eight persons, whose countenances indicated health of mind and body, arose to their feet.—*Review and Herald,* August 23, 1877.

Warn Against Presumption.—Parents, warn your children against the sin of presumption. Teach them that it is presumption to educate an appetite for tobacco, liquor, or any hurtful thing. Teach them that their bodies are God's property. They are His by creation and by redemption. They are not their own; for they have been bought with a price. Teach them that the body is the temple of God, and that it is not to be made strengthless and diseased by the indulgence of appetite.

The Lord did not create the disease and imbecility now seen in the bodies and minds of the human race. The enemy has done this. He desires to enfeeble the body, knowing that it is the only medium through which mind and soul can be developed for the upbuilding of a symmetrical character. Habits which are contrary to the laws of nature, war constantly against the soul.

God calls upon you to do a work which through His grace you can do. How many sound bodies are there which can be presented to God as a sacrifice that He will accept in His service? How many are standing forth in their God-given manhood and womanhood? How many can show a purity of tastes, appetites, and habits that will bear comparison with Daniel's? How many have calm nerves, clear brain, unimpaired judgment?—*Signs of the Times,* April 4, 1900.

3. Defiling the Temple of God

Inconvenient, Expensive, Uncleanly.—The use of tobacco is an inconvenient, expensive, uncleanly habit. The teachings of Christ, pointing to purity, self-denial, and temperance, all rebuke this defiling practice. . . . Is it for the glory of God for men to enfeeble the physical powers, confuse the brain, and yield the will to this narcotic poison?—*Christian Temperance and Bible Hygiene,* pages 17, 18.

Looking Through Clouded Windows.—The youth who has made a practice of using tobacco has defiled the whole man. The will has no longer the promptness and force which made him trustworthy and of value before he accepted the enemy's poison. . . . His mind need not have decayed. He need not have lost the inspiration that comes from God. But when the human agent works in perfect harmony with the destroyer, enervating the sinews and muscles, the fluids and solids, of the whole human structure, he is dulling the machinery through which the intellect works. He is clouding the windows through which he looks. He sees everything in a perverted light.—Manuscript 17, 1898.

Incense to His Satanic Majesty.—As I have seen men who claimed to enjoy the blessing of entire sanctification, while they were slaves to tobacco, spitting and defiling everything around them, I have thought, How would heaven appear with tobacco users in it? The lips that were taking the precious name of Christ were defiled by tobacco spittle, the breath was polluted with the stench, and even the linen was defiled; the soul that loved this uncleanness and enjoyed this poisonous atmosphere must also be defiled. The sign was hung upon the outside, testifying of what was within.

Men professing godliness offer their bodies upon Satan's altar, and burn the incense of tobacco to his satanic majesty. Does this statement seem severe? The offering must be presented to some deity. As God is pure and holy, and will accept nothing defiling in its character, He refuses this expensive, filthy, and unholy sacrifice; therefore we conclude that Satan is the one who claims the honor.—*Counsels on Health,* page 83.

The Pipe Versus Heaven.—I have seen many an example of the power of these habits. One woman I knew who was advised by her physician to smoke as a remedy for the asthma. To all appearance she had been a zealous Christian for many years, but she became so addicted to smoking that when urged to give it up as an unhealthful and defiling habit, she utterly refused to do so. She said, "When the matter comes before my mind distinctly, that I must give up my pipe or lose heaven, then I say, 'Farewell heaven;' I cannot surrender my pipe." This woman only put into words that which many express by their actions. God, the maker of heaven and earth, He who created man and claims the whole heart, the entire affections, is held subordinate to the disgusting, defiling nuisance, tobacco.—*Letter 8, 1893.*

That Christ should be discarded for these soul-and-body-destroying indulgences, is an amazement to the unfallen universe.—*Letter 8, 1893.*

Dulls Appreciation of Atonement and Eternal Things.—When we pursue a course of eating and drinking that lessens physical and mental vigor, or become the prey of habits that tend to the same results, we dishonor God, for we rob Him of the service He claims from us. Those who acquire and indulge the unnatural appetite for tobacco, do this at the expense of health. They are destroying nervous energy, lessening vital force, and sacrificing mental strength.

Those who profess to be the followers of Christ, yet have this terrible sin at their door, cannot have a high appreciation of the atonement and an elevated estimate of eternal things. Minds that are clouded and partially paralyzed by narcotics, are easily overcome by temptation, and cannot enjoy communion with God.—*Signs of the Times,* Jan. 6, 1876.

If Christ and the Apostles Were Here.—James says that the wisdom which is from above is "first pure." If he had seen his brethren using tobacco, would he not have denounced the practice as "earthly, sensual, devilish"?—*The Sanctified Life,* page 24.

Were Peter upon the earth now he would exhort the professed followers of Christ to abstain from fleshly lusts which war against the soul. And Paul would call upon the churches in general to cleanse themselves from all filthiness of the flesh and spirit, perfecting holiness in the fear of God. And Christ would drive from the temple those who are defiled by the use of tobacco, polluting the sanctuary of God by their tobaccoized breaths. He would say to these worshipers, as He did to the Jews, "My house shall be called of all nations the house of prayer; but ye have made it a den of thieves." We would say to such, Your unholy offerings of ejected quids of tobacco defile the temple, and are abhorred of God. Your worship is not acceptable, for your bodies which should be the temple for the Holy Ghost are defiled. You also rob the treasury of God of thousands of dollars through the indulgence of unnatural appetite.—*Signs of the Times,* Aug. 13, 1874.

Tobacco-Using Priests Would Have Suffered Death.—The priests, who ministered in sacred things, were commanded to wash their feet and their hands before entering the tabernacle in the presence of God to importune for Israel, that they might not desecrate the sanctuary. If the priests had entered the sanctuary with their mouths polluted with tobacco, they would have shared the fate of Nadab and Abihu. And yet professed Christians bow before God in their families to pray with their mouths defiled with the filth of tobacco. . . .

Be Ye Clean.—Men who have been set apart by the laying on of hands, to minister in sacred things, often stand in the desk with their mouths polluted, their lips stained, and their breath tainted with the defilements of tobacco. They speak to the people in Christ's stead. How can such service be acceptable to a holy God, who required the priests of Israel to make such special preparations before coming into His presence, lest His sacred holiness should consume them for dishonoring Him, as in the case of Nadab and Abihu?

These may be assured that the mighty God of Israel is still a God of cleanliness. They profess to be serving God while they are committing idolatry, by making a god of their appetite. Tobacco is their cherished idol. To it every high and sacred consideration must bow. They profess to be worshiping God, while at the same time they are violating the first commandment. They have other gods before the Lord. "Be ye clean that bear the vessels of the Lord."—*Spiritual Gifts,* vol. 4, pp. 127, 128.

He Will Not Defile God's Temple.—God desires all who believe in Him to feel the necessity of improvement. Every entrusted faculty is to be enlarged. Not one gift is to be laid aside. As God's husbandry and building, man is under His supervision in every sense of the word, and the better he becomes acquainted with his Maker, the more sacred will his life become in his estimation. He will not place tobacco in his mouth, knowing that it defiles God's temple. He will not drink wine or liquor, for, like tobacco, it degrades the whole being.—Manuscript 130, 1899.

4. An Economic Waste

God's Money Squandered.—The love of tobacco is a warring lust. Means are thereby squandered that would aid in the good work of clothing the naked, feeding the hungry, and sending the truth to poor souls out of Christ. What a record will appear when the accounts of life are balanced in the book of God! It will then appear that vast sums of money have been expended for tobacco and alcoholic liquors! For what? To ensure health and prolong life? Oh, no! To aid in the perfection of Christian character and a fitness for the society of holy angels? Oh, no! But to minister to a depraved, unnatural appetite for that which poisons and kills not only the user but those to whom he transmits his legacy of disease and imbecility.—*Signs of the Times,* Oct. 27, 1887.

All Must Give an Account.—Millions of dollars are spent for stimulants and narcotics. All this money rightfully belongs to God, and those who thus misappropriate His entrusted goods will someday be called to give an account of how they have used their Lord's goods.—Letter 243a, 1905.

Tobacco Users to Look Over the Record.—Have you considered your responsibility as God's stewards, for the means in your hands? How much of the Lord's money do you spend for tobacco? Reckon up what you have thus spent during your lifetime. How does the amount consumed by this defiling lust compare with what you have given for the relief of the poor and the spread of the gospel?

No human being needs tobacco, but multitudes are perishing for want of the means that by its use is worse than wasted. Have you not been misappropriating the Lord's goods? Have you not been guilty of robbery toward God and your fellow men? Know ye not that "ye are not your own? For ye are bought with a price; therefore glorify God in your body, and in your spirit, which are God's." 1 Corinthians 6:19, 20.—*The Ministry of Healing,* page 330.

Appetite Versus Natural Affection and Claims of God.—Those who are slaves to tobacco will see their families suffering for the conveniences of life, and for necessary food, yet they have not the power of will to forgo their tobacco. The clamors of appetite prevail over natural affection. Appetite, which they have in common with the brute, controls them. The cause of Christianity, and even humanity, would not in any case be met, if dependent upon those in the habitual use of tobacco and liquor. If they had means to use only in one direction, the treasury of God would not be replenished, but they would have their tobacco and liquor. The tobacco idolater will not deny his appetite for the cause of God.—*Review and Herald,* Sept. 8, 1874.

Taking the Lead in Self-Denial, Self-Sacrifice, and Temperance.—The man who has become the property of Jesus Christ, and whose body is the temple of the Holy Ghost, will not be enslaved by the pernicious habit of tobacco using. His powers belong to Christ, who has bought him with the price of blood. His property is the Lord's. How, then, can he be guiltless in expending every day the Lord's entrusted capital to gratify an appetite which has no foundation in nature?

An enormous sum is yearly squandered for this indulgence, while souls are perishing for the word of life. Professed Christians rob God in tithes and offerings, while they offer on the altar of destroying lust, in the use of tobacco, more than they give to relieve the poor or to supply the wants of God's cause. Those who are truly sanctified, will overcome every hurtful lust. Then all these channels of needless expense will be turned to the Lord's treasury, and Christians will take the lead in self-denial, in self-sacrifice, and in temperance. Then they will be the light of the world.—*The Sanctified Life,* pages 24, 25.

5. The Power of Example

The Older Ones Set the Example.—How often do we see boys not more than eight years old using tobacco! If you speak to them about it, they say, "My father uses it, and if it does him good, it will me." They point to the minister or the Sunday school superintendent, and say, "If such good men as they use it, surely I can." How can we expect anything else of the children, with their inherited tendencies, while the older ones set them such an example?—*Christian Temperance and Bible Hygiene,* page 18.

Popularity of the Tobacco Habit.—So powerful is the habit when once formed, that the use of tobacco becomes popular. An example of sin is set before youth, whose minds should be disabused of all thought that the use of the narcotic is not harmful. They are not told of its injurious effects on the physical, mental, and moral powers. . . .

If a follower of Christ allows himself to be led astray by the influence of others, and conforms to the fashionable dissipation of the world, he is under Satan's sway, and his sin is even greater than is the sin of avowed unbelievers,—the ungodly,—because he is standing under false colors. His life is inconsistent; professedly a Christian, in practice he is yielding to unnatural, sinful propensities that war against the purification and elevation necessary for spiritual superiority. . . .

Becoming conformed to the habit, in practice they are in fellowship with the world. All such who claim to be Christians, have no right to assume this name; for a Christian is one who is Christlike. When the judgment sits and all are judged according to the deeds done in the body, they will learn that they have misrepresented Christ in practical life, and have not made themselves a savor of life unto life, but a savor of death unto death. In fellowship with them will be a numerous company who have conformed to lustful practices; but numbers will neither excuse their iniquity, nor lessen their condemnation for destroying the brain nerve power and the physical health. All will be judged personally. They will stand before God to hear their sentence.—Manuscript 123, 1901.

Smoking Clergymen.—How many there are who minister in the sacred desk, in Christ's stead, and are beseeching men to be reconciled to God, and are exalting the free gospel, who are themselves slaves to appetite, and are defiled with tobacco. They are daily weakening their nerve brain power by the use of a filthy narcotic. And these men profess to be ambassadors for the holy Jesus.—*Health Reformer,* December, 1871.

No man can be a true minister of righteousness, and yet be under the inspiration of sensual appetites. He cannot indulge the habit of using tobacco, and yet win souls to the platform of true temperance. The cloud of smoke coming from his lips has no salutary effect upon liquor drinkers. The gospel sermon must come from lips undefiled by tobacco smoke. With pure, clean lips God's servants must tell the triumphs of the cross. The practice of using liquor, tobacco, tea, and coffee must be overcome by the converting power of God. There shall nothing enter into the kingdom of God that defileth.—Manuscript 86, 1897.

When clergymen throw their influence and example on the side of this injurious habit, what hope is there for young men? We must raise the standard of temperance higher and still higher. We must bear a clear, decided testimony against the use of intoxicating drinks and the use of tobacco.—Manuscript 82, 1900.

The Tobacco-Using Physician.—Many come under the physician's care who are ruining soul and body by the use of tobacco or intoxicating drink. The physician who is true to his responsibility must point out to these patients the cause of their suffering. But if he himself is a user of tobacco or intoxicants, what weight will be given to his words? With the consciousness of his own indulgence before him, will he not hesitate to point out the plague spot in the life of his patient? While using these things himself, how can he convince the youth of their injurious effects?

How can a physician stand in the community as an example of purity and self-control, how can he be an effectual worker in the temperance cause, while he himself is indulging a vile habit? How can he minister acceptably at the bedside of the sick and the dying, when his very breath is offensive, laden with the odor of liquor or tobacco?

While disordering his nerves and clouding his brain by the use of narcotic poisons, how can one be true to the trust reposed in him as a skillful physician? How impossible for him to discern quickly or to execute with precision!

If he does not observe the laws that govern his own being, if he chooses selfish gratification above soundness of mind and body, does he not thereby declare himself unfit to be entrusted with the responsibility of human lives?—*The Ministry of Healing,* pages 133, 134.

Father Disqualified for Parental Responsibilities.—Fathers, the golden hours which you might spend in getting a thorough knowledge of the temperament and character of your children, and the best method of dealing with their young minds, are too precious to be squandered in the pernicious habit of smoking, or in lounging about the dramshop.

The indulgence of this poisonous stimulant disqualifies the father to bring up his children in the nurture and admonition of the Lord. The directions given by God to the children of Israel were that the fathers should teach their children the statutes and precepts of His law, when they rose up, and when they sat down, when they went out, and when they came in.

This commandment of God is too little heeded; for Satan, through his temptations, has chained many fathers in the slavery of gross habits, and hurtful appetites. Their physical, mental, and moral powers are so paralyzed by these means that it is impossible for them to do their duty toward their families. Their minds are so besotted by the stupefying influences of tobacco or liquor that they do not realize their responsibility to train their children so that they may have moral power to resist temptation, to control appetite, to stand for the right, not to be influenced to evil, but to yield a strong influence for good.

Parents by a sinful indulgence of perverted appetite often place themselves in a condition of nervous excitability or exhaustion, where they are unable to discriminate between right and wrong, to manage their children wisely, and to judge correctly their motives and actions. They are in danger of magnifying little matters to mountains in their minds, while they pass lightly over grave sins. The father who has become a slave to abnormal appetite, who has sacrificed his God-given manhood to become a tobacco inebriate, cannot teach his children to control appetite and passion. It is impossible for him to thus educate them either by precept or example. How can the father whose mouth is filled with tobacco, whose breath poisons the atmosphere of home, teach his sons lessons of temperance and self-control? . . .

Held Accountable for Example and Influence.—When we approach the youth who are acquiring the habit of using tobacco, and tell them of its pernicious influence upon the system, they frequently fortify themselves by citing the example of their fathers, or that of certain Christian ministers, or good and pious members of the church. They say, "If it does them no harm, it certainly cannot injure me." What an account will professed Christian men have to render to God for their intemperance! Their example strengthens the temptations of Satan to pervert the senses of the young by the use of artificial stimulants; it seems to them not a very bad thing to do what respectable church members are in the habit of doing. But it is only a step from tobacco using to liquor drinking; in fact, the two vices usually go together.

Thousands learn to be drunkards from such influences as these. Too often the lesson has been unconsciously taught them by their own fathers. A radical change must be made in the heads of families before much progress can be made in ridding society of the monster of intemperance.—*Health Reformer,* September, 1877.

Tobacco User No Help to Inebriates.—As twin evils, tobacco and alcohol go together.—*Review and Herald,* July 9, 1901.

Those who use tobacco can make but a poor plea to the liquor inebriate. Two thirds of the drunkards in our land created an appetite for liquor by the use of tobacco.—*Signs of the Times,* Oct. 27, 1887.

Tobacco Users in Temperance Work.—Tobacco users cannot be acceptable workers in the temperance cause, for there is no consistency in their profession to be temperance men. How can they talk to the man who is destroying reason and life by liquor drinking, when their pockets are filled with tobacco, and they long to be free to chew and smoke and spit all they please? How can they with any degree of consistency plead for moral reforms before boards of health and from temperance platforms while they themselves are under the stimulus of tobacco? If they would have power to influence the people to overcome their love for stimulants, their words must come forth with pure breath and from clean lips.—*Testimonies,* vol. 5, p. 441.

What power can the tobacco devotee have to stay the progress of intemperance? There must be a revolution upon the subject of tobacco before the ax will be laid at the root of the tree. Tea, coffee, and tobacco, as well as alcoholic drinks, are different degrees in the scale of artificial stimulants.—*Christian Temperance and Bible Hygiene,* page 34.

Section IV

OTHER STIMULANTS AND NARCOTICS

1. Abstain From Fleshly Lusts

There Is Always a Reaction.—Under the head of stimulants and narcotics is classed a great variety of articles that, altogether used as food or drink, irritate the stomach, poison the blood, and excite the nerves. Their use is a positive evil. Men seek the excitement of stimulants, because, for the time, the results are agreeable. But there is always a reaction. The use of unnatural stimulants always tends to excess, and it is an active agent in promoting physical degeneration and decay.—*The Ministry of Healing,* page 325.

Peter's All-Inclusive Warning.—"Abstain from fleshly lusts, which war against the soul," is the language of the apostle Peter. Many regard this warning as applicable only to the licentious; but it has a broader meaning. It guards against every injurious gratification of appetite or passion. It is a most forcible warning against the use of such stimulants and narcotics as tea, coffee, tobacco, alcohol, and morphine. These indulgences may well be classed among the lusts that exert a pernicious influence upon moral character. The earlier these hurtful habits are formed, the more firmly will they hold their victim in slavery to lust, and the more certainly will they lower the standard of spirituality.—*Counsels on Diet and Foods,* pages 62, 63.

Lessens Physical and Mental Activity.—Never be betrayed into indulging in the use of stimulants: for this will result not only in reaction and loss of physical strength, but in a benumbed intellect.—*Testimonies,* vol. 4, p. 214.

Vital energy is imparted to the mind through the brain; therefore the brain should never be dulled by the use of narcotics or excited by the use of stimulants. Brain, bone, and muscle, are to be brought into harmonious action, that all may work as well-regulated machines, each part acting in harmony, not one being overtaxed.—Letter 100, 1898.

When those who are in the habit of using tea, coffee, tobacco, opium, or spirituous liquors, are deprived of the accustomed indulgence, they find it impossible to engage with interest and zeal in the worship of God. Divine grace seems powerless to enliven or spiritualize their prayers or their testimonies. These professed Christians should consider the source of their enjoyment. Is it from above, or from beneath?—*The Sanctified Life,* page 25.

Advanced Age of Some Users No Argument.—Those who use tea, coffee, opium, and alcohol, may sometimes live to old age, but this fact is no argument in favor of the use of these stimulants. What these persons might have accomplished, but failed to do because of their intemperate habits, the great day of God alone will reveal.—*Christian Temperance and Bible Hygiene,* page 35.

Not All Tempted Alike.—Some look with horror upon men who have been overcome with liquor, and are seen reeling and staggering in the street, while at the same time they are gratifying their appetite for things differing in their nature from spirituous liquor, but which injure the health, affect the brain, and destroy their high sense of spiritual things. The liquor drinker has an appetite for strong drink which he gratifies, while another has no appetite for intoxicating drinks to restrain, but he desires some other hurtful indulgence, and does not practice self-denial any more than the drunkard.—*Spiritual Gifts,* vol. 4, p. 125.

Satan's Counterfeit of the Tree of Life.—From beginning to end, the crime of tobacco using, of opium and drug medication, has its origin in perverted knowledge. It is through plucking and eating of poisonous fruit, through the intricacies of names that the common people do not understand, that thousands and ten thousands of lives are lost. This great knowledge, supposed by men to be so wonderful, God did not mean that man should have. They are using the poisonous productions that Satan himself has planted to take the place of the tree of life, whose leaves are for the healing of the nations. Men are dealing in liquors and narcotics that are destroying the human family.—Manuscript 119, 1898.

2. Tea and Coffee

The stimulating diet and drink of this day are not conducive to the best state of health. Tea, coffee, and tobacco are all stimulating, and contain poisons. They are not only unnecessary, but harmful, and should be discarded if we would add to knowledge, temperance.—*Review and Herald,* Feb. 21, 1888.

Stimulants—Not Foods.—Tea and coffee do not nourish the system. The relief obtained from them is sudden, before the stomach has time to digest them. This shows that what the users of these stimulants call strength is only received by exciting the nerves of the stomach, which convey the irritation to the brain, and this in turn is aroused to impart increased action to the heart and short-lived energy to the entire system. All this is false strength that we are the worse for having. They do not give a particle of natural strength.—*Testimonies,* vol. 2, p. 65.

The health is in no way improved by the use of those things which stimulate for a time, but afterward cause a reaction which leaves the system lower than before. Tea and coffee whip up the flagging energies for the time being; but when their immediate influence has gone, a feeling of depression is the result. These beverages have no nourishment whatever in themselves. The milk and sugar it contains constitute all the nourishment afforded by a cup of tea or coffee.—*Counsels on Diet and Foods,* page 425.

Because these stimulants produce for the time being such agreeable results, many conclude that they really need them and continue their use. But there is always a reaction. The nervous system, having been unduly excited, borrowed power for present use from its future resources of strength.—*Testimonies,* vol. 3, p. 487.

What Tea Does.—Tea . . . enters into the circulation and gradually impairs the energy of body and mind. It stimulates, excites, and quickens the motion of the living machinery, forcing it to unnatural action, and thus gives the tea drinker the impression that it is doing him great service, imparting to him strength. This is a mistake.

Tea draws upon the strength of the nerves and leaves them greatly weakened. When its influence is gone and the increased action caused by its use is abated, then what is the result? Languor and debility corresponding to the artificial vivacity the tea imparted.

When the system is already overtaxed and needs rest, the use of tea spurs up nature by stimulation to perform unwonted, unnatural action, and thereby lessens her power to perform and her ability to endure; and her powers give out long before Heaven designed they should. Tea is poisonous to the system. Christians should let it alone. . . . The second effect of tea drinking is headache, wakefulness, palpitation of the heart, indigestion, trembling of the nerves, with many other evils.—*Testimonies,* vol. 2, pp. 64, 65.

Coffee Still More Harmful.—The influence of coffee is in a degree the same as tea, but the effect upon the system is still worse. Its influence is exciting, and just in the degree that it elevates above par it will exhaust and bring prostration below par. Tea and coffee drinkers carry the marks upon their faces. . . . The glow of health is not seen upon the countenance.—*Testimonies,* vol. 2, pp. 64, 65.

Coffee is a hurtful indulgence. It temporarily excites the mind, . . . but the aftereffect is exhaustion, prostration, paralysis of the mental, moral, and physical powers. The mind becomes enervated, and unless through determined effort the habit is overcome, the activity of the brain is permanently lessened.—*Christian Temperance and Bible Hygiene,* page 34.

Effects of All Caffeine Drinks.—The action of coffee and many other popular drinks is similar. The first effect is exhilarating. The nerves of the stomach are excited; these convey irritation to the brain, and this in turn is aroused to impart increased action to the heart, and short-lived energy to the entire system. Fatigue is forgotten; the strength seems to be increased. The intellect is aroused, the imagination becomes more vivid.—*The Ministry of Healing,* page 326.

By this continual course of indulgence of appetite the natural vigor of the constitution becomes gradually and imperceptibly impaired. If we would preserve a healthy action of all the powers of the system, nature must not be forced to unnatural action. Nature will stand at her post of duty, and do her work wisely and efficiently, if the false props that have been brought in to take the place of nature are expelled.—*Review and Herald,* April 19, 1887.

Cause of Time Lost on Account of Sickness.—Many who have accustomed themselves to the use of stimulating drinks, suffer from headache and nervous prostration, and lose much time on account of sickness. They imagine they cannot live without the stimulus, and are ignorant of its effect upon health. What makes it the more dangerous is, that its evil effects are so often attributed to other causes.—*Christian Temperance and Bible Hygiene,* page 35.

Habit-Forming Beverages.—Tea and coffee are neither wholesome nor necessary. They are of no use as far as the health of the body is concerned. But practice in the use of these things becomes habit.—Manuscript 86, 1897.

An Unnatural Craving Produced.—The continued use of these nerve irritants is followed by headache, wakefulness, palpitation of the heart, indigestion, trembling, and many other evils; for they wear away the life forces. Tired nerves need rest and quiet instead of stimulation and overwork. Nature needs time to recuperate her exhausted energies. When her forces are goaded on by the use of stimulants, more will be accomplished for a time; but as the system becomes debilitated by their constant use, it gradually becomes more difficult to rouse the energies to the desired point. The demand for stimulants becomes more difficult to control, until the will is overborne, and there seems to be no power to deny the unnatural craving. Stronger and still stronger stimulants are called for, until exhausted nature can no longer respond.—*The Ministry of Healing,* pages 326, 327.

Preparing the System for Disease.—It is these hurtful stimulants that are surely undermining the constitution and preparing the system for acute diseases, by impairing Nature's fine machinery and battering down her fortifications erected against disease and premature decay.—*Testimonies,* vol. 1, pp. 548, 549.

The Whole System Suffers.—Through the use of stimulants, the whole system suffers. The nerves are unbalanced, the liver is morbid in its action, the quality and circulation of the blood are affected, and the skin becomes inactive and sallow. The mind, too, is injured. The immediate influence of these stimulants is to excite the brain to undue activity, only to leave it weaker and less capable of exertion. The aftereffect is prostration, not only mental and physical, but moral. As a result we see nervous men and women, of unsound judgment and unbalanced mind. They often manifest a hasty, impatient, accusing spirit, viewing the faults of others as through a magnifying glass, and utterly unable to discern their own defects.—*Christian Temperance and Bible Hygiene,* pages 35, 36.

The Tongue Is Loosened.—When these tea and coffee users meet together for social entertainment, the effects of their pernicious habit are manifest. All partake freely of the favorite beverages, and as the stimulating influence is felt, their tongues are loosened, and they begin the wicked work of talking against others. Their words are not few or well chosen. The tidbits of gossip are passed around, too often the poison of scandal as well. These thoughtless gossipers forget that they have a witness. An unseen Watcher is writing their words in the books of heaven. All these unkind criticisms, these exaggerated reports, these envious feelings, expressed under the excitement of the cup of tea, Jesus registers as against Himself. "Inasmuch as ye have done it unto one of the least of these My brethren, ye have done it unto Me."—*Christian Temperance and Bible Hygiene,* page 36.

An Economic Waste.—The money expended for tea and coffee is worse than wasted. They do the user only harm, and that continually.—*Christian Temperance and Bible Hygiene,* page 35.

Destructive Narcotics.—All should bear a clear testimony against tea and coffee, never using them. They are narcotics, injurious alike to the brain and to the other organs of the body.—*Counsels on Diet and Foods,* page 430.

Destroys Temple of God.—The drunkard sells his reason for a cup of poison. Satan takes control of his reason, affections, conscience. Such a man is destroying the temple of God. Tea drinking helps to do this same work. Yet how many there are who place these destroying agencies on their tables, thereby quenching the divine attributes.—*Manuscript 130, 1899.*

Use Inimical to Spiritual Life.—Tea and coffee drinking is a sin, an injurious indulgence, which, like other evils, injures the soul. These darling idols create an excitement, a morbid action of the nervous system.—*Counsels on Diet and Foods,* page 425.

Those who indulge a perverted appetite, do it to the injury of health and intellect. They cannot appreciate the value of spiritual things. Their sensibilities are blunted, and sin does not appear very sinful, and truth is not regarded of greater value than earthly treasure.—*Spiritual Gifts,* vol. 4, p. 129.

Less Susceptible to Holy Spirit's Influence.—To a user of stimulants, everything seems insipid without the darling indulgence. This deadens the natural sensibilities of both body and mind, and renders him less susceptible to the influence of the Holy Spirit. In the absence of the usual stimulant, he has a hungering of body and soul, not for righteousness, not for holiness, not for God's presence, but for his cherished idol. In the indulgence of hurtful lusts, professed Christians are daily enfeebling their powers, making it impossible to glorify God.—*The Sanctified Life,* page 25.

Fosters Desire for Stronger Stimulants.—By the use of tea and coffee an appetite is formed for tobacco, and this encourages the appetite for liquors.—*Testimonies,* vol. 3, p. 563.

Some Have Backslidden.—Some have backslidden and tampered with tea and coffee. Those who break the laws of health will become blinded in their minds and break the law of God.—*Review and Herald,* Oct. 21, 1884.

God's People Must Overcome.—Those who have received instruction regarding the evils of the use of flesh foods, tea and coffee, and rich and unhealthful food preparations, and who are determined to make a covenant with God by sacrifice, will not continue to indulge their appetite for food that they know to be unhealthful. God demands that the appetites be cleansed, and that self-denial be practiced in regard to those things which are not good. This is a work that will have to be done before His people can stand before Him a perfected people.—*Testimonies,* vol. 9, pp. 153, 154.

Determined Perseverance Will Bring Victory.—Those who use these slow poisons, like the tobacco user, think they cannot live without them, because they feel so very bad when they do not have these idols.

Why they suffer when they discontinue the use of these stimulants, is because they have been breaking down nature in her work of preserving the entire system in harmony and in health. They will be troubled with dizziness, headache, numbness, nervousness, and irritability. They feel as though they should go all to pieces, and some have not courage to persevere in abstaining from them till abused nature recovers, but again resort to the use of the same hurtful things. They do not give nature time to recover the injury they have done her, but for present relief return to these hurtful indulgences. Nature is continually growing weaker, and less capable of recovering. But if they will be determined in their efforts to persevere and overcome, abused nature will soon again rally, and perform her work wisely and well without these stimulants.—*Spiritual Gifts,* vol. 4, pp. 128, 129.

In some cases it is as difficult to break up this tea and coffee habit as it is for the inebriate to discontinue the use of liquor.—*Counsels on Health,* page 442.

A Pledge Embracing Tea and Coffee.—All these nerve irritants are wearing away the life forces; and the restlessness, the impatience, the mental feebleness caused by shattered nerves, become a warring element, ever working against spiritual progress. Shall Christians bring their appetite under the control of reason, or will they continue its indulgence because they feel so "let down" without it, like the drunkard without his stimulant? Shall not those who advocate temperance reform awake in regard to these injurious things also? And shall not the pledge embrace coffee and tea as hurtful stimulants?—*Counsels on Health,* page 442.

Some Need to Take This Step.—We hope to carry our brethren and sisters up to a still higher standard to sign the pledge to abstain from Java coffee and the herb that comes from China. We see that there are some who need to take this step in reform.—*Review and Herald,* April 19, 1887.

Proper Course at the Tables of Others—a Word to Colporteur Evangelists.—If you sit at their table, eat temperately, and only of food that will not confuse the mind. Keep yourself from all intemperance. Be yourself an object lesson, illustrating right principles. If they offer you tea to drink, tell them in simple words its injurious effect on the system.—Manuscript 23, 1890.

Following Jesus in the Path of Reform.—Jesus overcame on the point of appetite, and so may we. Let us move on, then, step by step, advancing in reform until all our habits shall be in accordance with the laws of life and health. The Redeemer of the world in the wilderness of temptation fought the battle upon the point of appetite in our behalf. As our surety He overcame, thus making it possible for man to overcome in His name. "To him that overcometh will I grant to sit with Me in My throne, even as I also overcame, and am set down with My Father in His throne."—*Review and Herald,* April 19, 1887.

3. Drugs

The Usual but Dangerous Course.—A practice that is laying the foundation of a vast amount of disease and of even more serious evils, is the free use of poisonous drugs. When attacked by disease, many will not take the trouble to search

Other Stimulants and Narcotics

out the cause of their illness. Their chief anxiety is to rid themselves of pain and inconvenience. So they resort to patent nostrums, of whose real properties they know little, or they apply to a physician for some remedy to counteract the result of their misdoing, but with no thought of making a change in their unhealthful habits. If immediate benefit is not realized, another medicine is tried, and then another. Thus the evil continues.—*The Ministry of Healing,* page 126.

Medicine at Any Cost.—The sick are in a hurry to get well, and the friends of the sick are impatient. They will have medicine, and if they do not feel that powerful influence upon their systems their erroneous views lead them to think they should feel, they impatiently change for another physician. The change often increases the evil. They go through a course of medicine equally as dangerous as the first.—*How to Live,* No. 3, p. 62.

The Sad Result.—By the use of poisonous drugs, many bring upon themselves lifelong illness, and many lives are lost that might be saved by the use of natural methods of healing. The poisons contained in many so-called remedies create habits and appetites that mean ruin to both soul and body. Many of the popular nostrums called patent medicines, and even some of the drugs dispensed by physicians, act a part in laying the foundation of the liquor habit, the opium habit, the morphine habit, that are so terrible a curse to society.—*The Ministry of Healing,* pages 126, 127.

Nervous System Deranged.—Drugs given to stupefy, whatever they may be, derange the nervous system.—*How to Live,* No. 3, p. 57.

A Penalty Fixed for Every Transgression.—God has formed laws which govern our constitutions, and these laws which He has placed in our being are divine, and for every transgression there is affixed a penalty, which must sooner or later be realized. The majority of diseases which the human family have been and still are suffering under, they have created by ignorance of their own organic laws. They seem indifferent in regard to the matter of health, and work perseveringly to tear themselves to pieces, and when broken down and debilitated in body and mind, send for the doctor and drug themselves to death.—*Counsels on Diet and Foods,* page 19.

Simple Living Versus the Drugstore.—Thousands who are afflicted might recover their health, if, instead of depending upon the drugstore for their life, they would discard all drugs, and live simply, without using tea, coffee, liquor, or spices, which irritate the stomach and leave it weak, unable to digest even simple food without stimulation. The Lord is willing to let His light shine forth in clear, distinct rays to all who are weak and feeble.—*Medical Ministry,* page 229.

A Reckless Course.—To use drugs while continuing evil habits, is certainly inconsistent, and greatly dishonors God by dishonoring the body which He has made. Yet for all this, stimulants and drugs continue to be prescribed, and freely used by human beings, while the hurtful indulgences that produce the disease are not discarded.—*Letter 19, 1892.*

Those who will gratify their appetite, and then suffer because, of their intemperance, and take drugs to relieve them, may be assured that God will not interpose to save health and life which is so recklessly periled. The cause has produced the effect. Many, as their last resort, follow the directions in the word of God, and request the prayers of the elders of the church for their restoration to health. God does not see fit to answer prayers offered in behalf of such, for He knows that if they should be restored to health, they would again sacrifice it upon the altar of unhealthy appetite.—*Spiritual Gifts,* vol. 4, p. 145.

A Sin Against the Children.—If those who take these drugs

Other Stimulants and Narcotics

were alone the sufferers, then the evil would not be as great. But parents not only sin against themselves in swallowing drug poisons, but they sin against their children. The vitiated state of their blood, the poison distributed throughout the system, the broken constitution, and various drug diseases, as the result of drug poisons, are transmitted to their offspring, and left them as a wretched inheritance, which is another great cause of the degeneracy of the race.—*How to Live,* No. 3, p. 50.

Easier to Use Drugs.—Make use of the remedies that God has provided. Pure air, sunshine, and the intelligent use of water are beneficial agents in the restoration of health. But the use of water is considered too laborious. It is easier to employ drugs than to use natural remedies.—*Healthful Living,* page 247.

Many parents substitute drugs for judicious nursing.—*Health Reformer,* September, 1866.

Educate Away From Drugs.—Drug medication, as it is generally practiced, is a curse. Educate away from drugs. Use them less and less, and depend more upon hygienic agencies; then nature will respond to God's physicians—pure air, pure water, proper exercise, a clear conscience. Those who persist in the use of tea, coffee, and flesh meats will feel the need of drugs, but many might recover without one grain of medicine if they would obey the laws of health. Drugs need seldom be used.—*Counsels on Health,* page 261.

The only hope of better things is in the education of the people in right principles. Let physicians teach the people that restorative power is not in drugs, but in nature. Disease is an effort of nature to free the system from conditions that result from a violation of the laws of health. In case of sickness, the cause should be ascertained. Unhealthful conditions should be changed, wrong habits corrected. Then nature is to be assisted in her effort to expel impurities and to re-establish right conditions in the system.—*The Ministry of Healing,* page 127.

Importance of Preventive Medicine.—The first labors of a physician should be to educate the sick and suffering in the very course they should pursue to prevent disease. The greatest good can be done by our trying to enlighten the minds of all we can obtain access to, as to the best course for them to pursue to prevent sickness and suffering, and broken constitutions, and premature death. But those who do not care to undertake work that taxes their physical and mental powers will be ready to prescribe drug medication, which lays a foundation in the human organism for a twofold greater evil than that which they claim to have relieved.—*Medical Ministry,* pages 221, 222.

People need to be taught that drugs do not cure disease. It is true that they sometimes afford present relief, and the patient appears to recover as the result of their use; this is because nature has sufficient vital force to expel the poison and to correct the conditions that cause the disease. Health is recovered in spite of the drug. But in most cases the drug only changes the form and location of the disease. Often the effect of the poison seems to be overcome for a time, but the results remain in the system, and work great harm at some later period.—*The Ministry of Healing,* page 126.

A Challenge to Conscientious Physicians.—A physician who has the moral courage to imperil his reputation in enlightening the understanding by plain facts, in showing the nature of disease and how to prevent it, and the dangerous practice of resorting to drugs, will have an uphill business, but he will live and let live. . . . He will, if a reformer, talk plainly in regard to the false appetites and ruinous self-indulgence, in dressing, in eating and drinking, in overtaxing to do a large amount of work in a given time, which has a ruinous influ-

Other Stimulants and Narcotics

ence upon the temper, the physical and mental powers. . . .

Right and correct habits, intelligently and perseveringly practiced, will be removing the cause for disease, and the strong drugs need not be resorted to.—*Medical Ministry,* page 222.

Study and Teach Laws of Preventive Medicine.—There is now positive need even with physicians, reformers in the line of treatment of disease, that greater painstaking effort be made to carry forward and upward the work for themselves, and to interestedly instruct those who look to them for medical skill to ascertain the cause of their infirmities. They should call their attention in a special manner to the laws which God has established, which cannot be violated with impunity. They dwell much on the working of disease, but do not, as a general rule, arouse the attention to the laws which must be sacredly and intelligently obeyed, to prevent disease.—*Medical Ministry,* page 223.

Medicines Which Leave Injurious Effects.—God's servants should not administer medicines which they know will leave behind injurious effects upon the system, even if they do relieve present suffering. Every poisonous preparation in the vegetable and mineral kingdoms, taken into the system, will leave its wretched influence, affecting the liver and lungs, and deranging the system generally.—*Spiritual Gifts,* vol. 4, p. 140.

Why Sanitariums Were Established.—Nothing should be put into the human system that will leave a baleful influence behind. And to carry out the light on this subject, to practice hygienic treatment, is the reason which has been given me for establishing sanitariums in various localities.—*Medical Ministry,* page 228.

Years ago the Lord revealed to me that institutions should be established for treating the sick without drugs. Man is

God's property, and the ruin that has been made of the living habitation, the suffering caused by the seeds of death sown in the human system, are an offense to God.—*Medical Ministry, page 229.*

Patients are to be supplied with good, wholesome food; total abstinence from all intoxicating drinks is to be observed; drugs are to be discarded, and rational methods of treatment followed. The patients must not be given alcohol, tea, coffee, or drugs; for these always leave traces of evil behind them. By observing these rules, many who have been given up by the physicians may be restored to health.—*Medical Ministry, page 228.*

Drugs Seldom Needed.—Many might recover without one grain of medicine, if they would live out the laws of health. Drugs need seldom be used. It will require earnest, patient, protracted effort to establish the work and to carry it forward upon hygienic principles. But let fervent prayer and faith be combined with your efforts, and you will succeed. By this work you will be teaching the patients, and others also, how to take care of themselves when sick, without resorting to the use of drugs.—*Medical Ministry, pages 259, 260.*

Our institutions are established that the sick may be treated by hygienic methods, discarding almost entirely the use of drugs. . . . There is a terrible account to be rendered to God by men who have so little regard for human life as to treat the body so ruthlessly in dealing out their drugs. . . . We are not excusable if through ignorance we destroy God's building by taking into our stomachs poisonous drugs under a variety of names we do not understand. It is our duty to refuse all such prescriptions. We wish to build a sanitarium where maladies may be cured by nature's own provisions, and where the people may be taught how to treat themselves when sick; where they will learn to eat temperately of wholesome food, and be educated to refuse all narcotics,—tea, coffee, fer-

Other Stimulants and Narcotics

mented wines, and stimulants of all kinds,—and to discard the flesh of dead animals.—Manuscript 44, 1896.

For the Most Effective Work.—The question of health reform is not agitated as it must and will be. A simple diet, and the entire absence of drugs, leaving nature free to recuperate the wasted energies of the body, would make our sanitariums far more effectual in restoring the sick to health.—Letter 73a, 1896.

Teach the Patients How to Co-operate With God.—The people must be educated to understand that it is a sin to destroy their physical, mental, and spiritual energies, and they must understand how to co-operate with God in their own restoration. Through faith in Christ they can overcome the habit of using health-destroying stimulants and narcotics.—Manuscript 12, 1900.

Section V

MILDER INTOXICANTS

1. Importance of Strictly Temperate Habits

Examples From Old and New Testament.—When the Lord would raise up Samson as a deliverer of His people, He enjoined upon the mother correct habits of life before the birth of her child. And the same prohibition was to be imposed, from the first, upon the child; for he was to be consecrated to God as a Nazarite from his birth.

The angel of God appeared to the wife of Manoah, and informed her that she should have a son; and in view of this He gave her the important directions: "Now therefore beware, I pray thee, and drink not wine nor strong drink, and eat not any unclean thing." Judges 13:4, 14.

God had important work for the promised child of Manoah to do, and it was to secure for him the qualifications necessary for this work, that the habits of both the mother and the child were to be so carefully regulated. "Neither let her drink wine or strong drink," was the angel's instruction for the wife of Manoah, "nor eat any unclean thing: all that I commanded her let her observe." The child will be affected for good or evil by the habits of the mother. She must herself be controlled by principle, and must practice temperance and self-denial, if she would seek the welfare of her child.

In the New Testament we find a no less impressive example of the importance of temperate habits.

John the Baptist was a reformer. To him was committed a great work for the people of his time. And in preparation for that work, all his habits were carefully regulated, even from his birth. The angel Gabriel was sent from heaven to instruct the parents of John in the principles of health reform. He "shall drink neither wine nor strong drink," said the heavenly messenger; "and he shall be filled with the Holy Ghost." Luke 1:15.

John separated himself from his friends, and from the luxuries of life, dwelling alone in the wilderness, and subsisting upon a purely vegetable diet. The simplicity of his dress—a garment woven of camel's hair—was a rebuke to the extravagance and display of the people of his generation, especially of the Jewish priests. His diet also, of locusts and wild honey, was a rebuke to the gluttony that everywhere prevailed.

The work of John was foretold by the prophet Malachi: "Behold, I will send you Elijah the prophet before the coming of the great and dreadful day of the Lord: and he shall turn the heart of the fathers to the children, and the heart of the children to their fathers." Malachi 4:5, 6. John the Baptist went forth in the spirit and power of Elijah, to prepare the way of the Lord, and to turn the people to the wisdom of the just. He was a representative of those living in the last days, to whom God has entrusted sacred truths to present before the people, to prepare the way for the second appearing of Christ. And the same principles of temperance which John practiced should be observed by those who in our day are to warn the world of the coming of the Son of man.

God has made man in His own image, and He expects man to preserve unimpaired the powers that have been imparted to him for the Creator's service. Then should we not heed His admonitions, and seek to preserve every power in the best condition to serve Him? The very best we can give to God is feeble enough.

Why is there so much misery in the world today? Is it because God loves to see His creatures suffer?—Oh, no! It is because men have become weakened by immoral practices. We mourn over Adam's transgression, and seem to think that our first parents showed great weakness in yielding to temptation; but if Adam's transgression were the only evil we had to meet, the condition of the world would be much better than it is. There has been a succession of falls since Adam's day.—*Christian Temperance and Bible Hygiene,* pages 37-39.

A Warning Regarding the Effect of Wine.—The history of Nadab and Abihu is also given as a warning to man, showing that the effect of wine upon the intellect is to confuse. And it will ever have this influence upon the minds of those who use it. Therefore God explicitly forbids the use of wine and strong drink.—*Signs of the Times,* July 8, 1880.

Nadab and Abihu would never have committed that fatal sin, had they not first become partially intoxicated by the free use of wine. They understood that the most careful and solemn preparation was necessary before presenting themselves in the sanctuary where the divine presence was manifested; but by intemperance they were disqualified for their holy office. Their minds became confused, and their moral perceptions dulled, so that they could not discern the difference between the sacred and the common.—*Patriarchs and Prophets,* pages 361, 362.

2. Psychological Effects of Mild Intoxicants

Inherited Tendencies Aroused by Wine and Cider.—For persons who have inherited an appetite for stimulants, it is by no means safe to have wine or cider in the house; for Satan is continually soliciting them to indulge. If they yield to his temptations, they do not know where to stop; appetite clamors for indulgence, and is gratified to their ruin. The brain is clouded; reason no longer holds the reins, but lays them on the neck of lust. Licentiousness abounds, and vices of almost every type are practiced as the result of indulging the appetite for wine and cider.—*Christian Temperance and Bible Hygiene,* pages 32, 33.

Cannot Grow in Grace.—It is impossible for one who loves these stimulants, and accustoms himself to their use, to grow in grace. He becomes gross and sensual; the animal passions control the higher powers of the mind, and virtue is not cherished.—*Christian Temperance and Bible Hygiene,* page 33.

Perversion of Mind Through Mild Intoxicants.—So gradually does Satan lead away from the strongholds of temperance, so insidiously do wine and cider exert their influence upon the taste, that the highway to drunkenness is entered upon all unsuspectingly. The taste for stimulants is cultivated; the nervous system is disordered; Satan keeps the mind in a fever of unrest; and the poor victim, imagining himself perfectly secure, goes on and on, until every barrier is broken down, every principle sacrificed. The strongest resolutions are undermined, and eternal interests are too weak to keep the debased appetite under the control of reason. Some are never really drunk, but are always under the influence of mild intoxicants. They are feverish, unstable in mind, not really delirious, but as truly unbalanced; for the nobler powers of the mind are perverted.—*Christian Temperance and Bible Hygiene,* page 33.

Unfermented Wine and Cider.—The pure juice of the grape, free from fermentation, is a wholesome drink.—*Manuscript 126, 1903.*

Cider and wine may be canned when fresh, and kept sweet a long time, and if used in an unfermented state, they will not dethrone reason.—*Review and Herald,* March 25, 1884.

Sweet Cider.—Do we know of what this palatable sweet cider is made? Those who manufacture apples into cider for the market are not very careful as to the condition of the fruit used, and in many cases the juice of decayed apples is expressed. Those who would not think of taking the poison of rotten apples into their system, will drink the cider made from them, and call it a luxury; but the microscope would reveal the fact that this pleasant beverage is often unfit for the human stomach, even when fresh from the press. If it is boiled, and care is taken to remove the impurities, it is less objectionable.

I have often heard people say, "Oh! this is only sweet cider; it is perfectly harmless, and even healthful." Several quarts, perhaps gallons, are carried home. For a few days it is sweet; then fermentation begins. The sharp flavor makes it all the more acceptable to many palates, and the lover of sweet wine or cider is loath to admit that his favorite beverage ever becomes hard and sour.—*Review and Herald,* March 25, 1884.

The Only Safe Course.—Persons who have inherited an appetite for unnatural stimulants should by no means have wine, beer, or cider in their sight, or within their reach; for this keeps the temptation constantly before them.—*The Ministry of Healing,* page 331.

If men would become temperate in all things, if they would touch not, taste not, handle not, tea, coffee, tobacco, wines, opium, and alcoholic drinks, reason would take the reins of government in her own hands, and hold the appetites and passions under control.

Through appetite, Satan controls the mind and the whole being. Thousands who might have lived, have passed into the grave, physical, mental, and moral wrecks, because they sacrificed all their powers to the indulgence of appetite.—*Christian Temperance and Bible Hygiene,* page 37.

3. The Intoxicating Effects of Wine and Cider

Persons may become just as really intoxicated on wine and cider as on stronger drinks, and the worst kind of inebriation is produced by these so-called milder drinks. The passions are more perverse; the transformation of character is greater, more determined, and obstinate. A few quarts of cider or sweet wine may awaken a taste for stronger drinks, and many who have become confirmed drunkards have thus laid the foundation of the drinking habit.—*Review and Herald,* March 25, 1884.

A Possible Precursor to Habitual Drunkenness.—A single glass of wine may open the door of temptation which will lead to habits of drunkenness.—*Testimonies,* vol. 4, p. 578.

Diseased Condition Resulting From Use of Cider.—A tendency to disease of various kinds, as dropsy, liver complaint, trembling nerves, and a determination of blood to the head, results from the habitual use of sour cider. By its use, many bring upon themselves permanent diseases. Some die of consumption or fall under the power of apoplexy from this cause alone. Some suffer from dyspepsia. Every vital function refuses to act, and the physicians tell them that they have liver complaint, when if they would break in the head of the cider barrel, and never give way to the temptation to replace it, their abused life forces would recover their vigor.—*Review and Herald,* March 25, 1884.

Effects of Wine After the Flood.—The world had become so corrupt through indulgence of appetite and debased passion in the days of Noah that God destroyed its inhabitants by the waters of the Flood. And as men again multiplied upon the earth, the indulgence in wine to intoxication, perverted the senses, and prepared the way for excessive meat eating and the strengthening of the animal passions. Men lifted themselves up against the God of Heaven; and their faculties and opportunities were devoted to glorifying themselves rather than honoring their Creator.—*Redemption; or the Temptation of Christ,* pages 21, 22.

Leads to Use of Stronger Drinks.—Cider drinking leads to the use of stronger drinks. The stomach loses its natural vigor, and something stronger is needed to arouse it to action. On one occasion when my husband and myself were traveling, we were obliged to spend several hours waiting for the train. While we were in the depot, a red-faced, bloated farmer came into the restaurant connected with it, and in a loud, rough voice asked, "Have you first-class brandy?" He was answered in the affirmative, and ordered half a tumbler. "Have you pepper sauce?" "Yes," was the answer. "Well, put in two large spoonfuls." He next ordered two spoonfuls of alcohol added, and concluded by calling for "a good dose of black pepper." The man who was preparing it asked, "What will you do with such a mixture?" He replied, "I guess that will take hold," and placing the full glass to his lips, drank the whole of this fiery compound. Said my husband, "That man has used stimulants until he has destroyed the tender coats of the stomach. I should suppose that they must be as insensible as a burnt boot."

Many, as they read this, will laugh at the warning of danger. They will say, "Surely the little wine or cider that I use cannot hurt me." Satan has marked such as his prey; he leads them on step by step, and they perceive it not until the chains of habit and appetite are too strong to be broken. We see the power that appetite for strong drink has over men; we see how many of all professions and of heavy responsibilities, men of exalted station, of eminent talents, of great attainments, of fine feelings, of strong nerves, and of high reasoning powers, sacrifice everything for the indulgence of appetite until they are reduced to the level of the brutes; and in very many cases their downward course commenced with the use of wine or cider. Knowing this, I take my stand decidedly in opposition to the manufacture of wine or cider to be used as a beverage. . . . If all would be vigilant and faithful in guarding the little openings made by the moderate use of the so-called harmless wine and cider, the highway to drunkenness would be closed up.—*Review and Herald,* March 25, 1884.

4. Wine in the Bible

The Wine at Cana Not Fermented.—The Bible nowhere sanctions the use of intoxicating wine. The wine that Christ made from water at the marriage feast of Cana was the pure juice of the grape. This is the "new wine . . . found in the cluster," of which the Scripture says, "Destroy it not; for a blessing is in it." Isaiah 65:8.

It was Christ who, in the Old Testament, gave the warning to Israel, "Wine is a mocker, strong drink is raging: and whosoever is deceived thereby is not wise." Proverbs 20:1. He Himself provided no such beverage. Satan tempts men to indulgence that will becloud reason and benumb the spiritual perceptions, but Christ teaches us to bring the lower nature into subjection. He never places before men that which would be a temptation. His whole life was an example of self-denial. It was to break the power of appetite that in the forty days' fast in the wilderness He suffered in our behalf the severest test that humanity could endure. It was Christ who directed that John the Baptist should drink neither wine nor strong drink. It was He who enjoined similar abstinence upon the wife of Manoah. Christ did not contradict His own teaching. The unfermented wine that He provided for the wedding guests was a wholesome and refreshing drink. This is the wine that was used by our Saviour and His disciples in the first Communion. It is the wine that should always be used on the Communion table as a symbol of the Saviour's blood. The sacramental service is designed to be soul-refreshing and life-giving. There is to be connected with it nothing that could minister to evil.—*The Ministry of Healing,* pages 333, 334.

Wine Recommended in Bible Not Intoxicating.—The Bible nowhere teaches the use of intoxicating wine, either as a beverage or as a symbol of the blood of Christ. We appeal to the natural reason whether the blood of Christ is better represented by the pure juice of the grape in its natural state, or after it has been converted into a fermented and intoxicating wine. . . . We urge that the latter should never be placed upon the Lord's table. . . . We protest that Christ never made intoxicating wine; such an act would have been contrary to all the teachings and example of His life. . . . The wine which Christ manufactured from water by a miracle of His power, was the pure juice of the grape.—*Signs of the Times,* Aug. 29, 1878.

5. Christians and the Production of Liquor-Making Products

Many who would hesitate to place liquor to a neighbor's lips, will engage in the raising of hops, and thus lend their influence against the temperance cause. I cannot see how, in the light of the law of God, Christians can conscientiously engage in the raising of hops or in the manufacture of wine and cider for the market.—*Christian Temperance and Bible Hygiene,* page 32.

Abstain From the Appearance of Evil.—When intelligent men and women who are professedly Christians plead that there is no harm in making wine or cider for the market because when unfermented it will not intoxicate, I feel sad at heart. I know there is another side to this subject that they refuse to look upon; for selfishness has closed their eyes to the terrible evils that may result from the use of these stimulants. I do not see how our brethren can abstain from all appearance of evil and engage largely in the business of hop raising, knowing to what use the hops are put.

Those who help to produce these beverages that encourage and educate the appetite for stronger stimulants will be rewarded as their works have been. They are transgressors of the law of God, and they will be punished for the sins which they commit and for those which they have influenced others to commit through the temptations which they have placed in their way.

Let all who profess to believe the truth for this time, and to be reformers, act in accordance with their faith. If one whose name is on the church book manufactures wine or cider for the market, he should be faithfully labored with, and, if he continues the practice, he should be placed under censure of the church. Those who will not be dissuaded from doing this work are unworthy of a place and a name among the people of God.

We are to be followers of Christ, to set our hearts and our influence against every evil practice. How should we feel in the day when God's judgments are poured out, to meet men who have become drunkards through our influence? We are living in the antitypical day of atonement, and our cases must soon come in review before God. How shall we stand in the courts of heaven, if our course of action has encouraged the use of stimulants that pervert reason and are destructive of virtue, purity, and the love of God?—*Testimonies,* vol. 5, pages 358, 359.

The Love of Money Not to Mislead.—I have a few acres of land that, when I purchased it, was set out to wine grapes; but I will not sell one pound of these grapes to any winery. The money I should get for them would increase my income; but rather than aid the cause of intemperance by allowing them to be converted into wine, I would let them decay upon the vines. . . .

The love of money will lead men to violate conscience. Perhaps that very money may be brought to the Lord's treasury; but He will not accept any such offering, it is an offense to Him. It was obtained by transgressing His law, which requires that a man love his neighbor as himself. It is no excuse for the transgressor to say that if he had not made wine or cider, somebody else would, and his neighbor might have become a drunkard just the same. Because some will place the bottle to their neighbor's lips, will Christians venture to stain their garments with the blood of souls,—to incur the curse pronounced upon those who place this temptation in the way of erring men? Jesus calls upon His followers to stand under His banner and aid in destroying the works of the devil.

The world's Redeemer, who knows well the state of society in the last days, represents eating and drinking as the sins that condemn this age. He tells us that as it was in the days of Noah, so shall it be when the Son of man is revealed. "They were eating and drinking, marrying and giving in marriage, until the day that Noah entered into the ark, and knew not until the Flood came, and took them all away." Just such a state of things will exist in the last days, and those who believe these warnings will use the utmost caution not to take a course that will bring them under condemnation.—*Review and Herald,* March 25, 1884.

In the Light of Scripture, Nature, and Reason.—In the light of what the Scriptures, nature, and reason teach concerning the use of intoxicants, how can Christians engage in the raising of hops for beermaking, or in the manufacture of wine or cider for the market? If they love their neighbor as themselves, how can they help to place in his way that which will be a snare to him?—*The Ministry of Healing,* page 334.

Brethren, let us look at this matter in the light of the Scriptures and exert a decided influence on the side of temperance in all things. Apples and grapes are God's gifts; they may be put to excellent use as healthful articles of food, or they may be abused by being put to a wrong use. Already God is blighting the grapevine and the apple crop because of men's sinful practices. We stand before the world as reformers; let us give no occasion for infidels or unbelievers to reproach our faith. Said Christ: "Ye are the salt of the earth," "the light of the world." Let us show that our hearts and consciences are under the transforming influence of divine grace, and that our lives are governed by the pure principles of the law of God, even though these principles may require the sacrifice of temporal interests.—*Testimonies,* vol. 5, p. 361.

6. Temperance and Total Abstinence

If anything is needed to quench thirst, pure water drunk some little time before or after the meal is all that nature requires. Never take tea, coffee, beer, wine, or any spirituous liquors. Water is the best liquid possible to cleanse the tissues. —*Review and Herald,* July 29, 1884.

The lesson here presented [of Daniel and his companions] is one which we would do well to ponder. Our danger is not from scarcity, but from abundance. We are constantly tempted to excess. Those who would preserve their powers unimpaired for the service of God, must observe strict temperance in the use of His bounties, as well as total abstinence from every injurious or debasing indulgence.

The rising generation are surrounded with allurements calculated to tempt the appetite. Especially in our large cities, every form of indulgence is made easy and inviting. Those who, like Daniel, refuse to defile themselves, will reap the reward of their temperate habits. With their greater physical stamina and increased power of endurance, they have a bank of deposit upon which to draw in case of emergency.—*Christian Temperance and Bible Hygiene,* pages 27, 28.

It is often urged that in order to win the youth from sensational or worthless literature, we should supply them with a better class of fiction. This is like trying to cure the drunkard by giving him, in the place of whisky or brandy, the milder intoxicants, such as wine, beer, or cider. The use of these would continually foster the appetite for stronger stimulants. The only safety for the inebriate, and the only safeguard for the temperate man, is total abstinence.—*The Ministry of Healing,* page 446.

Section VI

ACTIVATING PRINCIPLES OF A CHANGED LIFE

1. Only as the Life Is Changed

The Character Reshaped.—Our work for the tempted and fallen will achieve real success only as the grace of Christ reshapes the character and the man is brought into living connection with the infinite God. This is the purpose of all true temperance effort.—*Testimonies,* vol. 6, p. 111.

Christ Works From Within.—Men will never be truly temperate until the grace of Christ is an abiding principle in the heart. . . . Circumstances cannot work reform. Christianity proposes a reformation in the heart. What Christ works within, will be worked out under the dictation of a converted intellect. The plan of beginning outside and trying to work inward has always failed, and always will fail.—*Counsels on Diet and Foods,* page 35.

Power of Self-Control Must Be Regained.—One of the most deplorable effects of the original apostasy was the loss of man's power of self-control. Only as this power is regained, can there be real progress.

The body is the only medium through which the mind and the soul are developed for the upbuilding of character. Hence it is that the adversary of souls directs his temptations to the enfeebling and degrading of the physical powers. His success here means the surrender to evil of the whole being. The tendencies of our physical nature, unless under the dominion of a higher power, will surely work ruin and death.

Activating Principles of a Changed Life

The body is to be brought into subjection. The higher powers of the being are to rule. The passions are to be controlled by the will, which is itself to be under the control of God. The kingly power of reason, sanctified by divine grace, is to bear sway in our lives.—*The Ministry of Healing,* pages 129, 130.

Futility of Attempts to Stop by Degrees.—Shall those who have had more opportunities and much precious light, who enjoy the advantages of education, make the plea that they cannot cut away from unhealthful practices? Why do not those who have excellent reasoning powers reason from cause to effect? Why do they not advocate reform by planting their feet firmly on principle, determined not to taste alcoholic drink or to use tobacco? These are poisons, and their use is a violation of God's law. Some say, when an effort is made to enlighten them on this point, I will leave off by degrees. But Satan laughs at all such decisions. He says, They are secure in my power. I have no fear of them on that ground.

But he knows that he has no power over the man who, when sinners entice him, has moral courage to say "No" squarely and positively. Such a one has dismissed the companionship of the devil, and as long as he holds to Jesus Christ, he is safe. He stands where heavenly angels can connect with him, giving him moral power to overcome.—Manuscript 86, 1897.

A Hard Battle, but God Will Help.—Do you use tobacco or intoxicating liquor? Cast them from you; for they becloud your faculties. To give up the use of these things will mean a hard battle, but God will help you to fight this battle. Ask Him for grace to overcome, and then believe that He will give it to you, because He loves you. Do not allow worldly companions to draw you away from your allegiance to Christ. Rather let your mind be drawn from these companions to Christ. Tell them that you are seeking for heavenly treasure. You are not your own; you have been bought with a price, even the life of the Son of God, and you are to glorify God in your body and in your spirit, for they are His.—Letter 226, 1903.

Seek Help of God and the Righteous.—I have a message from the Lord for the tempted soul who has been under the control of Satan, but who is striving to break free. Go to the Lord for help. Go to those who you know love and fear God, and say, Take me under your care; for Satan tempts me fiercely. I have no power from the snare to go. Keep me with you every moment, until I have more strength to resist temptation.—Letter 166, 1903.

Personal Relationship With God.—Keep your wants, your joys, your sorrows, your cares, and your fears, before God. . . . "The Lord is very pitiful, and of tender mercy." His heart of love is touched by our sorrows, and even by our utterance of them. . . . Nothing that in any way concerns our peace is too small for Him to notice. There is no chapter in our experience too dark for Him to read; there is no perplexity too difficult for Him to unravel. No calamity can befall the least of His children, no anxiety harass the soul, no joy cheer, no sincere prayer escape the lips, of which our heavenly Father is unobservant, or in which He takes no immediate interest. "He healeth the broken in heart, and bindeth up their wounds." The relations between God and each soul are as distinct and full as though there were not another soul for whom He gave His beloved Son.—*Steps to Christ,* pages 104, 105.

2. Conversion the Secret of Victory

Indulgence Is Sin.—The indulgence of unnatural appetite, whether for tea, coffee, tobacco, or liquor, is intemperance, and is at war with the laws of life and health. By using these forbidden articles a condition of things is created in the system which the Creator never designed. This indulgence in any

Activating Principles of a Changed Life

of the members of the human family is sin. . . . Suffering, disease, and death are the sure penalty of indulgence.—*Evangelism,* page 266.

When the Holy Spirit Works Among Us.—The very first and the most important thing is to melt and subdue the soul by presenting our Lord Jesus Christ as the Sin Bearer, the sin-pardoning Saviour, making the gospel as clear as possible. When the Holy Spirit works among us, . . . souls who are unready for Christ's appearing are convicted. . . . The tobacco devotees sacrifice their idol and the liquor drinker his liquor. They could not do this if they did not grasp by faith the promises of God for the forgiveness of their sins.—*Evangelism,* page 264.

Man's Great Need.—Christ gave His life to purchase redemption for the sinner. The world's Redeemer knew that indulgence of appetite was bringing physical debility and deadening the perceptive faculties so that sacred and eternal things could not be discerned. He knew that self-indulgence was perverting the moral powers, and that man's great need was conversion,—in heart and mind and soul, from the life of self-indulgence to one of self-denial and self-sacrifice.—*Medical Ministry,* page 264.

Man Will Fail in His Own Strength.—The tobacco habit . . . beclouds so many minds. Why do you not give up this habit? Why not arise and say, I will serve sin and the devil no longer? Say, I will let alone this poisonous narcotic. You never can do it in your own strength. Christ says, "I am at thy right hand to help thee."—*Manuscript 9, 1893.*

Why So Many Fail.—Temptations to the indulgence of appetite possess a power which can be overcome only by the help that God can impart. But with every temptation we have the promise of God that there shall be a way of escape. Why, then, are so many overcome? It is because they do not put their trust in God. They do not avail themselves of the means provided for their safety. The excuses offered for the gratification of perverted appetite, are therefore of no weight with God.—*Christian Temperance and Bible Hygiene,* page 22.

The Only Remedy.—For every soul struggling to rise from a life of sin to a life of purity, the great element of power abides in the only "name under heaven given among men, whereby we must be saved." Acts 4:12. "If any man thirst," for restful hope, for deliverance from sinful propensities, Christ says, "let him come unto Me, and drink." John 7:37. The only remedy for vice is the grace and power of Christ.

The good resolutions made in one's own strength avail nothing. Not all the pledges in the world will break the power of evil habit. Never will men practice temperance in all things until their hearts are renewed by divine grace. We cannot keep ourselves from sin for one moment. Every moment we are dependent upon God. . . .

Christ lived a life of perfect obedience to God's law, and in this He set an example for every human being. The life that He lived in this world we are to live, through His power and under His instruction.

Perfect Obedience Required.—In our work for the fallen, the claims of the law of God and the need of loyalty to Him are to be impressed on mind and heart. Never fail to show that there is a marked difference between the one who serves God and the one who serves Him not. God is love, but He cannot excuse willful disregard for His commands. The enactments of His government are such that men do not escape the consequences of disloyalty. Only those who honor Him can He honor. Man's conduct in this world decides his eternal destiny. As he has sown, so he must reap. Cause will be followed by effect.

Nothing less than perfect obedience can meet the standard of God's requirement. He has not left His requirements indefinite. He has enjoined nothing that is not necessary in order to bring man into harmony with Him. We are to point sinners to His ideal of character, and to lead them to Christ, by whose grace only can this ideal be reached.

Victory Assured Through Christ's Sinless Life.—The Saviour took upon Himself the infirmities of humanity, and lived a sinless life, that men might have no fear that because of the weakness of human nature they could not overcome. Christ came to make us "partakers of the divine nature," and His life declares that humanity, combined with divinity, does not commit sin.

The Saviour overcame to show man how he may overcome. All the temptations of Satan, Christ met with the word of God. By trusting in God's promises, He received power to obey God's commandments, and the tempter could gain no advantage. To every temptation His answer was, "It is written." So God has given us His word wherewith to resist evil. Exceeding great and precious promises are ours, that by these we "might be partakers of the divine nature, having escaped the corruption that is in the world through lust." 2 Peter 1:4.

Bid the tempted one look not to circumstances, to the weakness of self, or to the power of temptation, but to the power of God's word. All its strength is ours. "Thy word," says the psalmist, "have I hid in mine heart, that I might not sin against Thee." "By the word of Thy lips I have kept me from the paths of the destroyer." Psalms 119:11; 17:4.

Linked With Christ Through Prayer.—Talk courage to the people; lift them up to God in prayer. Many who have been overcome by temptation are humiliated by their failures, and they feel that it is in vain for them to approach unto God; but this thought is of the enemy's suggestion. When they have sinned, and feel that they cannot pray, tell them that it is then the time to pray. Ashamed they may be, and deeply humbled; but as they confess their sins, He who is faithful and just will forgive their sins, and cleanse them from all unrighteousness.

Nothing is apparently more helpless, yet really more invincible, than the soul that feels its nothingness, and relies wholly on the merits of the Saviour. By prayer, by the study of His word, by faith in His abiding presence, the weakest of human beings may live in contact with the living Christ, and He will hold them by a hand that will never let go.—*The Ministry of Healing,* pages 179-182.

Health and Strength to the Overcomer.—When men who have indulged in wrong habits and sinful practices yield to the power of divine truth, the application of that truth to the heart revives the moral powers, which had seemed to be paralyzed. The receiver possesses stronger, clearer understanding than before he riveted his soul to the eternal Rock. Even his physical health improves by the realization of his security in Christ. The special blessing of God resting upon the receiver is of itself health and strength.—*Christian Temperance and Bible Hygiene,* page 13.

Power for Victory in Christ Alone.—Men have polluted the soul-temple, and God calls upon them to awake, and to strive with all their might to win back their God-given manhood. Nothing but the grace of God can convict and convert the heart; from Him alone can the slaves of custom obtain power to break the shackles that bind them. It is impossible for a man to present his body a living sacrifice, holy, acceptable to God, while continuing to indulge habits that are depriving him of physical, mental, and moral vigor. Again the apostle says, "Be not conformed to this world: but be ye transformed by the renewing of your mind, that ye may prove what is that good, and acceptable, and perfect, will of God." Romans 12:2.—*Christian Temperance and Bible Hygiene,* pages 10, 11.

In the Strength of Christ.—Christ fought the battle upon the point of appetite, and came off victorious; and we also can

Activating Principles of a Changed Life

conquer through strength derived from Him. Who will enter in through the gates into the city?—Not those who declare that they cannot break the force of appetite. Christ has resisted the power of him who would hold us in bondage; though weakened by His long fast of forty days, He withstood temptation, and proved by this act that our cases are not hopeless. I know that we cannot obtain the victory alone; and how thankful we should be that we have a living Saviour, who is ready and willing to aid us!

I recall the case of a man in a congregation that I was once addressing. He was almost wrecked in body and mind by the use of liquor and tobacco. He was bowed down from the effects of dissipation; and his dress was in keeping with his shattered condition. To all appearance he had gone too far to be reclaimed. But as I appealed to him to resist temptation in the strength of a risen Saviour, he rose tremblingly, and said, "You have an interest for me, and I will have an interest for myself." Six months afterward he came to my house. I did not recognize him. With a countenance beaming with joy, and eyes overflowing with tears, he grasped my hand, and said, "You do not know me, but you remember the man in an old blue coat who rose in your congregation, and said that he would try to reform?" I was astonished. He stood erect, and looked ten years younger. He had gone home from that meeting, and passed the long hours in prayer and struggle till the sun arose. It was a night of conflict, but, thank God, he came off a victor. This man could tell by sad experience of the bondage of these evil habits. He knew how to warn the youth of the dangers of contamination; and those who, like himself, had been overcome, he could point to Christ as the only source of help.—*Christian Temperance and Bible Hygiene,* pages 19, 20.

No Genuine Reform Apart From Christ.—Apart from divine power, no genuine reform can be effected. Human barriers against natural and cultivated tendencies are but as the sandbank against the torrent. Not until the life of Christ becomes a vitalizing power in our lives can we resist the temptations that assail us from within and from without.

Christ came to this world and lived the law of God, that man might have perfect mastery over the natural inclinations which corrupt the soul. The Physician of soul and body, He gives victory over warring lusts. He has provided every facility, that man may possess completeness of character.

When one surrenders to Christ, the mind is brought under the control of the law; but it is the royal law, which proclaims liberty to every captive. By becoming one with Christ, man is made free. Subjection to the will of Christ means restoration to perfect manhood.

Obedience to God is liberty from the thralldom of sin, deliverance from human passion and impulse. Man may stand conqueror of himself, conqueror of his own inclinations, conqueror of principalities and powers, and of "the rulers of the darkness of this world," and of "spiritual wickedness in high places." Ephesians 6:12.—*The Ministry of Healing,* pages 130, 131.

3. The Will the Key to Success

A Hand-to-Hand Battle.—When men are content to live merely for this world, the inclination of the heart unites with the suggestions of the enemy, and his bidding is done. But when they seek to leave the black banner of the power of darkness, and range themselves under the bloodstained banner of Prince Emmanuel, the struggle begins, and the warfare is carried on in the sight of the universe of heaven.

Every one who fights on the side of right, must fight hand to hand with the enemy. He must put on the whole armor of God, that he may be able to stand against the wiles of the devil.—Manuscript 47, 1896.

Man Must Do His Part.—God cannot save man, against his will, from the power of Satan's artifices. Man must work with his human power, aided by the divine power of Christ, to resist and to conquer at any cost to himself. In short, man must overcome as Christ overcame. And then, through the victory which it is his privilege to gain by the all-powerful name of Jesus, he may become an heir of God and joint heir with Christ.

This could not be the case if Christ alone did all the overcoming. Man must do *his* part. Man must be victor on his own account, through the strength and grace that Jesus gives him. Man must be a co-worker with Christ in the labor of overcoming, and then he will be partaker with Christ of His glory.—*Review and Herald,* Nov. 21, 1882.

"Show Thyself a Man."—The victims of evil habit must be aroused to the necessity of making an effort for themselves. Others may put forth the most earnest endeavor to uplift them, the grace of God may be freely offered, Christ may entreat, His angels may minister; but all will be in vain unless they themselves are roused to fight the battle in their own behalf.

The last words of David to Solomon, then a young man, and soon to receive the crown of Israel, were, "Be thou strong, . . . and show thyself a man." 1 Kings 2:2. To every child of humanity, the candidate for an immortal crown, are these words of inspiration spoken, "Be strong, and show thyself a man."

The self-indulgent must be led to see and feel that great moral renovation is necessary if they would be men. God calls upon them to arouse, and in the strength of Christ win back the God-given manhood that has been sacrificed through sinful indulgence.

He Can—He Must Resist Evil.—Feeling the terrible power of temptation, the drawing of desire that leads to indulgence, many a man cries in despair, "I cannot resist evil." Tell him that he can, that he must resist. He may have been overcome again and again, but it need not be always thus. He is weak in moral power, controlled by the habits of a life of sin. His promises and resolutions are like ropes of sand. The knowledge of his broken promises and forfeited pledges weakens his confidence in his own sincerity, and causes him to feel that God cannot accept him or work with his efforts. But he need not despair.

Those who put their trust in Christ are not to be enslaved by any hereditary or cultivated habit or tendency. Instead of being held in bondage to the lower nature, they are to rule every appetite and passion. God has not left us to battle with evil in our own finite strength. Whatever may be our inherited or cultivated tendencies to wrong, we can overcome through the power that He is ready to impart.

The Power of the Will.—The tempted one needs to understand the true force of the will. This is the governing power in the nature of man,—the power of decision, of choice. Everything depends on the right action of the will. Desires for goodness and purity are right, so far as they go; but if we stop here, they avail nothing. Many will go down to ruin while hoping and desiring to overcome their evil propensities. They do not yield the will to God. They do not *choose* to serve Him.

We Must Choose.—God has given us the power of choice; it is ours to exercise. We cannot change our hearts, we cannot control our thoughts, our impulses, our affections. We cannot make ourselves pure, fit for God's service. But we can *choose* to serve God, we can give Him our will; then He will work in us to will and to do according to His good pleasure. Thus our whole nature will be brought under the control of Christ.

Through the right exercise of the will, an entire change may be made in the life. By yielding up the will to Christ, we ally ourselves with divine power. We receive strength from above to hold us steadfast. A pure and noble life, a life of victory over appetite and lust, is possible to everyone who will unite his weak, wavering human will to the omnipotent, unwavering will of God.—*The Ministry of Healing,* pages 174-176.

If the Will Is Set Right.—The will is the governing power in the nature of man. If the will is set right, all the rest of the being will come under its sway. The will is not the taste or the inclination, but it is the choice, the deciding power, the kingly power, which works in the children of men unto obedience to God or to disobedience.

You will be in constant peril until you understand the true force of the will. You may believe and promise all things, but your promises and your faith are of no account until you put your will on the right side. If you will fight the fight of faith with your will power, there is no doubt that you will conquer.

When We Put the Will on the Side of Christ.—Your part is to put your will on the side of Christ. When you yield your will to His, He immediately takes possession of you, and works in you to will and to do of His good pleasure. Your nature is brought under the control of His Spirit. Even your thoughts are subject to Him. If you cannot control your impulses, your emotions, as you may desire, you can control the will, and thus an entire change will be wrought in your life. When you yield up your will to Christ, your life is hid with Christ in God. It is allied to the power which is above all principalities and powers. You have a strength from God that holds you fast to His strength; and a new life, even the life of faith, is possible to you.

You can never be successful in elevating yourself, unless your will is on the side of Christ, co-operating with the Spirit of God. Do not feel that you cannot; but say, "I can, I will."

And God has pledged His Holy Spirit to help you in every decided effort.

The Feeblest Cry for Help Is Heard.—Every one of us may know that there is a power working with our efforts to overcome. Why will not men lay hold upon the help that has been provided, that they may become elevated and ennobled? Why do they degrade themselves by the indulgence of perverted appetite? Why do they not rise in the strength of Jesus, and be victorious in His name? The very feeblest prayer that we can offer, Jesus will hear. He pities the weakness of every soul. Help for everyone has been laid upon Him who is mighty to save. I point you to Jesus Christ, the sinner's Saviour, who alone can give you power to overcome on every point.

Crowns for All Who Overcome.—Heaven is worth everything to us. We must not run any risk in this matter. We must take no venture here. We must know that our steps are ordered by the Lord. May God help us in the great work of overcoming. He has crowns for those that overcome. He has white robes for the righteous. He has an eternal world of glory for those who seek for glory, honor, and immortality. Everyone who enters the city of God will enter it as a conqueror. He will not enter it as a condemned criminal, but as a son of God. And the welcome given to everyone who enters there will be, "Come, ye blessed of My Father, inherit the kingdom prepared for you from the foundation of the world." Matthew 25:34.

Gladly would I speak words that would aid such trembling souls to fasten their grasp by faith upon the mighty Helper, that they might develop a character upon which God will be pleased to look. Heaven may invite them, and present its choicest blessings, and they may have every facility to develop a perfect character; but all will be in vain unless they are willing to help themselves. They must put forth their own

God-given powers, or they will sink lower and lower, and be of no account for good, either in time or in eternity.—*Christian Temperance and Bible Hygiene,* pages 147-149.

4. Enduring Victory

Importance of Living Healthfully.—Those who are struggling against the power of appetite should be instructed in the principles of healthful living. They should be shown that violation of the laws of health, by creating diseased conditions and unnatural cravings, lays the foundation of the liquor habit. Only by living in obedience to the principles of health can they hope to be freed from the craving for unnatural stimulants. While they depend upon divine strength to break the bonds of appetite, they are to co-operate with God by obedience to His laws, both moral and physical.

Employment; Self-Support.—Those who are endeavoring to reform should be provided with employment. None who are able to labor should be taught to expect food and clothing and shelter free of cost. For their own sake, as well as for the sake of others, some way should be devised whereby they may return an equivalent for what they receive. Encourage every effort toward self-support. This will strengthen self-respect and a noble independence. And occupation of mind and body in useful work is essential as a safeguard against temptation.

Disappointments; Dangers.—Those who work for the fallen will be disappointed in many who give promise of reform. Many will make but a superficial change in their habits and practices. They are moved by impulse, and for a time may seem to have reformed; but there is no real change of heart. They cherish the same self-love, have the same hungering for foolish pleasures, the same desire for self-indulgence. They have not a knowledge of the work of character building, and they cannot be relied upon as men of principle. They have debased their mental and spiritual powers by the gratification of appetite and passion, and this makes them weak. They are fickle and changeable. Their impulses tend toward sensuality. These persons are often a source of danger to others. Being looked upon as reformed men and women, they are trusted with responsibilities, and are placed where their influence corrupts the innocent.

Total Dependence on Christ the Only Solution.—Even those who are sincerely seeking to reform are not beyond the danger of falling. They need to be treated with great wisdom as well as tenderness. The disposition to flatter and exalt those who have been rescued from the lowest depths, sometimes proves their ruin. The practice of inviting men and women to relate in public the experience of their life of sin, is full of danger to both speaker and hearers. To dwell upon scenes of evil is corrupting to mind and soul. And the prominence given to the rescued ones is harmful to them. Many are led to feel that their sinful life has given them a certain distinction. A love of notoriety and a spirit of self-trust are encouraged that prove fatal to the soul. Only in distrust of self and dependence on the mercy of Christ can they stand.

The Rescued to Help Others.—All who give evidence of true conversion should be encouraged to work for others. Let none turn away a soul who leaves the service of Satan for the service of Christ. When one gives evidence that the Spirit of God is striving with him, present every encouragement for entering the Lord's service. "Of some have compassion, making a difference." Jude 22. Those who are wise in the wisdom that comes from God will see souls in need of help, those who have sincerely repented, but who without encouragement would hardly dare to lay hold of hope. The Lord will put it into the hearts of His servants to welcome these trembling, repentant ones to their loving fellowship. Whatever may have been their besetting sins, however low they may have fallen, when in contrition they come to Christ, He receives them. Then give them something to do for Him. If they desire to labor in uplifting others from the pit of destruction from which they themselves were rescued, give them opportunity. Bring them into association with experienced Christians, that they may gain spiritual strength. Fill their hearts and hands with work for the Master.

When light flashes into the soul, some who appear to be most fully given to sin will become successful workers for just such sinners as they themselves once were. Through faith in Christ, some will rise to high places of service, and be entrusted with responsibilities in the work of saving souls. They see where their own weakness lies, they realize the depravity of their nature. They know the strength of sin, the power of evil habit. They realize their inability to overcome without the help of Christ, and their constant cry is, "I cast my helpless soul on Thee."

These can help others. The one who has been tempted and tried, whose hope was well-nigh gone, but who was saved by hearing a message of love, can understand the science of soulsaving. He whose heart is filled with love for Christ because he himself has been sought for by the Saviour, and brought back to the fold, knows how to seek the lost. He can point sinners to the Lamb of God. He has given himself without reserve to God, and has been accepted in the Beloved. The hand that in weakness was held out for help has been grasped. By the ministry of such ones, many prodigals will be brought to the Father.—*The Ministry of Healing,* pages 176-179.

Helped by Helping Others.—One who is weakened, and even degraded by sinful indulgence, may become a son of God. It is in his power to be constantly doing good to others, and helping them to overcome temptation; and in so doing he will reap benefit to himself. He may be a bright and shining light in the world, and at last hear the benediction,

"Well done, good and faithful servant," from the lips of the King of glory.—*Christian Temperance and Bible Hygiene* page 149.

When Presented From the Standpoint of the Christian.— In Australia I met a man considered free from everything like intemperance, except for one habit. He used tobacco. He came to hear us at the tent, and one night after he went home, as he afterward told us, he wrestled against the habit of tobacco using, and obtained the victory. Some of his relatives had told him that they would give him fifty pounds if he would throw away his tobacco. He would not do it. "But," he said, "when you present the principles of temperance before us as you have done, I cannot resist them. You present before us the self-denial of One who gave His life for us. I do not know Him now, but I desire to know Him. I have never offered a prayer in my house. I have cast away my tobacco, but that is as far as I have gone."

We prayed with him, and after we left him we wrote to him and later visited him again. He finally reached the point where he gave himself to God, and he is becoming the very pillar of the church in the place where he lives. He is working with all his soul to bring his relatives to a knowledge of the truth.—*Evangelism,* pages 531, 532.

A Fisherman Gains the Victory.—In this place a fisherman has recently been converted to the truth. Although formerly a habitual user of the poisonous weed, he has, by the grace of God, determined to leave it alone for the future. The question was asked him, "Had you a hard struggle in giving it up?" "I should think I did," he answered, "but I saw the truth as it was presented to me. I learned that tobacco was unhealthful. I prayed to the Lord to help me to give it up, and He has helped me in a most marked manner. But I have not yet decided that I can give up my cup of tea. It braces me, and I know that I should have a severe headache did I not take it."

The evils of tea drinking were laid before him by Sister Sara McEnterfer. She encouraged him to have moral courage to try what giving up tea would do for him. He said, "I will." In two weeks he bore his testimony in meeting. "When I said that I would give up tea," he said, "I meant it. I did not drink it, and the result was a most severe headache. But I thought, Am I to keep using tea to ward off the headache? Must I be so dependent on it that when I let it alone I am in this condition? Now I know that its effects are bad. I will use it no more. I have not used it since, and I feel better every day. My headache no longer troubles me. My mind is clearer than it was. I can better understand the Scriptures as I read them."

I thought of this man, poor as far as worldly possessions are concerned, but with moral courage to cut loose from smoking and tea drinking, the habits of his boyhood. He did not plead for a little indulgence in wrongdoing. No; he decided that tobacco and tea were injurious, and that his influence must be on the right side. He has given evidence that the Holy Spirit is working on his mind and character to make him a vessel unto honor.—Manuscript 86, 1897.

Stand in His Strength.—The Lord has a remedy for every man who is beset by a strong appetite for strong drink or tobacco, or any other hurtful thing which destroys the brain power and defiles the body. He bids us come out from among them and be separate, and touch not the unclean thing. We are to set an example of Christian temperance. We are to do all in our power by self-denial and self-sacrifice, to control the appetite. And having done all, He bids us stand,—stand in His strength. He desires us to be victorious in every conflict with the enemy of our souls. He desires us to act understandingly, as wise generals in an army, as men who have perfect control over themselves.—Manuscript 38½, 1905.

5. Help for the Tempted

"Take My Yoke Upon You."—Jesus looked upon the distressed and heart-burdened, those whose hopes were blighted, and who with earthly joys were seeking to quiet the longing of the soul, and He invited all to find rest in Him.

Tenderly He bade the toiling people, "Take My yoke upon you, and learn of Me; for I am meek and lowly in heart: and ye shall find rest unto your souls." Matthew 11:29.

In these words, Christ was speaking to every human being. Whether they know it or not, all are weary and heavy-laden. All are weighed down with burdens that only Christ can remove. The heaviest burden that we bear is the burden of sin. If we were left to bear this burden, it would crush us. But the Sinless One has taken our place. "The Lord hath laid on Him the iniquity of us all." Isaiah 53:6.

He has borne the burden of our guilt. He will take the load from our weary shoulders. He will give us rest. The burden of care and sorrow also He will bear. He invites us to cast all our care upon Him; for He carries us upon His heart.

Christ Knows the Weaknesses of Humanity.—The Elder Brother of our race is by the eternal throne. He looks upon every soul who is turning his face toward Him as the Saviour. He knows by experience what are the weaknesses of humanity, what are our wants, and where lies the strength of our temptations; for He was "in all points tempted like as we are, yet without sin." Hebrews 4:15. He is watching over you, trembling child of God. Are you tempted? He will deliver. Are you weak? He will strengthen. Are you ignorant? He will enlighten. Are you wounded? He will heal. The Lord "telleth the number of the stars;" and yet "He healeth the broken in heart, and bindeth up their wounds." Psalm 147:4, 3.

Whatever your anxieties and trials, spread out your case before the Lord. Your spirit will be braced for endurance.

The way will be open for you to disentangle yourself from embarrassment and difficulty. The weaker and more helpless you know yourself to be, the stronger will you become in His strength. The heavier your burdens, the more blessed the rest in casting them upon your Burden Bearer.—*The Ministry of Healing,* pages 71, 72.

Power to Meet Every Temptation.—He who truly believes in Christ is made a partaker of the divine nature, and has power that he can appropriate under every temptation.—*Review and Herald,* Jan. 14, 1909.

Because man fallen could not overcome Satan with his human strength, Christ came from the royal courts of heaven to help him with His human and divine strength combined. Christ knew that Adam in Eden with his superior advantages might have withstood the temptations of Satan and conquered him. He also knew that it was not possible for man out of Eden, separated from the light and love of God since the Fall, to resist the temptations of Satan in his own strength. In order to bring hope to man, and save him from complete ruin, He humbled Himself to take man's nature, that with His divine power combined with the human He might reach man where he is. He obtained for the fallen sons and daughters of Adam that strength which it is impossible for them to gain for themselves, that in His name they might overcome the temptations of Satan.—*Redemption, or the Temptation of Christ,* page 44.

Help for Self-Inflicted Disease.—Many of those who came to Christ for help had brought disease upon themselves; yet He did not refuse to heal them. And when virtue from Him entered into these souls, they were convicted of sin, and many were healed of their spiritual disease as well as of their physical maladies.—*The Ministry of Healing,* page 73.

Power to Free the Captive.—Over the winds and the waves,

and over men possessed of demons, Christ showed that He had absolute control. He who stilled the tempest, and calmed the troubled sea, spoke peace to minds distracted and overborne by Satan.

In the synagogue at Capernaum, Jesus was speaking of His mission to set free the slaves of sin. He was interrupted by a shriek of terror. A madman rushed forward from among the people, crying out, "Let us alone; what have we to do with Thee, Thou Jesus of Nazareth? art Thou come to destroy us? I know Thee who Thou art, the Holy One of God."

Jesus rebuked the demon, saying, "Hold thy peace, and come out of him. And when the devil had thrown him in the midst, he came out of him, and hurt him not." Mark 1:24; Luke 4:35.

The cause of this man's affliction also was in his own life. He had been fascinated with the pleasures of sin, and had thought to make life a grand carnival. Intemperance and frivolity perverted the noble attributes of his nature, and Satan took entire control of him. Remorse came too late. When he would have sacrificed wealth and pleasure to regain his lost manhood, he had become helpless in the grasp of the evil one.

In the Saviour's presence he was roused to long for freedom; but the demon resisted the power of Christ. When the man tried to appeal to Jesus for help, the evil spirit put words into his mouth, and he cried out in an agony of fear. The demoniac partially comprehended that he was in the presence of One who could set him free; but when he tried to come within reach of that mighty hand, another's will held him; another's words found utterance through him.

The conflict between the power of Satan and his own desire for freedom was terrible. It seemed that the tortured man must lose his life in the struggle with the foe that had been the ruin of his manhood. But the Saviour spoke with author-

Activating Principles of a Changed Life

ity and set the captive free. The man who had been possessed stood before the wondering people in the freedom of self-possession.

With glad voice he praised God for deliverance. The eye that had so lately glared with the fire of insanity now beamed with intelligence, and overflowed with grateful tears. The people were dumb with amazement. As soon as they recovered speech they exclaimed one to another, "What is this? a new teaching! with authority He commandeth even the unclean spirits, and they obey Him." Mark 1:27, R.V.

Deliverance for Those in Need Today.—There are multitudes today as truly under the power of evil spirits as was the demoniac of Capernaum. All who willfully depart from God's commandments are placing themselves under the control of Satan. Many a man tampers with evil, thinking that he can break away at pleasure; but he is lured on and on, until he finds himself controlled by a will stronger than his own. He cannot escape its mysterious power. Secret sin or master passion may hold him a captive as helpless as was the demoniac at Capernaum.

Yet his condition is not hopeless. God does not control our minds without our consent; but every man is free to choose what power he will have to rule over him. None have fallen so low, none are so vile, but that they may find deliverance in Christ. The demoniac, in place of prayer, could utter only the words of Satan; yet the heart's unspoken appeal was heard. No cry from a soul in need, though it fail of utterance in words, will be unheeded. Those who consent to enter into covenant with God are not left to the power of Satan or to the infirmity of their own nature.

"Shall the prey be taken from the mighty, or the lawful captive delivered? . . . Thus saith the Lord, Even the captives of the mighty shall be taken away, and the prey of the terrible shall be delivered: for I will contend with him that contendeth with thee, and I will save thy children." Isaiah 49:24, 25.

Marvelous will be the transformation wrought in him who by faith opens the door of the heart to the Saviour.—*The Ministry of Healing, pages 91-93.*

The Saviour's Love for Ensnared Souls.—Jesus knows the circumstances of every soul. The greater the sinner's guilt, the more he needs the Saviour. His heart of divine love and sympathy is drawn out most of all for the one who is the most hopelessly entangled in the snares of the enemy. With His own blood He has signed the emancipation papers of the race.

Jesus does not desire those who have been purchased at such a cost to become the sport of the enemy's temptations. He does not desire us to be overcome and perish. He who curbed the lions in their den, and walked with His faithful witnesses amid the fiery flames, is just as ready to work in our behalf, to subdue every evil in our nature. Today He is standing at the altar of mercy, presenting before God the prayers of those who desire His help. He turns no weeping, contrite one away. Freely will He pardon all who come to Him for forgiveness and restoration. He does not tell to any all that He might reveal, but He bids every trembling soul take courage. Whosoever will, may take hold of God's strength, and make peace with Him, and He will make peace.

The souls that turn to Him for refuge, Jesus lifts above the accusing and the strife of tongues. No man or evil angel can impeach these souls. Christ unites them to His own divine-human nature.—*The Ministry of Healing, pages 89, 90.*

Precious Promises.—These precious words every soul that abides in Christ may make his own. He may say:

> "I will look unto the Lord;
> I will wait for the God of my salvation:
> My God will hear me.

Activating Principles of a Changed Life

> Rejoice not against me, O mine enemy;
> When I fall, I shall arise;
> When I sit in darkness,
> The Lord shall be a light unto me.

> "He will again have compassion on us,
> He will blot out our iniquities;
> Yea, Thou wilt cast all our sins into the depths of the sea!" Micah 7:7, 8, 19, Noyes's translation.

God has promised:

> "I will make a man more precious than fine gold;
> Even a man than the golden wedge of Ophir."
> Isaiah 13:12.

> "Though ye have lain among the pots,
> Yet shall ye be as the wings of a dove covered with silver,
> And her feathers with yellow gold." Psalm 68:13.

Those whom Christ has forgiven most will love Him most. These are they who in the final day will stand nearest to His throne.

"They shall see His face; and His name shall be in their foreheads." Revelation 22:4.—*The Ministry of Healing,* page 182.

Section VII

REHABILITATING THE INTEMPERATE

1. Counsel on How to Work

Temperance Work a Living Issue.—Every true reform has its place in the work of the gospel and tends to the uplifting of the soul to a new and nobler life. Especially does the temperance reform demand the support of Christian workers. They should call attention to this work, and make it a living issue. Everywhere they should present to the people the principles of true temperance, and call for signers to the temperance pledge. Earnest effort should be made in behalf of those who are in bondage to evil habits.

There is everywhere a work to be done for those who through intemperance have fallen. In the midst of churches, religious institutions, and professedly Christian homes, many of the youth are choosing the path to destruction. Through intemperate habits they bring upon themselves disease, and through greed to obtain money for sinful indulgence they fall into dishonest practices. Health and character are ruined. Aliens from God, outcasts from society, these poor souls feel that they are without hope either for this life or for the life to come. The hearts of the parents are broken. Men speak of these erring ones as hopeless; but not so does God regard them. He understands all the circumstances that have made them what they are, and He looks upon them with pity. This is a class that demand help. Never give them occasion to say, "No man cares for my soul."

Give First Attention to the Physical Condition.—Among the victims of intemperance are men of all classes and all professions. Men of high station, of eminent talents, of great attainments, have yielded to the indulgence of appetite, until they are helpless to resist temptation. Some of them who were once in the possession of wealth are without home, without friends, in suffering, misery, disease, and degradation. They have lost their self-control. Unless a helping hand is held out to them, they will sink lower and lower. With these self-indulgence is not only a moral sin, but a physical disease.

Often in helping the intemperate, we must, as Christ so often did, give first attention to their physical condition. They need wholesome, unstimulating food and drink, clean clothing, opportunity to secure physical cleanliness. They need to be surrounded with an atmosphere of helpful, uplifting Christian influence. In every city a place should be provided where the slaves of evil habit may receive help to break the chains that bind them. Strong drink is regarded by many as the only solace in trouble; but this need not be, if, instead of acting the part of the priest and Levite, professed Christians would follow the example of the good Samaritan.

Patience Needed in Dealing with Demon-Possessed Inebriate.—In dealing with the victims of intemperance we must remember that we are not dealing with sane men, but with those who for the time being are under the power of a demon. Be patient and forbearing. Think not of the repulsive, forbidding appearance, but of the precious life that Christ died to redeem. As the drunkard awakens to a sense of his degradation, do all in your power to show that you are his friend. Speak no word of censure. Let no act or look express reproach or aversion. Very likely the poor soul curses himself. Help him to rise. Speak words that will encourage faith. Seek to strengthen every good trait in his character. Teach him how to reach upward. Show him that it is possible for him to live so as to win the respect of his fellow men. Help him to see the value of the talents which God has given him, but which he has neglected to improve.

Although the will has been depraved and weakened, there is hope for him in Christ. He will awaken in the heart higher impulses and holier desires. Encourage him to lay hold of the hope set before him in the gospel. Open the Bible before the tempted, struggling one, and over and over again read to him the promises of God. These promises will be to him as the leaves of the tree of life. Patiently continue your efforts, until with grateful joy the trembling hand grasps the hope of redemption through Christ.

Continued Efforts Needed.—You must hold fast to those whom you are trying to help, else victory will never be yours. They will be continually tempted to evil. Again and again they will be almost overcome by the craving for strong drink; again and again they may fall; but do not, because of this, cease your efforts.

They have decided to make an effort to live for Christ; but their will power is weakened, and they must be carefully guarded by those who watch for souls as they that must give an account. They have lost their manhood, and this they must win back. Many have to battle against strong hereditary tendencies to evil. Unnatural cravings, sensual impulses, were their inheritance from birth. These must be carefully guarded against. Within and without, good and evil are striving for the mastery. Those who have never passed through such experiences cannot know the almost overmastering power of appetite, or the fierceness of the conflict between habits of self-indulgence and the determination to be temperate in all things. Over and over again the battle must be fought.

Not to Be Discouraged by Backsliding.—Many who are drawn to Christ will not have moral courage to continue the warfare against appetite and passion. But the worker must not be discouraged by this. Is it only those rescued from the lowest depths that backslide?

Remember that you do not work alone. Ministering angels unite in service with every truehearted son and daughter of God. And Christ is the Restorer. The Great Physician Himself stands beside His faithful workers, saying to the repentant soul, "Child, thy sins be forgiven thee." Mark 2:5, and A.R.V. margin.

Many Will Enter Heaven.—Many are the outcasts who will grasp the hope set before them in the gospel, and will enter the kingdom of heaven, while others who were blessed with great opportunities and great light which they did not improve will be left in outer darkness.—*The Ministry of Healing,* pages 171-174.

Good Impulses Beneath a Forbidding Exterior.—We become too easily discouraged over the souls who do not at once respond to our efforts. Never should we cease to labor for a soul while there is one gleam of hope. Precious souls cost our self-sacrificing Redeemer too dear a price to be lightly given up to the tempter's power.

We need to put ourselves in the place of the tempted ones. Consider the power of heredity, the influence of evil associations and surroundings, the power of wrong habits. Can we wonder that under such influences many become degraded? Can we wonder that they should be slow to respond to efforts for their uplifting?

Often, when won to the gospel, those who appeared coarse and unpromising will be among its most loyal adherents and advocates. They are not altogether corrupt. Beneath the forbidding exterior, there are good impulses that might be reached. Without a helping hand many would never recover themselves, but by patient, persistent effort they may be uplifted. Such need tender words, kind consideration, tangible help. They need that kind of counsel which will not extinguish the faint gleam of courage in the soul. Let the workers who come in contact with them consider this.

Fruits of the Miracle of Grace.—Some will be found whose minds have been so long debased that they will never in this life become what under more favorable circumstances they might have been. But the bright beams of the Sun of Righteousness may shine into the soul. It is their privilege to have the life that measures with the life of God. Plant in their minds uplifting, ennobling thoughts. Let your life make plain to them the difference between vice and purity, darkness and light. In your example let them read what it means to be a Christian. Christ is able to uplift the most sinful, and place them where they will be acknowledged as children of God, joint heirs with Christ to the immortal inheritance.

By the miracle of divine grace, many may be fitted for lives of usefulness. Despised and forsaken, they have become utterly discouraged; they may appear stoical and stolid. But under the ministration of the Holy Spirit, the stupidity that makes their uplifting appear so hopeless will pass away. The dull, clouded mind will awake. The slave of sin will be set free. Vice will disappear, and ignorance will be overcome. Through the faith that works by love the heart will be purified and the mind enlightened.—*The Ministry of Healing,* pages 168, 169.

2. The Temperance Worker

Personal Labor Called For.—Missionary work does not consist merely of preaching. It includes personal labor for those who have abused their health and have placed themselves where they have not moral power to control their appetites and passions. These souls are to be labored for as those more favorably situated. Our world is full of suffering ones. —*Evangelism,* page 265.

The Example of Self-Control.—Those who control themselves are fitted to labor for the weak and erring. They will deal with them tenderly and patiently. By their own example, they will show what is right, and then they will seek to place the erring where they will be under good influences.

"Even from the days of your fathers ye are gone away from Mine ordinances, and have not kept them. Return unto Me, and I will return unto you, saith the Lord of hosts. But ye said, Wherein shall we return?"

If any of you find others who are in uncertainty as to what they should do, you are to show them. Everyone should be engaged in the work of soulsaving. Everyone should be prepared to give instruction in regard to the science of salvation. —Manuscript 38½, 1905.

Be Compassionate and Sympathetic.—Let us seek to understand how to reach the people. There is no better way to do this than to be compassionate and sympathetic. If you know of those who are sick and in need of assistance, help them, try to relieve them in their distress. As you do this work, the power of the Lord will speak through it to the soul. —*General Conference Bulletin,* April 23, 1901.

Win by Sympathy and Love.—Persons are attracted by sympathy and love; and many may thus be won to the ranks of Christ and reform; but they cannot be forced or driven. Christian forbearance, candor, consideration, and courtesy toward all who do not see the truth as we do, will exert a powerful influence for good. We must learn not to move too fast, and require too much of those who are newly converted to the truth.—Manuscript 1, 1878.

Encouragement of Little Attentions.—In all our associations it should be remembered that in the experience of others there are chapters sealed from mortal sight. On the pages of memory are sad histories that are sacredly guarded from curious eyes. There stand registered long, hard battles with trying circumstances, perhaps troubles in the home life, that day by day weaken courage, confidence, and faith. Those who are fighting the battle of life at great odds may be strengthened and encouraged by little attentions that cost only a loving effort. To such the strong, helpful grasp of the hand by a true friend is worth more than gold or silver. Words of kindness are as welcome as the smile of angels.—*The Ministry of Healing,* page 158.

Offer Something Better—Don't Attack.—It is of little use to try to reform others by attacking what we may regard as wrong habits. Such effort often results in more harm than good. In His talk with the Samaritan woman, instead of disparaging Jacob's well, Christ presented something better. "If thou knewest the gift of God," He said, "and who it is that saith to thee, Give Me to drink; thou wouldst have asked of Him, and He would have given thee living water." John 4:10. He turned the conversation to the treasure He had to bestow, offering the woman something better than she possessed, even living water, the joy and hope of the gospel. This is an illustration of the way in which we are to work. We must offer men something better than that which they possess, even the peace of Christ, which passeth all understanding. We must tell them of God's holy law, the transcript of His character, and an expression of that which He wishes them to become. Show them how infinitely superior to the fleeting joys and pleasures of the world is the imperishable glory of heaven. Tell them of the freedom and rest to be found in the Saviour. "Whosoever drinketh of the water that I shall give him shall never thirst" (verse 14), He declared.

Lift up Jesus, crying, "Behold, the Lamb of God, that taketh away the sin of the world!" John 1:29, A.R.V. He alone can satisfy the craving of the heart, and give peace to the soul.

Unselfish, Kind, Courteous.—Of all people in the world, reformers should be the most unselfish, the most kind, the most courteous. In their lives should be seen the true goodness of unselfish deeds. The worker who manifests a lack of courtesy, who shows impatience at the ignorance or waywardness of others, who speaks hastily or acts thoughtlessly, may close the door to hearts so that he can never reach them.

As the dew and the still showers fall upon the withering plants, so let words fall gently when seeking to win men from error. God's plan is first to reach the heart. We are to speak the truth in love, trusting in Him to give it power for the reforming of the life. The Holy Spirit will apply to the soul the word that is spoken in love.

Naturally we are self-centered and opinionated. But when we learn the lessons that Christ desires to teach us, we become partakers of His nature; henceforth we live His life. The wonderful example of Christ, the matchless tenderness with which He entered into the feelings of others, weeping with those who wept, rejoicing with those who rejoiced, must have a deep influence upon the character of all who follow Him in sincerity. By kindly words and acts they will try to make the path easy for weary feet.—*The Ministry of Healing,* pages 156-158.

The Lost Coin—Precious Still.—The lost coin, in the Saviour's parable, though lying in the dirt and rubbish, was a piece of silver still. Its owner sought it because it was of value. So every soul, however degraded by sin, is in God's sight accounted precious. As the coin bore the image and superscription of the reigning power, so man at his creation bore the image and superscription of God. Though now marred and dim through the influence of sin, the traces of this inscription remain upon every soul. God desires to recover that soul, and to retrace upon it His own image in righteousness and holiness.

How little do we enter into sympathy with Christ on that which should be the strongest bond of union between us and Him,—compassion for depraved, guilty, suffering souls, dead in trespasses and sins! The inhumanity of man toward man is our greatest sin. Many think that they are representing the justice of God, while they wholly fail of representing His tenderness and His great love. Often the ones whom they meet with sternness and severity are under the stress of temptation. Satan is wrestling with these souls, and harsh, unsympathetic words discourage them, and cause them to fall a prey to the tempter's power.—*The Ministry of Healing,* page 163.

No Censure for the Straying Sheep.—The parable of the lost sheep is a forcible illustration of the Saviour's love for the erring. The Shepherd leaves the ninety and nine in the shelter of the fold, while He goes out to search for the one lost, perishing sheep; and when it is found, He places it upon His shoulder, and returns with rejoicing. He did not find fault with the straying sheep; He did not say, "Let him go if he will;" but He went forth amid frost and sleet and tempest, to save the one that was lost. And He patiently continued His search until the object of His solicitude was found.

Thus are we to treat the erring, wandering one. We should be ready to sacrifice our own ease and comfort when a soul for whom Christ died is in peril. Said Jesus, "Joy shall be in heaven over one sinner that repenteth, more than over ninety and nine just persons, which need no repentance." As joy was manifested at the recovery of the one lost sheep, so will exceeding joy and gratitude be manifested by the true servants of Christ when one soul is saved from death.—Manuscript 1, 1878.

Christ Will Show Us How.—We are called upon to work with more than human energy, to labor with the power that is in Jesus Christ. The One who stooped to take human nature is the One who will show us how to conduct the battle. Christ has left His work in our hands, and we are to wrestle with God, supplicating day and night for the power that is unseen. It is laying right hold of God through Jesus

Christ that will gain the victory.—*Testimonies,* vol. 6, p. 111.

Gratitude of the Saved.—The worth of a soul cannot be fully estimated by finite minds. How gratefully will the ransomed and glorified ones remember those who were instrumental in their salvation! No one will then regret his self-denying efforts and persevering labors, his patience, forbearance, and earnest heart-yearnings for souls that might have been lost had he neglected his duty or become weary in well-doing.—Manuscript 1, 1878.

Safeguards for the Worker.—The temptations to which we are daily exposed make prayer a necessity. Dangers beset every path. Those who are seeking to rescue others from vice and ruin are especially exposed to temptation. In constant contact with evil, they need a strong hold upon God, lest they themselves be corrupted. Short and decisive are the steps that lead men down from high and holy ground to a low level. In a moment decisions may be made that fix one's condition forever. One failure to overcome leaves the soul unguarded. One evil habit, if not firmly resisted, will strengthen into chains of steel, binding the whole man.

The reason why so many are left to themselves in places of temptation is that they do not set the Lord always before them. When we permit our communion with God to be broken, our defense is departed from us. Not all your good purposes and good intentions will enable you to withstand evil. You must be men and women of prayer. Your petitions must not be faint, occasional, and fitful, but earnest, persevering, and constant. It is not always necessary to bow upon your knees in order to pray. Cultivate the habit of talking with the Saviour when you are alone, when you are walking, and when you are busy with your daily labor. Let the heart be continually uplifted in silent petition for help, for light, for strength, for knowledge. Let every breath be a prayer.

Protection for Those Who Make God Their Trust.—As

workers for God we must reach men where they are, surrounded with darkness, sunken in vice, and stained with corruption. But while we stay our minds upon Him who is our sun and our shield, the evil that surrounds us will not bring one stain upon our garments. As we work to save the souls that are ready to perish, we shall not be put to shame if we make God our trust. Christ in the heart, Christ in the life, this is our safety. The atmosphere of His presence will fill the soul with abhorrence of all that is evil. Our spirit may be so identified with His that in thought and aim we shall be one with Him.—*The Ministry of Healing,* pages 509-511.

Section VIII

OUR BROAD TEMPERANCE PLATFORM

1. What True Temperance Embodies

Reaching the Highest Degree of Perfection.—"Whether therefore ye eat, or drink, or whatsoever ye do, do all to the glory of God."

Only one lease of life is granted us; and the inquiry with everyone should be, How can I invest my life so that it will yield the greatest profit? How can I do most for the glory of God and the benefit of my fellow men? For life is valuable only as it is used for the attainment of these objects.

Our first duty toward God and our fellow beings is that of self-development. Every faculty with which the Creator has endowed us should be cultivated to the highest degree of perfection, that we may be able to do the greatest amount of good of which we are capable. Hence that time is spent to good account which is directed to the establishment and preservation of sound physical and mental health. We cannot afford to dwarf or cripple a single function of mind or body by overwork or by abuse of any part of the living machinery. As surely as we do this, we must suffer the consequences.

Intemperance, in the true sense of the word, is at the foundation of the larger share of the ills of life, and it annually destroys its tens of thousands. For intemperance is not limited to the use of intoxicating liquors; it has a broader meaning, and includes the hurtful indulgence of any appetite or passion. —*Signs of the Times,* Nov. 17, 1890.

Excess in Eating, Drinking, Sleeping, and Seeing.—Excessive indulgence in eating, drinking, sleeping, or seeing, is sin. The harmonious healthy action of all the powers of body and mind results in happiness; and the more elevated and refined the powers, the more pure and unalloyed the happiness.—*Testimonies,* vol. 4, p. 417.

Temperance in the Food Eaten.—The principles of temperance must be carried further than the mere use of spirituous liquors. The use of stimulating and indigestible food is often equally injurious to health, and in many cases sows the seeds of drunkenness. True temperance teaches us to dispense entirely with everything hurtful, and to use judiciously that which is healthful. There are few who realize as they should how much their habits of diet have to do with their health, their character, their usefulness in this world, and their eternal destiny. The appetite should ever be in subjection to the moral and intellectual powers. The body should be servant to the mind, and not the mind to the body.—*Patriarchs and Prophets,* page 562.

Eating Too Frequently or Too Much.—Those who eat and work intemperately and irrationally, talk and act irrationally. It is not necessary to drink alcoholic liquors in order to be intemperate. The sin of intemperate eating—eating too frequently, too much, and of rich, unwholesome food—destroys the healthy action of the digestive organs, affects the brain, and perverts the judgment, preventing rational, calm, healthy thinking and acting.—*Christian Temperance and Bible Hygiene,* page 155.

Those who will not, after the light has come to them, eat and drink from principle, instead of being controlled by appetite, will not be tenacious in regard to being governed by principle in other things.—*Health Reformer,* August, 1866.

Temperance in Dressing, Also.—God's people are to learn

the meaning of temperance in all things. They are to practice temperance in eating and drinking and dressing. All self-indulgence is to be cut away from their lives. Before they can really understand the meaning of true sanctification and of conformity to the will of Christ, they must, by co-operating with God, obtain the mastery over wrong habits and practices.—*Medical Ministry,* page 275.

Temperance in Labor.—We should practice temperance in our labor. It is not our duty to place ourselves where we shall be overworked. Some may at times be placed where this is necessary, but it should be the exception, not the rule. We are to practice temperance in all things. If we honor the Lord by acting our part, He will on His part preserve our health. We should have a sensible control of all our organs. By practicing temperance in eating, in drinking, in dressing, in labor, and in all things, we can do for ourselves what no physician can do for us.—Manuscript 41, 1908.

Living on Borrowed Capital.—Intemperance in almost everything, exists on every hand. Those who make great exertions to accomplish just so much work in a given time, and continue to labor when their judgment tells them they should rest, are never gainers. They are living on borrowed capital. They are expending the vital force which they will need at a future time. And when the energy they have so recklessly used is demanded, they fail for want of it. The physical strength is gone, the mental powers fail. They realize that they have met with a loss, but do not know what it is. Their time of need has come, but their physical resources are exhausted.

Everyone who violates the laws of health must sometime be a sufferer to a greater or less degree. God has provided us with constitutional force, which will be needed at different periods of our lives. If we recklessly exhaust this force by continual overtaxation, we shall sometimes be losers. Our usefulness will be lessened, if not our life itself destroyed.—*Fundamentals of Christian Education,* pages 153, 154.

Evening Labor.—As a rule, the labor of the day should not be prolonged into the evening. . . . I have been shown that those who do this, often lose much more than they gain, for their energies are exhausted, and they labor on nervous excitement. They may not realize any immediate injury, but they are surely undermining their constitution.—*Counsels on Health,* page 99.

Temperance in Study.—Intemperance in study is a species of intoxication, and those who indulge in it, like the drunkard, wander from safe paths, and stumble and fall in the darkness. The Lord would have every student bear in mind that the eye must be kept single to the glory of God. He is not to exhaust and waste his physical and mental powers in seeking to acquire all possible knowledge of the sciences, but is to preserve the freshness and vigor of all his powers to engage in the work which the Lord has appointed him in helping souls to find the path of righteousness.—*Counsels to Parents, Teachers, and Students,* pages 405, 406.

Intemperance in Seeking Riches.—One of the most fruitful sources of shattered constitutions among men is a devotion to the getting of money, an inordinate desire for wealth. They narrow their lives to the single pursuit of money, sacrifice rest, sleep, and the comforts of life to this one object. Their naturally good constitutions are broken down, disease sets in as a consequence of the abuse of their physical powers, and death closes the scene of a perverted life. Not a dollar of his wealth can that man take with him who has obtained it at such a terrible price. Money, palaces, and rich apparel avail him nothing now; his lifework is worse than useless.—*Health Reformer,* April, 1877.

To Guard Every Fiber of the Being.—Every organ, every

fiber of the being, is to be sacredly guarded from every harmful practice, if we would not be among the number that Christ represents as walking in the same dishonorable path as did the inhabitants of the world before the Flood. Those in this number will be appointed to destruction, because they have persisted in carrying lawful habits to extremes, and have created and indulged habits that have no foundation in nature, and that become a warring lust. . . .

The mass of the inhabitants of this world are destroying for themselves the true basis of the highest earthly interest. They are destroying their power of self-control, and making themselves incapable of appreciating eternal realities. Willingly ignorant of their own structure, they lead their children in the same path of self-indulgence, causing them to suffer the penalty of the transgression of nature's laws. . . .

Our habits of eating and drinking show whether we are of the world or among the number that the Lord by His mighty cleaver of truth has separated from the world. These are His peculiar people, zealous of good works.—Manuscript 86, 1897.

Temperance in All Things.—In order to preserve health, temperance in all things is necessary,—temperance in labor, temperance in eating and drinking. Our heavenly Father sent the light of health reform to guard against the evils resulting from a debased appetite, that those who love purity and holiness may know how to use with discretion the good things He has provided for them, and that by exercising temperance in daily life, they may be sanctified through the truth. —*Christian Temperance and Bible Hygiene,* page 52.

The advocates of temperance should place their standard on a broader platform. They would then be laborers together with God. With every iota of their influence they should encourage the spread of reform principles.—Manuscript 86, 1897.

2. The Body the Temple

The Christian's Responsibility.—"Know ye not," Paul asks, "that ye are the temple of God, and that the Spirit of God dwelleth in you? If any man defile the temple of God, him shall God destroy; for the temple of God is holy, which temple ye are." Man is God's workmanship, His masterpiece, created for a high and holy purpose; and on every part of the human tabernacle God desires to write His law. Every nerve and muscle, every mental and physical endowment, is to be kept pure.

God designs that the body shall be a temple for His Spirit. How solemn then is the responsibility resting on every soul. . . . How many there are, blessed with reason and intelligence, talents which should be used to the glory of God, who willfully degrade soul and body. Their lives are a continual round of excitement. Cricket and football matches and horse racing absorb the attention. The liquor curse, with its world of woe, is defiling the temple of God. . . . By the use of liquor and tobacco men are debasing the life given them for high and holy purposes. Their practices are represented by wood, hay, and stubble. Their God-given powers are perverted, their senses degraded, to minister to the desires of the carnal mind.

The drunkard sells himself for a cup of poison. Satan takes control of his reason, his affections, his conscience. Such a man is destroying the temple of God. Tea drinking helps to do this work. Yet how many there are who place destroying agencies on their tables.

No Right to Cripple One Organ of Mind or Body.—No man or woman has any right to form habits which lessen the healthful action of one organ of mind or body. He who perverts his powers is defiling the temple of the Holy Spirit. The Lord will not work a miracle to restore to soundness those who continue to use drugs which so degrade soul, mind, and body that sacred things are not appreciated. Those who give themselves up to the use of tobacco and liquor do not appreciate their intellect. They do not realize the value of the faculties God has given them. They allow their powers to wither and decay.

God desires all who believe in Him to feel the necessity of improvement. Every intrusted faculty is to be improved. Not one is to be neglected. As God's husbandry and building, man is under His supervision in every sense of the word; and the better he becomes acquainted with his Maker, the more sacred will his life become in his estimation. . . .

God asks His children to live a pure, holy life. He has given His Son that we may reach this standard. He has made every provision necessary to enable man to live, not for animal satisfaction, like the beasts that perish, but for God and heaven. . . .

God Keeps an Account.—The physical penalty of disregarding the laws of nature will appear in the form of sickness, ruined constitutions, and even death itself. But a settlement is also to be made, by and by, with God. He keeps an account of every work, whether it is good or evil, and in the day of judgment every man will receive according to his work. Every transgression of the laws of physical life is a transgression of the laws of God; and punishment must and will follow every such transgression.

The human house, God's building, requires close, watchful guardianship. . . . The physical life is to be carefully educated, cultivated, and developed, that through men and women the divine nature may be revealed in its fullness. God expects men to use the intellect He has given them. He expects them to use every reasoning power for Him. They are to give the conscience the place of supremacy that has been assigned to it. The mental and physical powers, with the affections, are to be so cultivated that they can reach the highest efficiency.—*Review and Herald,* Nov. 6, 1900.

When Guided by an Enlightened Conscience.—The apostle Paul writes: "Know ye not that they which run in a race run all, but one receiveth the prize? So run, that ye may obtain. And every man that striveth for the mastery is temperate in all things. Now they do it to obtain a corruptible crown; but we an incorruptible."—*Signs of the Times,* Oct. 2, 1907.

The apostle Paul here mentions the foot races, with which the Corinthians were familiar. The contestants in these races were subjected to the most severe discipline in order to fit them for the trial of their strength. Their diet was simple. Luxurious food and wine were prohibited. Their food was carefully selected. They studied to know what was best adapted to render them healthful and active, and to impart physical vigor and endurance, that they might put as heavy a tax as possible upon their strength. Every indulgence that would tend to weaken the physical powers was forbidden.—*Signs of the Times,* Jan. 27, 1909.

If heathen men, who were not controlled by enlightened conscience, who had not the fear of God before them, would submit to deprivation and the discipline of training, denying themselves of every weakening indulgence merely for a wreath of perishable substance and the applause of the multitude, how much more should they who are running the Christian race in the hope of immortality and the approval of High Heaven be willing to deny themselves unhealthful stimulants and indulgences, which degrade the morals, enfeeble the intellect, and bring the higher powers into subjection to the animal appetites and passions.

Multitudes in the world are witnessing this game of life, the Christian warfare. And this is not all. The Monarch of the universe and the myriads of heavenly angels are spectators of this race; they are anxiously watching to see who will be successful overcomers, and win the crown of glory that fadeth not away. With intense interest God and heavenly angels mark the self-denial, the self-sacrifice, and the agonizing efforts of those who engage to run the Christian race. The reward given to every man will be in accordance with the persevering energy and faithful earnestness with which he performs his part in the great contest.

In the games referred to, but one was sure of the prize. In the Christian race, says the apostle, "I so run not as uncertainly." We are not to be disappointed at the end of the race. To all those who fully comply with the conditions in God's word, and have a sense of their responsibility to preserve physical vigor and activity of body, that they may have well-balanced minds and healthy morals, the race is not uncertain. They all may gain the prize, and win and wear the crown of immortal glory that fadeth not away. . . .

Promises to the Overcomer.—The world should be no criterion for us. It is fashionable to indulge the appetite in luxurious food and unnatural stimulants, thus strengthening the animal propensities and crippling the growth and development of the moral faculties. There is no encouragement given to any of the sons or daughters of Adam that they may become victorious overcomers in the Christian warfare unless they decide to practice temperance in all things. If they do this, they will not fight as one that beateth the air.

If Christians will keep the body in subjection, and bring all their appetites and passions under the control of enlightened conscience, feeling it a duty that they owe to God and to their neighbors to obey the laws which govern health and life, they will have the blessing of physical and mental vigor. They will have moral power to engage in the warfare against Satan; and in the name of Him who conquered appetite in their behalf, they may be more than conquerors on their own account. This warfare is open to all who will engage in it.
—*Signs of the Times,* Oct. 2, 1907.

3. Temperance and Spirituality

The Surrender to Satan.—Man, through yielding to Satan's temptations to indulge intemperance, brings the higher faculties in subjection to the animal appetites and passions, and when these gain the ascendancy, man, who was created a little lower than the angels, with faculties susceptible of the highest cultivation, surrenders to the control of Satan. And he gains easy access to those who are in bondage to appetite. Through intemperance, some sacrifice one half, and others two thirds, of their physical, mental, and moral powers, and become playthings for the enemy.

Those who would have clear minds to discern Satan's devices, must have their physical appetites under the control of reason and conscience. The moral and vigorous action of the higher powers of the mind are essential to the perfection of Christian character, and the strength or the weakness of the mind has very much to do with our usefulness in this world, and with our final salvation.

The ignorance that has prevailed in regard to God's law in our physical nature, is deplorable. Intemperance of any kind is a violation of the laws of our being. Imbecility is prevailing to a fearful extent. Sin is made attractive by the covering of light which Satan throws over it, and he is well pleased when he can hold the Christian world in their daily habits under the tyranny of custom, like the heathen, and allow appetite to govern them.

Strength of Body and Intellect Sacrificed.—If men and women of intelligence have their moral powers benumbed through intemperance of any kind, they are, in many of their habits, elevated but little above the heathen. Satan is constantly drawing the people from saving light, to custom and fashion, irrespective of physical, mental, and moral health. The great enemy knows that if appetite and passion predominate, the health of body and strength of intellect are sacrificed upon the altar of self-gratification, and man is brought to speedy ruin. If enlightened intellect holds the reins, controlling the animal propensities and keeping them in subjection to the moral powers, Satan well knows that his power to overcome with his temptations is very small.

To Meet the Demands of Fashion.—In our day, people talk of the dark ages, and boast of progress. But with this progress wickedness and crime do not decrease. We deplore the absence of natural simplicity, and the increase of artificial display. Health, strength, beauty, and long life, which were common in the so-called "Dark Ages," are rare now. Nearly everything desirable is sacrificed to meet the demands of fashionable life.

A large share of the Christian world have no right to call themselves Christians. Their habits, their extravagance, and general treatment of their own bodies, are violations of physical law, and contrary to the Bible. They are working out for themselves, in their course of life, physical suffering, and mental and moral feebleness.

Through his devices, Satan, in many respects, has made the domestic life one of care and complicated burdens, in order to meet the demands of fashion. His purpose in doing this is to keep minds occupied so fully with the things of this life that they can give but little attention to their highest interest. Intemperance in eating and in dressing has so engrossed the minds of the Christian world that they do not take time to become intelligent in regard to the laws of their being, that they may obey them. To profess the name of Christ is of but little account if the life does not correspond with the will of God, revealed in His word. . . .

When Sanctification Is Impossible.—A large proportion of all the infirmities that afflict the human family, are the results of their own wrong habits, because of their willing ignorance, or of their disregard of the light which God has given in relation to the laws of their being. It is not possible for us to glorify God while living in violation of the laws of life. The heart cannot possibly maintain consecration to God while the lustful appetite is indulged. A diseased body and disordered intellect, because of continual indulgence in hurtful lust, make sanctification of the body and spirit impossible.

The apostle understood the importance of the healthful conditions of the body for the successful perfection of Christian character. He says, "I keep under my body, and bring it into subjection: lest that by any means, when I have preached to others, I myself should be a castaway."—*Redemption; or the Temptation of Christ,* pages 57-62.

Habits, Tastes, and Inclinations to Be Educated.—Nothing can be more offensive to God than to cripple or abuse the gifts lent us to be devoted to His service. It is written, "Whether therefore ye eat, or drink, or whatsoever ye do, do all to the glory of God."

In every important work, there are times of crisis, when there is great need that those connected with the work should have clear minds. There must be men who realize, as did the apostle Paul, the importance of practicing temperance in all things. There is work for us to do—stern, earnest work for our Master. All our habits, tastes, and inclinations must be educated in harmony with the laws of life and health. By this means we may secure the very best physical condition, and have mental clearness to discern between the evil and the good.

Intemperance of any kind benumbs the perceptive organs, and so weakens the brain nerve power that eternal things are not appreciated, but are placed on a level with common things. The higher powers of the mind, designed for noble purposes, are brought into slavery to the baser passions. If the physical habits are not right, the mental and moral powers cannot be strong; for great sympathy exists between the physical and

Our Broad Temperance Platform

the moral. The apostle Peter understood this, and raised his voice of warning: "Dearly beloved, I beseech you as strangers and pilgrims, abstain from fleshly lusts, which war against the soul."

Higher Interests Imperiled.—Thus the word of God plainly warns us that unless we abstain from fleshly lusts, the physical nature will be brought into conflict with the spiritual. Lustful indulgence wars against health and peace. A warfare is instituted between the higher and the lower attributes of the man. The lower propensities, strong and active, oppress the soul. The highest interests of the being are imperiled by the indulgence of unsanctified appetite.—*Signs of the Times,* Jan. 27, 1909.

A Lesson for Seventh-day Adventists.—The case of Aaron's sons has been placed upon record for the benefit of God's people, and should teach those especially who are preparing for the second coming of Christ, that the indulgence of a depraved appetite destroys the fine feelings of the soul, and so affects the reasoning powers which God has given to man, that spiritual and holy things lose their sacredness. Disobedience looks pleasing, instead of exceeding sinful.—*Signs of the Times,* July 8, 1880.

To Overcome Every Hurtful Practice.—The principles of temperance are far-reaching; and there is danger that those who have received great light on this subject will fail to appreciate this light. God requires that His people living in these last days, overcome every hurtful practice, presenting their bodies a living sacrifice, holy, acceptable unto Him, that they may win a seat at His right hand.

It is our duty to take ourselves in hand, and strive to bring our minds, our wills, and our tastes into conformity with the requirements of our Creator. The grace of God alone can enable us to do this: by its power our lives may be brought into harmony with right principles. We shall reap that which we sow, and only those who bring themselves into subjection to the will of God are truly wise.—Letter 69, 1896.

Controlled by Enlightened Conscience.—If Christians would bring all their appetites and passions under the control of enlightened conscience, feeling it a duty they owe to God and to their neighbor to obey the laws which govern life and health, they would have the blessing of physical and mental vigor; they would have moral power to engage in the warfare against Satan; and in the name of Him who conquered in their behalf, they might be more than conquerors on their own account.—*Christian Temperance and Bible Hygiene,* pages 39, 40.

Why Many Will Fall.—We want our sisters who are now injuring themselves by wrong habits to put them away and come to the front and be workers in reform. The reason why many of us will fall in the time of trouble is because of laxity in temperance and indulgence of appetite.

Moses preached a great deal on this subject, and the reason the people did not go through to the promised land was because of repeated indulgence of appetite. Nine tenths of the wickedness among the children of today is caused by intemperance in eating and drinking. Adam and Eve lost Eden through the indulgence of appetite, and we can only regain it by the denial of the same.—*Review and Herald,* Oct. 21, 1884.

So Run That Ye May Obtain.—There are precious victories to gain; and the victors in this contest against appetite and every worldly lust will receive a crown of life that fadeth not away, a blessed home in that city whose gates are of pearl and whose foundations are of precious stones. Is not this prize worth striving for? Is it not worth every effort that we can make? Then let us so run that we may obtain.—*Signs of the Times,* Sept. 1, 1887.

4. Daniel's Example

We can have no right understanding of the subject of temperance until we consider it from a Bible standpoint. And nowhere shall we find a more comprehensive and forcible illustration of true temperance and its attendant blessings than is afforded by the history of the prophet Daniel and his associates in the court of Babylon.—*Signs of the Times,* Dec. 6, 1910.

When the people of Israel, their king, nobles, and priests, were carried into captivity, four of their number were selected to serve in the court of the king of Babylon. One of these was Daniel, who early gave promise of the remarkable ability developed in later years. These youth were all of princely birth, and are described as "children in whom was no blemish, but well favored, and skillful in all wisdom, and cunning in knowledge, and understanding science, and such as had ability in them." Perceiving the superior talents of these youthful captives, King Nebuchadnezzar determined to prepare them to fill important positions in His kingdom. That they might be fully qualified for their life at court, according to Oriental custom, they were to be taught the language of the Chaldeans, and to be subjected for three years to a thorough course of physical and intellectual discipline.

The youth in this school of training were not only to be admitted to the royal palace, but it was provided that they should eat of the meat and drink of the wine which came from the king's table. In all this the king considered that he was not only bestowing great honor upon them, but securing for them the best physical and mental development that could be attained.

Meeting the Test.—Among the viands placed before the king were swine's flesh and other meats which were declared unclean by the law of Moses, and which the Hebrews had been expressly forbidden to eat. There Daniel was brought to a severe test. Should he adhere to the teachings of his fathers concerning meats and drinks, and offend the king, and probably lose not only his position but his life? or should he disregard the commandment of the Lord, and retain the favor of the king, thus securing great intellectual advantages and the most flattering worldly prospects?

Daniel did not long hesitate. He decided to stand firm in his integrity, let the result be what it might. He "purposed in his heart that he would not defile himself with the portion of the king's meat, nor with the wine which he drank."

Not Narrow or Bigoted.—There are many among professed Christians today who would decide that Daniel was too particular, and would pronounce him narrow and bigoted. They consider the matter of eating and drinking as of too little consequence to require such a decided stand,—one involving the probable sacrifice of every earthly advantage. But those who reason thus will find in the day of judgment that they turned from God's express requirements, and set up their own opinion as a standard of right and wrong. They will find that what seemed to them unimportant was not so regarded of God. His requirements should be sacredly obeyed. Those who accept and obey one of His precepts because it is convenient to do so, while they reject another because its observance would require a sacrifice, lower the standard of right, and by their example lead others to lightly regard the holy law of God. "Thus saith the Lord" is to be our rule in all things.

A Faultless Character.—Daniel was subjected to the severest temptations that can assail the youth of today; yet he was true to the religious instruction received in early life. He was surrounded with influences calculated to subvert those who would vacillate between principle and inclination; yet the word of God presents him as a faultless character. Daniel dared not trust to his own moral power. Prayer was to him a necessity. He made God his strength, and the fear of God was continually before him in all the transactions of his life.

Daniel possessed the grace of genuine meekness. He was true, firm, and noble. He sought to live in peace with all, while he was unbending as the lofty cedar wherever principle was involved. In everything that did not come in collision with his allegiance to God, he was respectful and obedient to those who had authority over him; but he had so high a sense of the claims of God that the requirements of earthly rulers were held subordinate. He would not be induced by any selfish consideration to swerve from his duty.

The character of Daniel is presented to the world as a striking example of what God's grace can make of men fallen by nature and corrupted by sin. The record of his noble, self-denying life is an encouragement to our common humanity. From it we may gather strength to nobly resist temptation, and firmly, and in the grace of meekness, stand for the right under the severest trial.

God's Approval Dearer Than Life.—Daniel might have found a plausible excuse to depart from his strictly temperate habits; but the approval of God was dearer to him than the favor of the most powerful earthly potentate,—dearer even than life itself. Having by his courteous conduct obtained favor with Melzar, the officer in charge of the Hebrew youth, Daniel made a request that they might not eat of the king's meat, or drink of his wine. Melzar feared that should he comply with this request, he might incur the displeasure of the king, and thus endanger his own life. Like many at the present day, he thought that an abstemious diet would render these youth pale and sickly in appearance, and deficient in muscular strength, while the luxurious food from the king's table would make them **ruddy and beautiful, and would pro**mote physical and mental activity.

Daniel requested that the matter be decided by a ten days' trial,—the Hebrew youth during this brief period being permitted to eat of simple foods, while their companions partook of the king's dainties. The request was finally granted, and then Daniel felt assured that he had gained his case. Although but a youth, he had seen the injurious effects of wine and luxurious living upon physical and mental health.

God Vindicates His Servants.—At the end of the ten days the result was found to be quite the opposite of Melzar's expectations. Not only in personal appearance, but in physical activity and mental vigor, those who had been temperate in their habits exhibited a marked superiority over their companions who had indulged appetite. As a result of this trial, Daniel and his associates were permitted to continue their simple diet during the whole course of their training for the duties of the kingdom.

The Lord regarded with approval the firmness and self-denial of these Hebrew youth, and His blessing attended them. He "gave them knowledge and skill in all learning and wisdom: and Daniel had understanding in all visions and dreams." At the expiration of the three years of training, when their ability and acquirements were tested by the king, he "found none like Daniel, Hananiah, Mishael, and Azariah: therefore stood they before the king. And in all matters of wisdom and understanding, that the king inquired of them, he found them ten times better than all the magicians and astrologers that were in all his realm."

Self-Control a Condition of Sanctification.—The life of Daniel is an inspired illustration of what constitutes a sanctified character. It presents a lesson for all, and especially for the young. A strict compliance with the requirements of God is beneficial to the health of body and mind. In order to reach the highest standard of moral and intellectual attainments, it is necessary to seek wisdom and strength from God, and to observe strict temperance in all the habits of life. In the experience of Daniel and his companions we have an instance of the triumph of principle over temptation to indulge the appetite. It shows us that through religious principle young men may triumph over the lusts of the flesh, and remain true to God's requirements, even though it cost them a great sacrifice.

What if Daniel and his companions had made a compromise with those heathen officers, and had yielded to the pressure of the occasion, by eating and drinking as was customary with the Babylonians? That single instance of departure from principle would have weakened their sense of right and their abhorrence of wrong. Indulgence of appetite would have involved the sacrifice of physical vigor, clearness of intellect, and spiritual power. One wrong step would probably have led to others, until, their connection with Heaven being severed, they would have been swept away by temptation.

God has said, "Them that honor Me I will honor." While Daniel clung to his God with unwavering trust, the Spirit of prophetic power came upon him. While he was instructed of man in the duties of court life, he was taught of God to read the mysteries of future ages, and to present to coming generations, through figures and similitudes, the wonderful things that would come to pass in the last days.—*The Sanctified Life,* pages 15-19.

The Hebrew youth did not act presumptuously, but in firm reliance upon God. They did not choose to be singular, but they would be so rather than dishonor God.—*Prophets and Kings,* page 483.

The Reward for Temperance for Us, Too.—The Hebrew captives were men of like passions with ourselves. Amid the seductive influences of the luxurious courts of Babylon, they stood firm. The youth of today are surrounded with allurements to self-indulgence. Especially in our large cities, every form of sensual gratification is made easy and inviting. Those who, like Daniel, refuse to defile themselves, will reap the reward of temperate habits. With their greater physical stamina and increased power of endurance, they have a bank of deposit upon which to draw in case of emergency.

Right physical habits promote mental superiority. Intellectual power, physical stamina, and length of life depend upon immutable laws. Nature's God will not interfere to preserve men from the consequences of violating nature's requirements. He who strives for the mastery must be temperate in all things. Daniel's clearness of mind and firmness of purpose, his power in acquiring knowledge and in resisting temptation, were due in a great degree to the plainness of his diet, in connection with his life of prayer.

There is much sterling truth in the adage, "Every man is the architect of his own fortune." While parents are responsible for the stamp of character, as well as for the education and training, of their sons and daughters, it is still true that our position and usefulness in the world depend, to a great degree, upon our own course of action. Daniel and his companions enjoyed the benefits of correct training and education in early life, but these advantages alone would not have made them what they were. The time came when they must act for themselves,—when their future depended upon their own course. Then they decided to be true to the lessons given them in childhood. The fear of God, which is the beginning of wisdom, was the foundation of their greatness.—*Youth's Instructor,* July 9, 1903.

5. The Food on Our Tables

Tracing Intemperance to Their Own Tables.—Many mothers who deplore the intemperance that exists everywhere, do not look deep enough to see the cause. Too often it may be traced to the home table. Many a mother, even among those who profess to be Christians, is daily setting before her household rich and highly seasoned food, which tempts the appetite and encourages overeating.—*Christian Temperance and Bible Hygiene,* pages 75, 76.

After a time, through continued indulgence, the digestive organs become weakened, and the food taken does not satisfy the appetite. Unhealthy conditions are established, and there is a craving for more stimulating food. Tea, coffee, and flesh meats produce an immediate effect. Under the influence of these poisons the nervous system is excited, and, in some cases, for the time being, the intellect seems to be invigorated and the imagination to be more vivid. Because these stimulants produce for the time being such agreeable results, many conclude that they really need them and continue their use. . . .

The appetite is educated to crave something stronger which will have a tendency to keep up and increase the agreeable excitement, until indulgence becomes habit, and there is a continual craving for stronger stimulus, as tobacco, wines, and liquors.—*Testimonies,* vol. 3, pp. 487, 488.

Healthful Food, Simply Prepared.—Every mother should carefully guard her table, and allow nothing to come upon it which will have the slightest tendency to lay the foundation of intemperate habits. Food should be prepared in as simple a manner as possible, free from condiments and spices, and even from an undue amount of salt.

You who have at heart the good of your children, and who would see them come up with unperverted tastes and appetites, must perseveringly urge your way against popular sentiments and practices. If you would have them prepared to be useful on earth and to obtain the eternal reward in the kingdom of glory, you must teach them to obey the laws of God, both in nature and revelation, instead of following the customs of the world.

Painstaking effort, prayer and faith, when united with a correct example, will not be fruitless. Bring your children to

God in faith, and seek to impress their susceptible minds with a sense of their obligations to their heavenly Father. It will require lesson upon lesson, line upon line, precept upon precept, here a little and there a little.—*Review and Herald,* Nov. 6, 1883.

Half the Mothers Deplorably Ignorant.—Not one half the mothers know how to cook or what to set before their children. They place before their little nervous children these rich substances that burn in the throat and all the way down to the tender coats of the stomach, making it like a burnt boot, so it does not recognize healthful food. The little ones will come to the table, and they cannot eat this, or they cannot eat that. They take control and get just what they want whether it is for their good or not.

I would recommend letting them go without for at least three days until they are hungry enough to enjoy good wholesome food. I would risk their starving. I have never placed on my table things which I did not allow my children to partake of. I would place before them just what I myself would eat. The children would eat of this food and never think of asking for things not on the table. We should not indulge the appetite of our children by placing before them these rich foods.—Manuscript 3, 1888.

Paving the Way for Intemperance.—The tables of our American people are generally prepared in a manner to make drunkards.—*Testimonies,* vol. 3, p. 563.

Those who believe present truth should refuse to drink tea or coffee, for these excite a desire for stronger stimulant. They should refuse to eat flesh meat, for this, too, excites a desire for strong drink. Wholesome food, prepared with taste and skill, should be our diet now.—*Evangelism,* page 265.

Meat Stimulates.—The immediate results of meat eating may be apparently to invigorate the system, but this is no reason for its being considered the best article of diet. The moderate use of brandy will have the same effect for the time being, but when its exciting influence is gone there follows a sense of languor and debility. Those who depend upon simple and nutritious food, that is comparatively unstimulating in its effects, can endure more labor in the course of months and years than the meat eater or the liquor drinker. They who work in the open air will feel less injury from the use of flesh-meats than those of sedentary habits, for sun and air are great helps to digestion, and do much to counteract the effect of wrong habits of eating and drinking.

The Effects of Stimulants.—All stimulants hurry the human machinery too fast, and although, for the time, activity and vigor may seem to be increased, in proportion to the irritating influence employed, there must be a reaction; a debility will follow corresponding in degree to the unnatural excitement that has been produced.

When this debility is felt, something to stimulate and tone up the system is again used to give immediate relief from disagreeable languor. Nature is gradually educated to rely upon this oft-repeated remedy, until her powers are enfeebled by being often aroused to unnatural action. All persons should become acquainted with the laws of their being. It should be an important subject of study, how to live, how to regulate labor, and how to eat and drink in reference to health.

The more simply and naturally we live the better shall we be able to resist epidemic and disease. If our habits are good and the system is not weakened by unnatural action, Nature will furnish all the stimulus that we require. . . .

Appetite an Unsafe Guide.—The rule which some recommend, is to eat whenever there is a sense of hunger, and to eat until satisfied. This course will lead to disease and numerous evils. Appetite at the present day is not generally natural, therefore is not a correct index to the wants of the system.

It has been pampered and misdirected until it has become morbid and can no longer be a safe guide. Nature has been abused, her efforts crippled by wrong habits and indulgence in sinful luxuries, until taste and appetite are alike perverted.

It is unnatural to have a craving for flesh meats. It was not thus in the beginning. The appetite for meat has been made and educated by man. Our Creator has furnished us, in vegetables, grains, and fruits, all the elements of nutrition necessary to health and strength. Flesh meats composed no part of the food of Adam and Eve before their fall. If fruits, vegetables, and grains are not sufficient to meet the wants of man, then the Creator made a mistake in providing for Adam. . . .

That Israel Might Preserve Physical and Moral Strength.—God did not withhold meat from the Hebrews in the wilderness simply to show His authority, but for their good, that they might preserve physical and moral strength. He knew that the use of animal food strengthens the animal passions and enfeebles the intellect. He knew that the gratification of the appetite of the Hebrews for flesh meats, would weaken their moral powers, and induce such an irritable disposition that the vast army would become insubordinate, that they would lose the high sense of their moral obligations, and refuse to be controlled by the wise laws of Jehovah. Violence and rebellion would exist among them, making it impossible for them to be a pure and happy people in the land of Canaan. God knew what was best for the children of Israel, therefore He deprived them in a great measure of flesh meats.

Satan tempted them to consider this unjust and cruel. He caused them to lust after forbidden things, because he saw that through the indulgence of perverted appetite they would become carnally minded and could be easily brought to do his will; the lower organs would be strengthened, while the intellectual and moral powers would be weakened.

Satan is no novice in the business of destroying souls. He well knows that if he can lead men and women into wrong habits of eating and drinking, he has gained, in a great degree, the control of their minds and baser passions. In the beginning man ate of the fruits of the earth, but sin brought into use the flesh of dead animals as food. This diet works directly against the spirit of true refinement and moral purity. The substance of that which is taken into the stomach, passes into the circulation, and is converted into flesh and blood. . . .

God requires that His people should be temperate in all things. The example of Christ, during that long fast in the wilderness, should teach His followers to repulse Satan when he comes under the guise of appetite. Then may they have influence to reform those who have been led astray by indulgence, and have lost moral power to overcome the weakness and sin that has taken possession of them. Thus may Christians secure health and happiness, in a pure, well-ordered life and a mind clear and untainted before God.—*Signs of the Times,* Jan. 6, 1876.

Reform as the New Convert Sees It.—When the message comes to those who have not heard the truth for this time, they see that a great reformation must take place in their diet. They see that they must put away flesh food, because it creates an appetite for liquor, and fills the system with disease. By meat eating, the physical, mental, and moral powers are weakened. Man is built up from that which he eats. Animal passions bear sway as the result of meat eating, tobacco using, and liquor drinking.—*Counsels on Diet and Foods,* pages 268, 269.

Intemperance in Variety of Dishes.—I go farther. Temperance should be practiced in the cooking of the food and in the variety of dishes provided, that the mother may be spared all the labor possible. A great variety of food is not essential for the sustenance of life; instead, it injures the digestive organs, causing a war in the stomach. With the blessing of God, plain, simple food will sustain life, and be the best for the entire being.

Few realize that generally more food than necessary is placed in the stomach. But the extra food eaten is a tax on the stomach, and injures the whole human structure.—*Manuscript 50, 1893.*

Overeating Is Intemperance.—Intemperance is seen in the quantity as well as in the quality of food eaten.—*Counsels on Health,* page 576.

Intemperance embraces much. With some it consists of eating too largely of food which, if taken in proper quantities, would not be objectionable. All that is taken into the stomach above the actual need of the system becomes a dangerous element. It decays in the stomach, and causes dyspepsia. Continual overeating uses up the vital forces, and deprives the brain of power to do its work.—*Manuscript 155, 1899.*

One who indulges freely in eating, who overloads the digestive organs until they are unable properly to care for the food eaten, is also an intemperate man, and he will find it impossible to discern clearly spiritual things.—*Manuscript 41, 1908.*

Our heavenly Father would have us use with discretion the good things He has provided for us.—*Signs of the Times,* Jan. 27, 1909.

An Important Place in Our Salvation.—Those who are not health reformers treat themselves unfairly and unwisely. By the indulgence of appetite they do themselves fearful injury. Some may think that the question of diet is not important enough to be included in the question of religion. But such make a great mistake. God's word declares, "Whether therefore ye eat, or drink, or whatsoever ye do, do all to the glory of God." The subject of temperance, in all its bearings, has an important place in the working out of our salvation.—*Evangelism,* page 265.

If men and women perseveringly live in accordance with the laws of life and of health, they will realize the blessed results of an entire health reform.—*Signs of the Times,* Jan. 6, 1876.

All Are Being Proved.—It is of great importance that individually we act well our part, and have an intelligent understanding of what we should eat and drink, and how we should live to preserve health. All are being proved to see whether they will accept the principles of health reform or follow a course of self-indulgence.—*Counsels on Diet and Foods,* page 34.

6. Total Abstinence Our Position

The Only Safe Course.—The only safe course is to touch not, taste not, handle not, tea, coffee, wines, tobacco, opium, and alcoholic drinks. The necessity for the men of this generation to call to their aid the power of the will, strengthened by the grace of God, in order to withstand the temptations of Satan and resist the least indulgence of perverted appetite is twice as great as it was several generations ago. But the present generation have less power of self-control than had those who lived then.—*Testimonies,* vol. 3, p. 488.

Let us never partake of a glass of alcoholic liquor. Let us never touch it.—Manuscript 38½, 1905.

The Will to Touch Not, Taste Not, and Handle Not.—If all would be vigilant and faithful in guarding the little openings made by the moderate use of the so-called harmless wine and cider, the highway to drunkenness would be closed up. What is needed in every community is firm purpose, and a will to touch not, taste not, handle not; then the temperance reformation would be strong, permanent, and thorough.—*Review and Herald,* March 25, 1884.

Abstain strictly from all stimulating food or drink. You are God's property. You are not to abuse any organ of the body. You are to care wisely for your body, that there may be a perfect development of the whole man. Is it not an act of ingratitude on your part to do anything so to weaken your vital forces that you are unable properly to represent Him or to do the work He has for you to do?—Letter 236, 1903.

Temperance Principles Stem From God's Law.—If men strictly and conscientiously kept the law of God, there would be no drunkards, no tobacco inebriates, no distress, penury, and crime. Liquor saloons would be closed for want of patronage, and nine tenths of all misery existing in the world would come to an end. Young men would walk forth with erect and noble forms, free and elastic step, clear eye, and healthy complexions.

When ministers, from their pulpits, make loyalty to the law of God disreputable; when they join with the world in making it unpopular; when these teachers of the people indulge in the social glass, and the defiling narcotic, tobacco, what depth of vice may not be expected from the youth of this generation? . . . You have heard much in regard to the authority and sanctity of the law of the Ten Commandments. God is the author of that law, which is the foundation of His government in heaven and on earth. All enlightened nations have based their laws upon this grand foundation of all law; yet the legislators and ministers, who are recognized as the leaders and teachers of the people, live in open violation of the principles inculcated in those holy statutes.

Many ministers preach Christ from the pulpit, and then do not hesitate to benumb their senses by wine tippling, or even indulging in brandy and other liquors. The Christian standard says, "Touch not; taste not; handle not;" and the laws of our physical being repeat the solemn injunction with emphasis. It is the duty of every Christian minister to lay this truth plainly before his people, teaching it both by precept and example. . . .

The Christian church is pronounced to be the salt of the earth, the light of the world. Can we apply this to the churches of today, many of whose members are using, not only the defiling narcotic, tobacco, but intoxicating wine, and spirituous liquor, and are placing the wine cup to their neighbor's lips? The church of Christ should be a school in which the inexperienced youth should be educated to control their appetites, from a moral and religious standpoint. They should there be taught how unsafe it is to tamper with temptation, to dally with sin; that there is no such thing as being a moderate and temperate drinker; that the path of the tippler is ever downward. They should be exhorted to "look not thou upon the wine when it is red," which "at the last biteth like a serpent, and stingeth like an adder."—*Signs of the Times,* Aug. 29, 1878.

Total Abstinence Our Platform.—When temperance is presented as a part of the gospel, many will see their need of reform. They will see the evil of intoxicating liquors and that total abstinence is the only platform on which God's people can conscientiously stand.—*Testimonies,* vol. 7, p. 75.

7. Relation to Church Membership

A Living, Working Element in the Church.—In the family circle and in the church we should place Christian temperance on an elevated platform. It should be a living, working element, reforming habits, dispositions, and characters. Intemperance lies at the foundation of all the evil in our world.—Manuscript 50, 1893.

Those We Cannot Take Into the Church.—God grant that

we may be wide awake to this awful evil. May He help us to labor with all our power to save men and women and youth from this effort of the enemy to ensnare them. We do not take into the church those who use liquor or tobacco. We cannot admit such ones. But we can try to help them to overcome. We can tell them that by giving up these harmful practices, they will make their families and themselves happier. Those whose hearts are filled with the Spirit of God will feel no need for stimulants.—*Review and Herald,* June 15, 1905.

The True Convert Abandons Defiling Habits and Appetites.—Men and women have many habits that are antagonistic to the principles of the Bible. The victims of strong drink and tobacco are corrupted, body, soul, and spirit. Such ones should not be received into the church until they give evidence that they are truly converted, that they feel the need of the faith that works by love and purifies the soul. The truth of God will purify the true believer. He who is thoroughly converted will abandon every defiling habit and appetite. By total abstinence he will overcome his desire for health-destroying indulgences.—*Evangelism,* page 264.

8. Seventh-day Adventists Spiritual Leaders

Preserve Mental Vigor and Give Power of Endurance.—There is a solemn responsibility upon all, especially upon ministers who teach the truth, to overcome on the point of appetite. The usefulness of ministers of Christ would be much greater if they had control of their appetites and passions; and their mental and moral powers would be stronger if they should combine physical labor with mental exertion. They could, with strictly temperate habits, with mental and physical labor combined, accomplish a far greater amount of labor and preserve clearness of mind. If they should pursue such a course their thoughts and words would flow more freely, their religious exercises would be more energized, and the impressions made upon their hearers would be more marked.

Intemperance in eating, even of food of the right quality, will have a prostrating influence upon the system, and will blunt the keener and holier emotions. Strict temperance in eating and drinking is highly essential for the healthy preservation and vigorous exercise of all the functions of the body. Strictly temperate habits, combined with the exertion of the muscles as well as the exercise of the mind, will preserve both mental and physical vigor, and give power of endurance to those engaged in the ministry, to editors, and to all others whose habits are sedentary.—*Health Reformer,* August, 1875.

Follow Christ's Example.—Ministers of Christ, professing to be His representatives, should follow His example, and above all others should form habits of strictest temperance. They should keep the life and example of Christ before the people by their own lives of self-denial, self-sacrifice, and active benevolence. Christ overcame appetite in man's behalf, and in His stead they are to set others an example worthy of imitation. Those who do not feel the necessity of engaging in the work of overcoming upon the point of appetite will fail to secure precious victories which they might have gained and will become slaves to appetite and lust, which are filling the cup of iniquity of those who dwell upon the earth."
—*Testimonies,* vol. 3, p. 490.

Spiritual Vision Impaired.—I am instructed to say to my brethren in the ministry: By intemperance in eating you disqualify yourselves for seeing clearly the difference between sacred and common fire. And by this intemperance you also reveal your disregard for the warnings that the Lord has given you. His word to you is: "Who is among you that feareth the Lord, that obeyeth the voice of His servant, that walketh in darkness, and hath no light? let him trust in the name of the Lord, and stay upon his God. Behold, all ye that kindle a fire, that compass yourselves about with sparks: walk in the light of your fire, and in the sparks that ye have kindled. This shall ye have of Mine hand; ye shall lie down in sorrow." Isaiah 50:10, 11.—*Testimonies,* vol. 7, p. 258.

An Aid to Clear Thinking.—We have no right to overtax either the mental or the physical powers so that we are easily excited and led to speak words which dishonor God. The Lord desires us to be always calm and forbearing. Whatever others may do, we are to represent Christ doing as He would do under similar circumstances.

Every day one in a position of trust has decisions to make on which depend results of great importance. He has often to think rapidly, and this can be done successfully only by those who practice strict temperance. The mind strengthens under the correct treatment of the physical and the mental powers. If the strain is not too great, it acquires new vigor with every taxation.—*Testimonies,* vol. 7, p. 199.

Qualifications for Men Chosen for Responsible Positions.—It means much to be true to God. He has claims upon all who are engaged in His service. He desires that mind and body be preserved in the best condition of health, every power and endowment under the divine control, and as vigorous as careful, strictly temperate habits can make them. We are under obligation to God to make an unreserved consecration of ourselves to Him, body and soul, with all the faculties appreciated as His entrusted gifts, to be employed in His service. All our energies and capabilities are to be constantly strengthened and improved during this probationary period. Only those who appreciate these principles, and have been trained to care for their bodies intelligently and in the fear of God, should be chosen to take responsibilities in this work. Those who have been long in the truth, yet who cannot distinguish between the pure principles of righteousness and the principles of evil, whose understanding in regard to justice, mercy, and the love of God is clouded, should be relieved of responsibilities. Every church needs a clear, sharp testimony, giving the trumpet a certain sound.—*Signs of the Times,* Oct. 2, 1907.

Health Workers to Be Temperate.—He [the physician] sees that those who are taking the nurses' course should be given a thorough education in the principles of health reform, that they should be taught to be strictly temperate in all things, because carelessness in regard to the laws of health is inexcusable in those set apart to teach others how to live.—*Testimonies,* vol. 7, p. 74.

Educate, Educate, Educate.—Because the principles of health and temperance are so important, and are so often misunderstood, neglected, or unknown, we should educate ourselves, that we may not only bring our own lives into harmony with these principles, but teach them to others. The people need to be educated, line upon line, precept upon precept. The matter must be kept fresh before them. Nearly every family needs to be stirred up. The mind must be enlightened and the conscience aroused to the duty of practicing the principles of true reform.

Ministers especially should become intelligent on this question. As shepherds of the flock, they will be held accountable for willing ignorance and disregard of nature's laws. Let them find out what constitutes true hygienic reform, and teach its principles, both by precept, and by a quiet, consistent example. They should not ignore their duty in this matter, not be turned aside because some may call them extremists. At conventions, institutes, and other large and important meetings, instruction should be given upon health and temperance. Bring into service all the talent at command, and follow up the work with publications on the subject. "Educate, educate, educate," should be the watchword.—Undated Manuscript 9.

Section IX

LAYING THE FOUNDATION OF INTEMPERANCE

1. Prenatal Influence

Where Reform Should Begin.—The efforts of our temperance workers are not sufficiently far-reaching to banish the curse of intemperance from our land. Habits once formed are hard to overcome. The reform should begin with the mother before the birth of her children; and if God's instructions were faithfully obeyed, intemperance would not exist.

It should be the constant effort of every mother to conform her habits to God's will, that she may work in harmony with Him to preserve her children from the health- and life-destroying vices of the present day. Let mothers place themselves without delay in right relations to their Creator, that they may by His assisting grace build around their children a bulwark against dissipation and intemperance.—*Counsels on Diet and Foods,* pages 225, 226.

The Habits of the Father and the Mother.—As a rule, every intemperate man who rears children, transmits his inclinations and evil tendencies to his offspring.—*Review and Herald,* Nov. 21, 1882.

The child will be affected for good or evil by the habits of the mother. She must herself be controlled by principle, and must practice temperance and self-denial, if she would seek the welfare of her child.—*Counsels on Diet and Foods,* page 218.

The Birthright of Evil Tendencies.—The thoughts and feelings of the mother will have a powerful influence upon the legacy she gives her child. If she allows her mind to dwell upon her own feelings, if she indulges in selfishness, if she is peevish and exacting, the disposition of her child will testify to the fact. Thus many have received as a birthright almost unconquerable tendencies to evil. The enemy of souls understands this matter much better than do many parents. He will bring his temptations to bear upon the mother, knowing that if she does not resist him, he can through her affect her child. The mother's only hope is in God. She may flee to Him for strength and grace; and she will not seek in vain.—*Signs of the Times,* Sept. 13, 1910.

God's Message to Every Mother.—The carefulness with which the mother should guard her habits of life is taught in the Scriptures. When the Lord would raise up Samson as a deliverer for Israel, "the angel of Jehovah" appeared to the mother, with special instruction concerning her habits, and also for the treatment of her child. "Beware," he said, "and now drink no wine nor strong drink, neither eat any unclean thing." Judges 13:13, 7.

The effect of parental influences is by many parents looked upon as a matter of little moment; but heaven does not so regard it. The message sent by an angel of God, and twice given in the most solemn manner, shows it to be deserving of our most careful thought.

In the words spoken to the Hebrew mother, God speaks to all mothers in every age. "Let her beware," the angel said; "all that I commanded her let her observe." The well-being of the child will be affected by the habits of the mother. Her appetites and passions are to be controlled by principle. There is something for her to shun, something for her to work against, if she fulfills God's purpose for her in giving her a child. If before the birth of her child she is self-indulgent, if she is selfish, impatient, and exacting, these traits will be reflected in the disposition of the child. Thus many children have received as a birthright almost unconquerable tendencies to evil. But if the mother unswervingly adheres to right principles, if she is temperate and self-denying, if she is kind, gentle and unselfish, she may give her child these same precious traits of character. Very explicit was the command prohibiting the use of wine by the mother. Every drop of strong drink taken by her to gratify appetite endangers the physical, mental, and moral health of her child, and is a direct sin against her Creator.—*The Ministry of Healing,* pages 372, 373.

Accountable for the Welfare of Future Generations.—If women of past generations had always moved from high considerations, realizing that future generations would be ennobled or debased by their course of action, they would have taken their stand, that they could not unite their life interest with men who were cherishing unnatural appetites for alcoholic drinks, and tobacco which is a slow, but sure and deadly poison, weakening the nervous system, and debasing the noble faculties of the mind. If men would remain wedded to these vile habits, women should have left them to their life of single blessedness, to enjoy these companions of their choice. Women should not have considered themselves of so little value as to unite their destiny with men who had no control over their appetites, but whose principal happiness consisted in eating and drinking, and gratifying their animal passions.

Women have not always followed the dictates of reason instead of impulse. They have not felt in a high degree the responsibilities resting upon them, to form such life connections as would not enstamp upon their offspring a low degree of morals, and a passion to gratify debased appetites, at the expense of health, and even life. God will hold them accountable in a large degree for the physical health and moral characters thus transmitted to future generations.—*How to Live,* No. 2, pp. 27, 28.

The Newborn Child.—The inquiry of fathers and mothers should be, "What shall we do unto the child that shall be born unto us?" We have brought before the reader what God has said concerning the course of the mother before the birth of her children. But this is not all. The angel Gabriel was sent from the heavenly courts to give directions for the care of children after their birth, that parents might fully understand their duty.

About the time of Christ's first advent the angel Gabriel came to Zacharias with a message similar to that given to Manoah. The aged priest was told that his wife should bear a son, whose name should be called John. "And," said the angel, "thou shalt have joy and gladness; and many shall rejoice at his birth. For he shall be great in the sight of the Lord, and shall drink neither wine nor strong drink; and he shall be filled with the Holy Ghost." This child of promise was to be brought up with strictly temperate habits. An important work of reform was to be committed to him, to prepare the way for Christ.

Intemperance in every form existed among the people. Indulgence in wine and luxurious food was lessening physical strength, and debasing the morals to such an extent that the most revolting crimes did not appear sinful. The voice of John was to sound forth from the wilderness in stern rebuke for the sinful indulgences of the people, and his own abstemious habits were also to be a reproof of the excesses of his time.—*Counsels on Diet and Foods,* page 225.

2. The Strength of Inherited Tendencies

Insatiable Cravings Transmitted.—Both parents transmit their own characteristics, mental and physical, their dispositions and appetites, to their children. As the result of parental intemperance, children often lack physical strength and mental and moral power. Liquor drinkers and tobacco users may, and do, transmit their insatiable craving, their inflamed blood and irritable nerves, to their children. The licentious often bequeath their unholy desires, and even loathsome diseases, as a legacy to their offspring. And as the children have less power to resist temptation than have the parents, the tendency is for each generation to fall lower and lower.—*Patriarchs and Prophets,* page 561.

To the Third and Fourth Generation.—Our ancestors have bequeathed to us customs and appetites which are filling the world with disease. The sins of the parents, through perverted appetite, are with fearful power visited upon the children to the third and fourth generations. The bad eating of many generations, the gluttonous and self-indulgent habits of the people, are filling our poorhouses, our prisons, and our insane asylums. Intemperance in drinking tea and coffee, wine, beer, rum, and brandy, and the use of tobacco, opium, and other narcotics, has resulted in great mental and physical degeneracy, and this degeneracy is constantly increasing.—*Review and Herald,* July 29, 1884.

The Legacy to Oncoming Generations.—Wherever the habits of the parents are contrary to physical law, the injury done to themselves will be repeated in the future generations. —Manuscript 3, 1897.

The race is groaning under a weight of accumulated woe, because of the sins of former generations. And yet with scarcely a thought or care, men and women of the present generation indulge intemperance by surfeiting and drunkenness, and thereby leave, as a legacy for the next generation, disease, enfeebled intellects, and polluted morals."—*Testimonies,* vol. 4, p. 31.

Counteracting Inherited Tendencies.—Parents may have transmitted to their children tendencies to appetite and passion, which will make more difficult the work of educating and training these children to be strictly temperate and to have pure and virtuous habits. If the appetite for unhealthy food and for stimulants and narcotics has been transmitted to them as a legacy from their parents, what a fearfully solemn responsibility rests upon the parents to counteract the evil tendencies which they have given to their children! How earnestly and diligently should the parents work to do their duty, in faith and hope, to their unfortunate offspring!—*Testimonies,* vol. 3, pp. 567, 568.

To Breast the Tide of Evil.—Many suffer in consequence of the transgression of their parents. While they are not responsible for what their parents have done, it is nevertheless their duty to ascertain what are and what are not violations of the laws of health. They should avoid the wrong habits of their parents, and by correct living, place themselves in better conditions.—*The Ministry of Healing,* page 234.

Greater Moral Power Now Required.—The necessity for the men of this generation to call to their aid the power of the will, strengthened by the grace of God, in order to withstand the temptations of Satan, and resist the least indulgence of perverted appetite, is far greater than it was several generations ago. But the present generation have less power of self-control than had those who lived then. Those who indulged in these stimulants transmitted their depraved appetites and passions to their children, and greater moral power is now required to resist intemperance in all its forms. The only perfectly safe course is to stand firm, observing strict temperance in all things, and never venturing into the path of danger.—*Christian Temperance and Bible Hygiene,* page 37.

3. Formation of Behavior Patterns

Begin With Infancy.—Let parents begin a crusade against intemperance at their own firesides, in their own families, in the principles they teach their children to follow from their very infancy, and they may hope for success.—*Testimonies, vol. 3, p. 567.*

Diligently Teach.—Teach your children from the cradle to practice self-denial and self-control. . . . Impress upon their tender minds the truth that God does not design that we should live for present gratification merely, but for our ultimate good. Teach them that to yield to temptation is weak and wicked; to resist, noble and manly. These lessons will be as seed sown in good soil, and they will bear fruit that will make your hearts glad.—*The Ministry of Healing, page 386.*

Importance of an Early Start.—Too much importance cannot be placed upon the early training of children. The lessons learned, the habits formed, during the years of infancy and childhood, have more to do with the formation of the character and the direction of the life than have all the instruction and training of afteryears.—*The Ministry of Healing, page 380.*

Far-Reaching Influence of Early Habits.—The character is formed, to a great extent, in early years. The habits then established have more influence than any natural endowment, in making men either giants or dwarfs in intellect; for the very best talents may, through wrong habits, become warped and enfeebled. The earlier in life one contracts hurtful habits, the more firmly will they hold their victim in slavery, and the more certainly will they lower his standard of spirituality.—*Counsels on Health, pages 112, 113.*

Difficult to Unlearn Established Habits.—It is a most difficult matter to unlearn the habits which have been indulged through life. The demon of intemperance is of giant strength, and is not easily conquered. . . . It will pay you, mothers, to use the precious hours which are given you by God in forming the character of your children, and in teaching them to adhere strictly to the principles of temperance in eating

Laying the Foundation of Intemperance

and drinking.—*Christian Temperance and Bible Hygiene,* page 79.

Creating Early Appetites for Liquor.—Teach your children to abhor stimulants. How many are ignorantly fostering in them an appetite for these things! In Europe I have seen nurses putting the glass of wine or beer to the lips of the innocent little ones, thus cultivating in them a taste for stimulants. As they grow older, they learn to depend more and more on these things, till little by little they are overcome, drift beyond the reach of help, and at last fill a drunkard's grave.—*Counsels on Diet and Foods,* page 235.

The First Three Years.—Let selfishness, anger, and self-will have its course for the first three years of a child's life, and it will be hard to bring it to submit to wholesome discipline. Its disposition has become soured; it delights in having its own way; parental control is distasteful. These evil tendencies grow with its growth, until in manhood supreme selfishness and a lack of self-control place him at the mercy of the evils that run riot in our land.—*Health Reformer,* April, 1877.

Weighty Responsibility of Parents.—How difficult it is to obtain the victory over appetite when once it is established. How important that parents bring their children up with pure tastes and unperverted appetites. Parents should ever remember that upon them rests the responsibility of training their children in such a way that they will have moral stamina to resist the evil that will surround them when they go out into the world.

Christ did not ask His Father to take the disciples out of the world, but to keep them from the evil in the world, to keep them from yielding to the temptations which they would meet on every hand. This prayer fathers and mothers should offer for their children. But shall they plead with God, and then leave their children to do as they please? God cannot keep children from evil if the parents do not co-operate with Him. Bravely and cheerfully parents should take up their work, carrying it forward with unwearying endeavor.—*Review and Herald,* July 9, 1901.

Those who indulge a child's appetite, and do not teach him to control his passions, may afterward see, in the tobacco-loving, liquor-drinking slave, whose senses are benumbed, and whose lips utter falsehood and profanity, the terrible mistake they have made.—*Counsels on Health,* page 114.

Molding the Character to Resist Temptation.—The first steps in intemperance are usually taken in childhood or early youth. Stimulating food is given to the child, and unnatural cravings are awakened. These depraved appetites are pandered to as they develop. The taste continually becomes more perverted; stronger stimulants are craved and are indulged in, till soon the slave of appetite throws aside all restraint. The evil commenced early in life, and could have been prevented by the parents. We witness strenuous efforts in our country to put down intemperance; but it is found a hard matter to overpower and chain the strong, full-grown lion.

If half the efforts that are put forth to stay this giant evil were directed toward enlightening parents as to their responsibility in forming the habits and characters of their children, a thousandfold more good might result than from the present course of combating only the full-grown evil. The unnatural appetite for spirituous liquors is created at home, in many cases at the very tables of those who are most zealous to lead out in the temperance campaigns. . . .

Parents should not lightly regard the work of training their children. They should employ much time in careful study of the laws which regulate our being. They should make it their first object to learn the proper manner of dealing with their children, that they may secure to them sound minds in sound bodies. Too many parents are controlled by custom, instead of sound reason and the claims of God. Many who profess to be followers of Christ are sadly neglectful of home duties. They do not perceive the sacred importance of the trust which God has placed in their hands, so to mold the characters of their children that they will have moral stamina to resist the many temptations that ensnare the feet of youth.—*Signs of the Times,* Nov. 17, 1890.

Commence With the Cradle.—If parents had done their duty in spreading the table with wholesome food, discarding irritating and stimulating substances, and at the same time had taught their children self-control, and educated their characters to develop moral power, we should not now have to handle the lion of intemperance. After habits of indulgence have been formed, and grown with their growth and strengthened with their strength, how hard then for those who have not been properly trained in youth to break up their wrong habits and learn to restrain themselves and their unnatural appetites. How hard to teach such ones and make them feel the necessity of Christian temperance, when they reach maturity. The temperance lessons should commence with the child rocked in the cradle.—*Review and Herald,* May 11, 1876.

The Final Reckoning.—When parents and children meet at the final reckoning, what a scene will be presented! Thousands of children who have been slaves to appetite and debasing vice, whose lives are moral wrecks, will stand face to face with the parents who made them what they are. Who but the parents must bear this fearful responsibility? Did the Lord make these youth corrupt? Oh, no! He made them in His image, a little lower than the angels.—*Testimonies,* vol. 3, p. 568.

4. Parental Example and Guidance

Responsible for Character.—But few parents realize that their children are what their example and discipline have made them, and that they are responsible for the characters their children develop.—*The Health Reformer,* December, 1872.

There is work for mothers in helping their children to form correct habits and pure tastes. Educate the appetite; teach the children to abhor stimulants. Bring your children up to have moral stamina to resist the evil that surrounds them. Teach them that they are not to be swayed by others, that they are not to yield to strong influences, but to influence others for good.—*The Ministry of Healing,* pages 334, 335.

The Mother an Example.—Woman is to fill a more sacred and elevated position in the family than the king upon his throne. Her great work is to make her life a living example which she would wish her children to copy.—*Testimonies,* vol. 3, p. 566.

Temperance in All Details of Home Life.—Parents should so conduct themselves that their lives will be a daily lesson of self-control and forbearance to their household. . . . We urge that the principles of temperance be carried into all the details of home life; that the example of parents should be a lesson of temperance.—*Signs of the Times,* April 20, 1882.

God Will Supplement the Parents' Endeavors.—When you take up your duties as a parent, in the strength of God, with a firm determination never to relax your efforts, nor to leave your post of duty, in striving to make your children what God would have them, then God looks down upon you with approbation. He knows that you are doing the best you can, and He will increase your power. He will Himself do the part of the work that the mother or father cannot do; He will work with the wise, patient, well-directed efforts of the God-fearing mother. Parents, God does not propose to do the work that He has left for you to do in your home. You must not give up to indolence and be slothful servants, if you would have your children saved from the perils that surround them in the world.—*Review and Herald,* July 10, 1888.

5. Teaching Self-Denial and Self-Control

Begin With Babyhood.—Self-denial and self-control should be taught to the children, and enforced upon them, so far as consistent, from babyhood. And first it is important that the little ones be taught that they eat to live, not live to eat; that appetite must be held in abeyance to the will; and that the will must be governed by calm, intelligent reason.—*Signs of the Times,* April 20, 1882.

Teach Principles of Reform.—Fathers and mothers, watch unto prayer. Guard strictly against intemperance in every form. Teach your children the principles of true health reform. Teach them what things to avoid in order to preserve health. Already the wrath of God has begun to be visited upon the children of disobedience. What crimes, what sins, what iniquitous practices, are being revealed on every hand! —*Testimonies,* vol. 9, p. 160.

Teach the True Object of Life.—Explicit instructions have been given in the word of God. Let these principles be carried out by the mother, with the co-operation and support of the father, and let children be trained from infancy to habits of self-control. Let them be taught that it is not the object of life to indulge sensual appetites, but to honor God and to bless their fellow men.

Fathers and mothers, labor earnestly and faithfully, relying on God for grace and wisdom. Be firm and yet mild. In all your commands aim to secure the highest good of your children, and then see that these commands are obeyed. Your energy and decision must be unwavering, yet ever in subjection to the Spirit of Christ. Then indeed may we hope to see "our sons may be as plants grown up in their youth; that our daughters may be as cornerstones, polished after the similitude of a palace."—*Signs of the Times,* Sept. 13, 1910.

Parents to Blame if Children Are Drunkards.—There is a general mourning that intemperance prevails to such a fearful extent; but we fasten the primal cause upon fathers and mothers who have provided upon their tables the means by which the appetites of their children are educated for exciting stimulants. They themselves have sown in their children the seeds of intemperance, and it is *their* fault if they become drunkards. —*Health Reformer,* May, 1877.

The food is often such as to excite a desire for stimulating drinks. Luxurious dishes are placed before the children,— spiced foods, rich gravies, cakes, and pastries. This highly seasoned food irritates the stomach, and causes a craving for still stronger stimulants. Not only is the appetite tempted with unsuitable food, of which the children are allowed to eat freely at their meals, but they are permitted to eat between meals, and by the time they are twelve or fourteen years of age they are often confirmed dyspeptics.

You have perhaps seen a picture of the stomach of one who is addicted to strong drink. A similar condition is produced under the irritating influence of fiery spices. With the stomach in such a state, there is a craving for something more to meet the demands of the appetite, something stronger, and still stronger. Next you find your sons out on the street learning to smoke.—*Counsels on Diet and Foods,* pages 235, 236.

Highway of Intemperance.—In their ignorance or carelessness, parents give their children the first lessons in intemperance. At the table, loaded with injurious condiments, rich food, and spiced knickknacks, the child acquires a taste for that which is hurtful to him, which tends to irritate the tender

Laying the Foundation of Intemperance

coats of the stomach, inflame the blood, and strengthen the animal passions. The appetite soon craves something stronger, and tobacco is used to gratify that craving. This indulgence only increasing the unnatural longing for stimulants, liquor drinking is soon resorted to, and drunkenness follows. This is the course of the great highway to intemperance.—*Review and Herald,* Sept. 6, 1877.

Moral Powers Paralyzed.—Through the channel of appetite, the passions are inflamed, and the moral powers are paralyzed, so that parental instruction in the principles of morality and true goodness falls upon the ear without affecting the heart. The most fearful warnings and threatenings of the word of God are not powerful enough to arouse the benumbed intellect and awaken the violated conscience.

The indulgence of appetite and passion fever and debilitate the mind, and disqualify for education. Our youth need a physiological education as well as other literary and scientific knowledge. It is important for them to understand the relation that their eating and drinking, and general habits, have to health and life. As they understand their own frames, they will know how to guard against debility and disease. With a sound constitution, there is hope of accomplishing almost anything. Benevolence, love, and piety, can be cultivated. A want of physical vigor will be manifested in the weakened moral powers. The apostle says, "Let not sin therefore reign in your mortal body, that ye should obey it in the lusts thereof."—*Health Reformer,* December, 1872.

It Is Somebody's Business.—You should study temperance in all things. You must study it in what you eat and in what you drink. And yet you say: "It is nobody's business what I eat, or what I drink, or what I place upon my table." It is somebody's business, unless you take your children and shut them up, or go into the wilderness where you will not be a burden upon others, and where your unruly, vicious children will not corrupt the society in which they mingle.—*Testimonies,* vol. 2, p. 362.

Educate for Moral Independence.—Parents should educate their children to have moral independence, not to follow impulse and inclination, but to exercise their reasoning powers, and to act from principle. Let mothers inquire, not for the latest fashion, but for the path of duty and usefulness, and direct the steps of their children therein. Simple habits, pure morals, and a noble independence in the right course, will be of more value to the youth than the gifts of genius, the endowments of learning, or the external polish which the world can give them. Teach your children to walk in the ways of righteousness, and they, in turn, will lead others into the same path. Thus may you see at last that your life has not been in vain, for you have been instrumental in bringing precious fruit to the garner of God.—*Review and Herald,* Nov. 6, 1883.

Parents to Study the Laws of Life.—Parents should make it their first business to understand the laws of life and health, that nothing shall be done by them in the preparation of food, or through any other habits, which will develop wrong tendencies in their children. How carefully should mothers study to prepare their tables with the most simple, healthful food, that the digestive organs may not be weakened, the nervous forces unbalanced, and the instruction which they should give their children counteracted by the food placed before them. This food either weakens or strengthens the organs of the stomach and has much to do in controlling the physical and moral health of the children, who are God's blood-bought property. What a sacred trust is committed to parents to guard the physical and moral constitutions of their children so that the nervous system may be well balanced, and the soul not be endangered!—*Testimonies,* vol. 3, p. 568.

Children Also to Understand Physiology.—Parents should seek to awaken in their children an interest in the study of

Laying the Foundation of Intemperance 185

physiology. From the first dawn of reason the human mind should become intelligent in regard to the physical structure. We may behold and admire the work of God in the natural world, but the human habitation is the most wonderful. It is therefore of the highest importance that among the studies selected for children, physiology occupy an important place. All children should study it. And then parents should see to it that practical hygiene is added.

Children are to be trained to understand that every organ of the body and every faculty of the mind is the gift of a good and wise God, and that each is to be used to His glory. Right habits in eating and drinking and dressing must be insisted upon. Wrong habits render the youth less susceptible to Bible instruction. The children are to be guarded against the indulgence of appetite, and especially against the use of stimulants and narcotics.—*Counsels to Teachers,* pages 125, 126.

Prepared to Meet Temptation.—Children should be trained and educated so that they may calculate to meet with difficulties, and expect temptations and dangers. They should be taught to have control over themselves, and to nobly overcome difficulties; and if they do not willfully rush into danger, and needlessly place themselves in the way of temptation; if they avoid evil influences and vicious society, and then are unavoidably compelled to be in dangerous company, they will have strength of character to stand for the right and preserve principle, and will come forth in the strength of God with their morals untainted. The moral powers of youth who have been properly educated, if they make God their trust, will be equal to stand the most powerful test.—*Health Reformer,* December, 1872.

If right principles in regard to temperance were implanted in the youth who are to form and mold society, there would be little necessity for temperance crusades. Firmness of character, moral control, would prevail, and in the strength of

Jesus the temptations of these last days would be resisted.—*Christian Temperance and Bible Hygiene,* page 79.

6. Youth and the Future

An Index to the Future.—The youth of today are a sure index to the future of society; and as we view them, what can we hope for that future? The majority are fond of amusement and averse to work. They lack moral courage to deny self and to respond to the claims of duty. They have but little self-control, and become excited and angry on the slightest occasion. Very many in every age and station of life are without principle or conscience; and with their idle, spendthrift habits they are rushing into vice and are corrupting society, until our world is becoming a second Sodom.—*Christian Temperance and Bible Hygiene,* page 45.

The Time to Establish Good Habits.—If correct and virtuous habits are formed in youth, they will generally mark the course of the possessor through life. In most cases, it will be found that those who in later life reverence God and honor the right, learned that lesson before there was time for the world to stamp its image of sin upon the soul. Those of mature age are generally as insensible to new impressions as is the hardened rock; but youth is impressible. Youth is the time to acquire knowledge for daily practice through life; a right character may then be easily formed. It is the time to establish good habits, to gain and to hold the power of self-control. Youth is the sowing time, and the seed sown determines the harvest, both for this life and the life to come.—*Counsels on Health,* page 113.

To Be Temperate Is to Be Manly.—The only way in which any can be secure against the power of intemperance, is to abstain wholly from wine, beer, and strong drinks. We must teach our children that in order to be manly they must let these things alone. God has shown us what constitutes true manliness. It is he that overcometh who will be honored, and whose name will not be blotted out of the book of life.—*Christian Temperance and Bible Hygiene,* page 37.

In our large cities there are saloons on the right hand and on the left, tempting passers-by to indulge an appetite which, once established, is exceedingly hard to overcome. The youth should be trained never to touch tobacco or intoxicating drink. Alcohol robs men of their reasoning powers.—*Review and Herald,* June 15, 1905.

Nadab and Abihu Had Formed the Habit of Drinking.— Anything that lessens the physical power enfeebles the mind, and makes it less clear to discriminate between good and evil, between right and wrong. This principle is illustrated in the case of Nadab and Abihu. God gave them a most sacred work to perform, permitting them to come near to Himself in their appointed service; but they had a habit of drinking wine, and they entered upon the holy service in the sanctuary with confused minds. . . . "And there went out fire from the Lord, and devoured them, and they died before the Lord."—*Fundamentals of Christian Education,* pages 427, 428.

A Warning to Parents and Youth.—Parents and children should be warned by the history of Nadab and Abihu. Appetite, indulged, perverted the reasoning powers, and led to the breaking of an express command, which brought the judgment of God upon them. Notwithstanding children may not have had the right instruction, and their characters not have been properly molded, God proposes to connect them with Himself as He did Nadab and Abihu, if they will heed His commands. If they will with faith and courage bring their will in submission to the will of God, He will teach them, and their lives may be like the pure white lily, full of fragrance on the stagnant waters. They must resolve in the strength of Jesus to control inclination and passion, and every day win victories over Satan's temptations. This is the way God has marked out for men to serve His high purposes.—*Signs of the Times,* July 8, 1880.

The One Worthy of Honor.—The young man who is determined to keep his appetite under the control of God, and who refuses the first temptation to drink intoxicating liquor, saying courteously, but firmly, "No, thank you," is the one who is worthy of honor. Let young men take their stand as total abstainers, even though the men standing high in the world have not the moral courage to take their stand boldly against a habit that is ruinous to health and life.—Letter 166, 1903.

The Influence of One Consecrated Youth.—One youth who has been instructed by right home training, will bring solid timbers into his character building, and by his example and life, if his powers are rightly employed, he will become a power in our world to lead others upward and onward in the path of righteousness. The salvation of one soul is the salvation of many souls.—*Review and Herald,* July 10, 1888.

Weaving a Web of Habits.—Remember that you are daily weaving for yourself a web of habits. If these habits are according to the Bible rule, you are going every day in steps heavenward, growing in grace and the knowledge of the truth; and like Daniel, God will give you wisdom as He gave to him. You will not choose the paths of selfish gratification. Practice habits of strictest temperance, and be careful to keep sacred the laws which God has established to govern your physical being. God has claims upon your powers, therefore careless inattention to the laws of health is sin. The better you observe the laws of health, the more clearly can you discern temptations, and resist them, and the more clearly can you discern the value of eternal things.—*Youth's Instructor,* Aug. 25, 1886, p. 135.

Laying the Foundation of Intemperance

Daniel's Example.—No young man or young woman could be more sorely tempted than were Daniel and his companions. To these four Hebrew youth were apportioned wine and meat from the king's table. But they chose to be temperate. They saw that perils were on every side, and that if they resisted temptation, they must make most decided efforts on their part, and trust the results with God. The youth who desire to stand as Daniel stood must exert their spiritual powers to the very utmost, co-operating with God, and trusting wholly in the strength that He has promised to all who come to Him in humble obedience.

There is a constant warfare to be maintained between virtue and vice. The discordant elements of the one, and the pure principles of the other, are at work striving for the mastery. Satan is approaching every soul with some form of temptation on the point of indulgence of appetite. Intemperance is fearfully prevalent. Look where we will, we behold this evil fondly cherished.

Honorable to Refuse.—The followers of Jesus will never be ashamed to practice temperance in all things. Then why should any young man blush with shame to refuse the wine cup or the foaming mug of beer? A refusal to indulge perverted appetite is an honorable act. To sin is unmanly; to indulge in injurious habits of eating and drinking is weak, cowardly, debased; but to deny perverted appetite is strong, brave, noble. In the Babylonian court, Daniel was surrounded by allurements to sin, but by the help of Christ he maintained his integrity. He who cannot resist temptation, when every facility for overcoming has been placed within his reach, is not registered in the books of heaven as a man.

"Dare to be a Daniel, dare to stand alone!" Have courage to do the right. A cowardly and silent reserve before evil associates, while you listen to their devices, makes you one with them. "Come out from among them, and be ye separate, saith the Lord, and touch not the unclean thing; and I will receive you, and will be a Father unto you, and ye shall be My sons and daughters."

Moral Courage Needed.—At all times and on all occasions it requires moral courage to adhere to the principles of strict temperance. We may expect that by following such a course we shall surprise those who do not totally abstain from all stimulants; but how are we to carry forward the work of reform if we conform to the injurious habits and practices of those with whom we associate? . . .

In the name and strength of Jesus every youth may conquer the enemy today on the point of perverted appetite. My dear young friends, advance step by step, until all your habits shall be in harmony with the laws of life and health. He who overcame in the wilderness of temptation declares: "To him that overcometh will I grant to sit with Me in My throne, even as I also overcame, and am set down with My Father in His throne."—*The Youth's Instructor,* July 16, 1903.

Not Removed From Temptation.—Daniel loved, feared, and obeyed God. Yet he did not flee away from the world to avoid its corrupting influence. In the providence of God he was to be in the world yet not of the world. With all the temptations and fascinations of court life surrounding him, he stood in the integrity of his soul, firm as a rock in his adherence to principle. He made God his strength and was not forsaken of Him in his time of greatest need.—*Testimonies,* vol. 4, pp. 569, 570.

The Result of Faithful Home Training.—Daniel's parents had trained him in his childhood to habits of strict temperance. They had taught him that he must conform to nature's laws in all his habits; that his eating and drinking had a direct influence upon his physical, mental, and moral nature, and that he was accountable to God for his capabilities; for he held them all as a gift from God, and must not, by any course of

Laying the Foundation of Intemperance

action, dwarf or cripple them. As the result of this teaching, the law of God was exalted in his mind, and reverenced in his heart. During the early years of his captivity, Daniel was passing through an ordeal which was to familiarize him with courtly grandeur, with hypocrisy, and with paganism. A strange school indeed to fit him for a life of sobriety, industry, and faithfulness! And yet he lived uncorrupted by the atmosphere of evil with which he was surrounded.

The experience of Daniel and his youthful companions illustrates the benefits that may result from an abstemious diet, and shows what God will do for those who will co-operate with Him in the purifying and uplifting of the soul. They were an honor to God, and a bright and shining light in the court of Babylon.

God's Call to Us.—In this history we hear the voice of God addressing us individually, bidding us gather up all the precious rays of light upon this subject of Christian temperance, and place ourselves in right relation to the laws of health.

We want a share in the eternal inheritance. We want a place in the city of God, free from every impurity. All heaven is watching to see how we are fighting the battle against temptation. Let all who profess the name of Christ so walk before the world that they may teach by example as well as precept the principles of true living. "I beseech you therefore, brethren, by the mercies of God, that ye present your bodies a living sacrifice, holy, acceptable unto God, which is your reasonable service."—*Christian Temperance and Bible Hygiene,* pages 23, 24.

Students to Take Care.—The character of the food and the manner in which it is eaten exert a powerful influence on the health. Many students have never made a determined effort to control the appetite, or to observe proper rules in regard to eating. Some eat too much at their meals, and some eat between meals whenever the temptation is presented.

The need of carefulness in habits of diet should be impressed on the minds of all students. I have been instructed that those attending our schools are not to be served with flesh foods or with preparations of food that are known to be unwholesome. Nothing that will serve to encourage a desire for stimulants should be placed on the table. I appeal to all to refuse to eat those things that will injure the health. Thus they can serve the Lord by sacrifice.—*Counsels to Teachers,* pages 297, 298.

Assert Your Manly Liberty.—Young men, who think that you cannot eat the simple wholesome food provided at the Health Institute and that you must go down to the restaurant and get something to gratify your appetite, it is time for you to arouse and assert your manly liberty.—Manuscript 3, 1888.

Enter Not Into Temptation.—Will you allow temporal, earthly employment to lead you into temptation? Will you doubt your Lord, who loves you? Will you neglect the work given you, of doing service for God? Your associations are with a class who are earthly, sensual, and devilish. You have breathed moral malaria, and you are in serious danger of failing where you might win if you would place yourself in right relation with Jesus, making His life and character your criterion. Now, in order to escape the corruption that is in the world through lust, you must be a partaker of the divine nature. It is your duty to keep your soul in the atmosphere of heaven.

You should not place yourself where you will be corrupted by dissolute companionship. As one who loves your soul I beseech you to shun, as far as possible, the company of the profligate, the licentious, and the ungodly. Pray, "Lead us not into temptation," that is, "Do not, O Lord, suffer us to be overcome when assailed by temptation." Watch and pray lest ye enter into temptation. There is a difference between being tempted, and entering into temptation.—Letter 8, 1893.

Jesus Social and Temperate.—Jesus rebuked intemperance, self-indulgence, and folly; yet He was social in His nature. He accepted invitations to dine with the learned and noble, as well as the poor and afflicted. On these occasions, His conversation was elevating and instructive, holding His hearers entranced. He gave no license to scenes of dissipation and revelry, yet innocent happiness was pleasing to Him. A Jewish marriage was a solemn and impressive occasion, the pleasure and joy of which were not displeasing to the Son of man.—*Redemption; or the Miracles of Jesus,* pages 13, 14.

Direct, but Do Not Repress.—The word of God does not condemn or repress man's activity, but tries to give it a right direction. While the world is filling mind and soul with excitement, the Lord puts the Bible into your hands, for you to study, to appreciate, and to heed as a guide to your steps. The word is your light.—Letter 8, 1893.

Section X

PREVENTIVE MEASURES

1. Education in Temperance

What We Can Do.—What can be done to press back the inflowing tide of evil? Let laws be enacted and rigidly enforced prohibiting the sale and the use of ardent spirits as a beverage. Let every effort be made to encourage the inebriate's return to temperance and virtue. But even more than this is needed to banish the curse of inebriety from our land. Let the appetite for intoxicating liquors be removed, and their use and sale is at an end.—*Gospel Workers,* page 388.

The Rich Harvest From Educational Efforts.—Men of different vocations and different stations in life have been overcome by the pollutions of the world, by the use of strong drink, by indulgence in the lusts of the flesh, and have fallen under temptation. While these fallen ones excite our pity and demand our help, should not some attention be given also to those who have not yet descended to these depths, but who are setting their feet in the same path?—*Testimonies,* vol. 6, p. 256.

If half the efforts that are put forth to stay this giant evil were directed toward enlightening parents as to their responsibility in forming the habits and characters of their children, a thousandfold more good might result than from the present course of combating only the full-grown evil. The unnatural appetite for spirituous liquors is created at home, in many cases at the very tables of those who are most zealous to lead out in the temperance campaigns. We bid all workers in the good cause, Godspeed; but we invite them to look deeper into the causes of the evil they war against, and labor more thoroughly and consistently in the work of reform."—*Signs of the Times,* Nov. 17, 1890.

What to Teach.—It must be kept before the people that the right balance of the mental and moral powers depends in a great degree on the right condition of the physical system. All narcotics and unnatural stimulants that enfeeble and degrade the physical nature tend to lower the tone of the intellect and morals. . . .

Temperance reformers have a work to do in educating the people in these lines. Teach them that health, character, and even life, are endangered by the use of stimulants, which excite the exhausted energies to unnatural, spasmodic action.—*The Ministry of Healing,* page 335.

Be Brave and Overcome.—The physical life is to be carefully educated, cultivated, and developed, that through men and women the divine nature may be revealed in its fullness. God expects men to use the intellect He has given them. He expects them to use every reasoning power for Him. They are to give the conscience the place of supremacy that has been assigned it. The mental and physical powers, with the affections, are to be so cultivated that they can reach the highest efficiency. . . .

Is God pleased to see any of the organs and faculties He has given to man neglected, misused, or deprived of the health and efficiency it is possible for them to acquire through exercise? Then cultivate the gift of faith. Be brave, and overcome every practice which mars the soul-temple. We are wholly dependent on God, and our faith is strengthened by still believing, though we cannot see God's purpose in His dealing with us, or the consequence of this dealing. Faith points forward and upward to things to come, laying hold of the only power that can make us complete in Him. "Let him take hold of My strength, that he may make peace with Me," God declares, "and he shall make peace with Me."—Manuscript 130, 1899.

No Subject of Greater Interest.—God has sent His warning message to arouse men and women to their danger and peril. But thousands, yes, millions, are disregarding the word which points out their danger. They eat food which is ruinous to health. They refuse to see that by eating improper food, and drinking intoxicating liquor, they are binding themselves in slavery. They violate the laws of life and health until appetite holds them in its chains. . . .

No subject which is presented to the inhabitants of our cities should command so large an interest as that which concerns physical health. True temperance calls for total abstinence from strong drink. It calls also for reform in dietetic habits, in dressing, in sleeping. Those who indulge appetite are not pleased to hear that it rests with them to decide whether they will be invalids. They need to wake up and reason from cause to effect. They need to realize that they are disease producers because of their ignorance upon the subject of proper eating, drinking, and dressing.—Manuscript 155, 1899.

The Secret of a Permanent Work.—We have seen that the victories gained by the "Temperance Crusade" are not often permanent. In those places where the excitement ran highest and apparently the most was accomplished in closing liquor saloons and reclaiming inebriates, after the lapse of a few months, intemperance prevailed to a greater extent than before the effort to suppress it was made.

The reason of this is evident. The work is not deep and thorough. The ax is not laid at the root of the tree. The roots of intemperance lie deeper than mere liquor drinking. In order to make the temperance movement a success, the work of reform must begin at our tables.—*Signs of the Times,* Jan. 6, 1876.

Presented in Strength and Clarity.—Let the people be shown what a blessing the practice of health principles will be to them. Let them see what God designed men and women to become. Point to the great sacrifice made for the uplifting and ennobling of the human race. With the Bible in hand, present the requirements of God. Tell the hearers that He expects them to use the powers of mind and body in a way that will honor Him. Show them how the enemy is trying to drag human beings down by leading them to indulge perverted appetite.

Clearly, plainly, earnestly, tell them how thousands of men and women are using God's money to corrupt themselves and to make this world a hell. Millions of dollars are spent for that which makes men mad. Present this matter so clearly that its force cannot but be seen. Then tell your hearers of the Saviour, who came to this world to save men and women from all sinful practices. "God so loved the world, that He gave His only-begotten Son, that whosoever believeth in Him should not perish, but have everlasting life."

Ask those who attend the meetings to help you in the work that you are trying to do. Show them how evil habits result in diseased bodies and diseased minds—in wretchedness that no pen can describe. The use of intoxicating liquor is robbing thousands of their reason. And yet the sale of this liquor is legalized. Tell them that they have a heaven to win and a hell to shun. Ask them to sign the pledge. The commission of the great I AM is to be your authority. Have the pledges prepared, and present them at the close of the meeting.—*Evangelism,* page 530.

2. Signing the Pledge

Every Seventh-day Adventist to Sign.—From the light God has given me, every member among us should sign the pledge and be connected with the temperance association.—*Review and Herald,* Oct. 21, 1884.

Sign and Encourage Others to Sign.—Here is a work opened before the young, the middle-aged, and the aged. When the temperance pledge is presented to you, sign it. More than this, resolve to put all your powers against the evil of intemperance, and encourage others who are trying to do a work of reform in the world.—*Review and Herald,* Jan. 14, 1909.

Every Youth to Sign Every Pledge Presented.—Intemperance and profanity and licentiousness are sisters. Let every God-fearing youth gird on the armor and press to the front. Put your names on every temperance pledge presented. Thus you lend your influence in favor of signing the pledge, and induce others to sign it. Let no weak excuse deter you from taking this step. Work for the good of your own souls and for good of others.—*The Youth's Instructor,* July 16, 1903.

The Drunkard to Sign.—Temperance workers try to induce the drunkard to sign a pledge that henceforth he will not use intoxicating liquor. This is well.—Manuscript 102, 1904.

The Drunkard's Children to Sign. An Appeal.—Let not one drop of wine or liquor pass your lips, for in its use is madness and woe. Pledge yourself to entire abstinence, for it is your only safety. . . . Let not one son by his words and his example become Satan's agent to tempt one of the members of the family to lead to indulge and awaken the demon appetite which spoiled the life of the father and sent him prematurely to the grave.—Manuscript 25, 1893.

Those in High Positions to Sign.—To those in high positions we are to present the total abstinence pledge, asking them to give the money they would otherwise spend for the harmful indulgences of liquor and tobacco to the establishment of institutions where children and youth may be prepared to fill positions of usefulness in the world.—*Testimonies,* vol. 7, p. 58.

Sign at Our Camp Meetings.—At our camp meetings we should call attention to this work and make it a living issue. We should present to the people the principles of true temperance and call for signers to the temperance pledge.—*Testimonies,* vol. 6, p. 110.

Offer No Excuse.—Let no excuse be offered when you are asked to put your name to the temperance pledge, but sign every pledge presented, and induce others to sign with you. Work for the good of your own souls, and the good of others. Never let an opportunity pass to cast your influence on the side of strict temperance.—*Counsels on Health,* page 441.

Failure to Sign Leaves Bars Down.—After the discourse Sunday evening, the pledge was circulated, and one hundred and thirty-seven names were attached. We were sorry to learn that some few names were withheld for that which we consider was no reason that would justify a true child of God. Their excuse was that their work called them into places where wine would be passed to them (as is customary in this country), and they could not refuse to take it for fear of offending those for whom they worked. I thought that here was a very good opportunity for them to lift the cross, and let their light shine forth as God's peculiar people whom He was purifying unto Himself. . . .

At all times and on all occasions it requires moral courage to resist temptation on the point of appetite. We may expect such practice will be a surprise to those who do not practice habits of total abstinence from all stimulants; but how are we to carry forward the work of reform if we are to conform to the habits and practices of those with whom we associate? Here is the very opportunity to manifest that we are a peculiar people, zealous of good works.

The beer drinkers will present their glasses of beer, and those who claim to be children of God may plead the same excuse for not signing the temperance pledge,—because they will be treated with beer, and it will not be agreeable to refuse. These excuses may be carried to any length, but they are not of any weight; and we were sorry that any who claimed to believe the truth should refuse to sign the pledge—refuse to put barriers about their souls and fortify themselves against temptation. They choose to leave the bars down, so that they can readily step over and accept temptation without making the effort to resist it. . . .

No Courage to Say, "I Have Signed the Pledge."—Those who claim to believe the truth have not all taken their position in relation to temperance which it is their sacred duty to do. There have been those who have stood aloof from decided committal on the side of temperance, and for what reason? Some say that if wine or beer is passed to them, they have not the moral courage to say, I have signed the pledge not to taste of fermented wine or beer or strong drink. Shall the names of those stand registered in the books of heaven as defending the indulgence of appetite?—*Review and Herald,* April 19, 1887.

Importance of Prominent Men Signing the Pledge.—I dreamed that there was a large company assembled together in the open air, and a tall young man that I have often seen in my dreams, when important matters are under consideration, was sitting near the chairman of the meeting. This young man arose and passed to the men that seemed to be at the head of the company and said, "Here is a paper I wish you to attach your names to, every one of you." He presented it to Brother A first. He looked at it and read aloud, "You here pledge yourselves to abstain from all fermented wines and spirituous liquors of any kind, and use your influence to induce all others that you can to follow your example."

I thought Brother A shook his head, saying it was not necessary for him to attach his name to the paper. He understood his duty and should advocate the cause of temperance all the same, but felt not called upon to bind himself, for there were exceptions in all these things.

He handed the same paper to Brother B, who took the paper, looked it over carefully and said, "I am of the same mind of Brother A. Sometimes I feel the need of something to stimulate me when I am weak and nervous, and I don't want to pledge myself that under no circumstances will I use wine or liquors."

There was a sad, grieved look expressed in the countenance. He passed on to others. There were about twenty or thirty who followed the example of Brethren A and B. He then returned to the first two and handed them the paper and said in a firm, decided manner, yet a low tone, "You, both of you, are in the greatest danger of being overcome upon the point of appetite. The work of reformation must commence at your tables and then be carried out conscientiously in every place under all and every circumstance. Your eternal destiny depends upon the decision you now make. You both have strong points of character and are weak in some directions. See what your influence has done." I saw the names of all who had refused to sign written upon the back of the pledge. . . .

Again he presented the paper and in an authoritative manner said, "Sign this paper or resign your positions. Not only sign, but upon your honor carry out your decisions. Be true to your principles. As God's messenger I come to you and demand your names. Neither of you have seen the necessity of health reform, but when the plagues of God shall be all around you, you will then see the principles of health reform and strict temperance in all things,—that temperance alone is the foundation of all the graces that come from God, the foundation of all victories to be gained. Refuse to sign this and you will never have another solicitation. You both need your spirits humbled, softened, and let mercy, tender compassion, and dutiful tenderness take the place of coarseness, harshness, set and determined will to carry out your ideas at any cost. . . .

I thought, with trembling hands the names were given and the entire thirty signed their names.

Then one of the most solemn addresses was given upon temperance. The subject was taken up from the table. "Here," said the speaker, "is the appetite created for love of strong liquor. Appetite and passion are the ruling sins of the age. Appetite, the way it is indulged, influences the stomach and excites the animal propensities. . . .

The stomach becomes diseased, then the appetite is morbid and continually craving something to stimulate, something to "hit the spot"! Some acquire the disgusting habit of tea and coffee, and go still further using tobacco, which benumb the tender organs of the stomach and lead them to crave something stronger than tobacco. They go still further to the use of liquor.—Manuscript 2, 1874.

An Early Experience in Pledge Signing.—Monday morning, June 2, 1879, while in attendance at a camp meeting held at Nevada, Missouri, we assembled under the tent to attend the organization of a temperance association. There was a fair representation of our people present. Elder Butler spoke, and confessed that he had not been as forward in the temperance reform as he should have been. He stated that he had always been a strictly temperance man, discarding the use of liquor, tea, and coffee, but he had not signed the pledge being circulated among our people. But he was now convinced that in not doing so he was hindering others who ought to sign it. He then placed his name under Colonel Hunter's; my husband placed his name beneath Brother Butler's, I wrote mine next, and Brother Farnsworth's followed. Thus the work was well started.

My husband continued to talk while the pledge was circulating. Some hesitated, thinking that the platform was too broad in including tea and coffee; but finally their names were given, pledging themselves to total abstinence.

Brother Hunter, who was then called upon to speak, responded by giving a very impressive testimony as to how the truth found him, and what it had done for him. He stated that he had drunk liquor enough to float a ship, and that now he wanted to accept the whole truth, reform and all. He had given up liquor and tobacco, and this morning he had drunk his last cup of coffee. He believed the testimonies were of God, and he wished to be led by the will of God expressed in them.

As the result of the meeting, one hundred and thirty-two names were signed to the teetotal pledge, and a decided victory was gained in behalf of temperance.—*Manuscript 79, 1907.*

Work Everywhere.—Give prominence to the temperance reform, and call for signers to the temperance pledge. Everywhere call attention to this work, and make it a living issue. —*Manuscript 52, 1900.*

3. Removing the Temptation

The Dark Blot Remains.—Notwithstanding thousands of years of experience and progress, the same dark blot which stained the first pages of history remains to disfigure our modern civilization. Drunkenness, with all its woes, is found everywhere we go. In spite of the noble efforts of temperance workers, the evil has gained ground. License laws have been enacted, but legal regulation has not stayed its progress, except in comparatively limited territory.—*Christian Temperance and Bible Hygiene, page 29.*

Fruitage of License Laws.—For a paltry sum, men are licensed to deal out to their fellow men the potion that shall rob them of all that makes this life desirable and of all hope of the life to come. Neither the lawmaker nor the liquor seller is ignorant of the result of his work. At the hotel bar, in the beer garden, at the saloon, the slave of appetite expends his means for that which is destructive to reason, health, and happiness. The liquor seller fills his till with the money that should provide food and clothing for the family of the poor drunkard.

This is the worst kind of robbery. Yet men in high position in society and in the church lend their influence in favor of license laws! And why?—because they can obtain higher rent for their buildings by letting them to liquor dealers? because it is desirable to secure the political support of their liquor interests? because these professed Christians are themselves secretly indulging in the alluring poison? Surely, a noble, unselfish love for humanity would not authorize men to entice their fellow creatures to destruction.

The laws to license the sale of spirituous liquors have filled our towns and cities, yes, even our villages and secluded hamlets, with snares and pitfalls for the poor, weak slave of appetite. Those who seek to reform are daily surrounded with temptation. The drunkard's terrible thirst clamors for indulgence. On every side are the fountains of destruction. Alas, how often is his moral power overborne! how often are his convictions silenced! He drinks and falls. Then follow nights of debauchery, days of stupor, imbecility, and wretchedness. Thus, step by step, the work goes on, until the man who was once a good citizen, a kind husband and father, seems changed to a demon.

Suppose those officials who at the beginning of [the year] granted license to liquor dealers, could [at the end of the year] behold a faithful picture of the results of the traffic carried on under that license. It is spread out before them in its startling and frightful details, and they know that all is true to life. There are fathers, mothers, and children falling beneath the murderer's hand; there are the wretched victims of cold and hunger and of vile and loathsome disease, criminals immured in gloomy dungeons, victims of insanity tortured by visions of fiends and monsters. There are gray-haired parents mourning for once noble, promising sons and lovely daughters, now gone down to an untimely grave. . . .

Day by day the cries of agony wrenched from the lips of the drunkard's wife and children go up to Heaven. And all this that the liquor seller may add to his gains! And his hellish work is performed under the broad seal of the law! Thus society is corrupted, workhouses and prisons are crowded with paupers and criminals, and the gallows is supplied with victims. The evil ends not with the drunkard and his unhappy family. The burdens of taxation are increased, the morals of the young are imperiled, the property and even the life of every member of society is endangered. But the picture may be presented never so vividly, and yet it falls short of the reality. No human pen or pencil can fully delineate the horrors of intemperance.

Were the only evil arising from the sale of ardent spirits the cruelty and neglect manifested by intemperate parents toward their children, this alone should be enough to condemn and destroy the traffic. Not only does the drunkard render the life of his children miserable, but by his sinful example he leads them also into the path of crime. How can Christian men and women tolerate this evil? Should barbarous nations steal our children and abuse them as intemperate parents abuse their offspring, all Christendom would be aroused to put an end to the outrage. But in a land professedly governed by Christian principles, the suffering and sin entailed upon innocent and helpless childhood by the sale and use of intoxicating liquors are considered a necessary evil!—*Review and Herald,* Nov. 8, 1881.

Under the Protection of the Law.—The licensing of the liquor traffic is advocated by many as tending to restrict the drink evil. But the licensing of the traffic places it under the protection of law. The government sanctions its existence, and thus fosters the evil which it professes to restrict. Under the protection of license laws, breweries, distilleries, and wineries are planted all over the land, and the liquor seller plies his work beside our very doors.

Often he is forbidden to sell intoxicants to one who is drunk or who is known to be a confirmed drunkard; but the work of making drunkards of the youth goes steadily forward. Upon the creating of the liquor appetite in the youth the very life of the traffic depends. The youth are led on, step by step, until the liquor habit is established, and the thirst is created that at any cost demands satisfaction. Less harmful would it be to grant liquor to the confirmed drunkard, whose ruin, in most cases, is already determined, than to permit the flower of our youth to be lured to destruction through this terrible habit.

By the licensing of the liquor traffic, temptation is kept constantly before those who are trying to reform. Institutions have been established where the victims of intemperance may be helped to overcome their appetite. This is a noble work; but so long as the sale of liquor is sanctioned by law, the intemperate receive little benefit from inebriate asylums. They cannot remain there always. They must again take their place in society. The appetite for intoxicating drink, though subdued, is not wholly destroyed; and when temptation assails them, as it does on every hand, they too often fall an easy prey.

The man who has a vicious beast, and who, knowing its disposition, allows it liberty, is by the laws of the land held accountable for the evil the beast may do. In the laws given to Israel the Lord directed that when a beast known to be vicious caused the death of a human being, the life of the owner should pay the price of his carelessness or malignity. On the same principle the government that licenses the liquor seller should be held responsible for the results of his traffic. And if it is a crime worthy of death to give liberty to a vicious beast, how much greater is the crime of sanctioning the work of the liquor seller!

Licenses are granted on the plea that they may bring a revenue to the public treasury. But what is this revenue when compared with the enormous expense incurred for the criminals, the insane, the paupers, that are the fruit of the liquor traffic! A man under the influence of liquor commits a crime; he is brought into court; and those who legalized the traffic are forced to deal with the result of their own work. They authorized the sale of the draft that would make a sane man mad; and now it is necessary for them to send the man to prison or to the gallows, while often his wife and children are left destitute, to become the charge of the community in which they live.

Considering only the financial aspect of the question, what folly it is to tolerate such a business! But what revenue can compensate for the loss of human reason, for the defacing and deforming of the image of God in man, for the ruin of children, reduced to pauperism and degradation, to perpetuate in their children the evil tendencies of their drunken fathers?—*The Ministry of Healing,* pages 342-344.

What Prohibition May Accomplish.—The man who has formed the habit of using intoxicants is in a desperate situation. His brain is diseased, his will power is weakened. So far as any power in himself is concerned, his appetite is uncontrollable. He cannot be reasoned with or persuaded to deny himself. Drawn into the dens of vice, one who has resolved to quit drink is led to seize the glass again, and with the first taste of the intoxicant every good resolution is overpowered, every vestige of will destroyed. . . . By legalizing the traffic, the law gives its sanction to this downfall of the soul, and refuses to stop the trade that fills the world with evil.

Must this always continue? Will souls always have to struggle for victory, with the door of temptation wide open before them? Must the curse of intemperance forever rest like a blight upon the civilized world? Must it continue to sweep, every year, like a devouring fire over thousands of happy homes? When a ship is wrecked in sight of shore, people do not idly look on. They risk their lives in the effort to rescue men and women from a watery grave. How much greater the demand for effort in rescuing them from the drunkard's fate!

It is not the drunkard and his family alone who are imperiled by the work of the liquor seller, nor is the burden of taxation the chief evil which his traffic brings on the community. We are all woven together in the web of humanity. The evil that befalls any part of the great human brotherhood brings peril to all.

Many a man who through love of gain or ease would have nothing to do with restricting the liquor traffic, has found, too late, that the traffic had to do with him. He has seen his own children besotted and ruined. Lawlessness runs riot. Property is in danger. Life is unsafe. Accidents by sea and by land multiply. Diseases that breed in the haunts of filth and wretchedness make their way to lordly and luxurious homes. Vices fostered by the children of debauchery and crime infect the sons and daughters of refined and cultured households.

There is no man whose interests the liquor traffic does not imperil. There is no man who for his own safeguard should not set himself to destroy it.—*The Ministry of Healing,* pages 344, 345.

There can never be a right state of society while these evils exist. And no real reform will be effected until the law shall close up liquor saloons, not only on Sunday, but on all days of the week. The closing of these saloons would promote public order and domestic happiness.—*Signs of the Times,* Feb. 11, 1886.

The honor of God, the stability of the nation, the well-being of the community, of the home, and of the individual, demand that every possible effort be made in arousing the people to the evil of intemperance. Soon we shall see the result of this terrible evil as we do not see it now. Who will put forth a determined effort to stay the work of destruction? As yet the contest has hardly begun. Let an army be formed to stop the sale of the drugged liquors that are making men mad. Let the danger from the liquor traffic be made plain, and a public sentiment be created that shall demand its prohibition. Let the drink-maddened men be given an opportunity to escape from their thralldom. Let the voice of the nation demand of its lawmakers that a stop be put to this infamous traffic.—*The Ministry of Healing,* page 346.

4. Diversion and Harmless Substitutes

Influence of Idleness, Lack of Aim, Evil Associations.—In order to reach the root of intemperance we must go deeper than the use of alcohol or tobacco. Idleness, lack of aim, or evil associations, may be the predisposing cause.—*Education,* pages 202, 203.

Influence of an Attractive Home.—Have your home as attractive as you can have it. Put back the drapery and let heaven's doctor in, which is sunlight. You want peace and quiet in your homes. You want your children to have beautiful characters. Make home so attractive that they will not want to go to the saloon.—*Manuscript 27, 1893.*

The Holding Power of an Attractive Home.—How many parents are lamenting the fact that they cannot keep their children at home, that they have no love for home. At an early age they have a desire for the company of strangers; and as soon as they are old enough, they break away from that which appears to them to be bondage and unreasonable restraint, and will neither heed a mother's prayers nor a father's counsels. Investigation would generally reveal that the sin lay at the door of the parents. They have not made home what it ought to be,—attractive, pleasant, radiant with the sunshine of kind words, pleasant looks, and true love.

The secret of saving your children lies in making your home lovely and attractive. Indulgence in parents will not bind the children to God nor to home; but a firm, godly influence to properly train and educate the mind would save many children from ruin.—*Review and Herald,* Dec. 9, 1884.

Let home be a place where cheerfulness, courtesy, and love exist. . . . If the home life is what it should be, the habits formed there will be a strong defense against the assaults of temptation when the young shall leave the shelter of home for the world.—*Counsels on Health,* page 100.

Country Homes and Useful Labor.—One of the surest safeguards for the young is useful occupation. Had they been trained to industrious habits, so that all their hours were usefully employed, they would have no time for repining at their lot or for idle daydreaming. They would be in little danger of forming vicious habits or associations. Let the youth be taught from childhood that there is no excellence without great labor. . . .

Every youth should make the most of his talents, by improving to the utmost present opportunities. He who will do this, may reach almost any height in moral and intellectual attainments. But he must possess a brave and resolute spirit. He will need to close his ears to the voice of pleasure; he must often refuse the solicitations of young companions. He must stand on guard continually, lest he be diverted from his purpose.

Many parents remove from their country homes to the city, regarding it as a more desirable or profitable location. But by making this change they expose their children to many and great temptations. The boys have no employment, and they obtain a street education, and go on from one step in depravity to another, until they lose all interest in anything that is good and pure and holy. How much better had the parents remained with their families in the country, where the influences are most favorable for physical and mental strength....

Through the neglect of parents, the youth in our cities are corrupting their ways and polluting their souls before God. This will ever be the fruit of idleness. The almshouses, the prisons, and the gallows publish the sorrowful tale of the neglected duties of parents.—*Review and Herald,* Sept. 13, 1881.

Substitute Innocent Pleasures for Sinful Amusements.— Youth cannot be made as sedate and grave as old age, the child as sober as the sire. While sinful amusements are condemned, as they should be, let parents, teachers, and guardians of youth provide in their stead innocent pleasures, which shall not taint or corrupt the morals. Do not bind down the young to rigid rules and restraints that will lead them to feel themselves oppressed and to break over and rush into paths of folly and destruction. With a firm, kindly, considerate hand, hold the lines of government, guiding and controlling their minds and purposes, yet so gently, so wisely, so lovingly, that they still will know that you have their best good in view. —*Review and Herald,* Dec. 9, 1884.

*To Provide Interesting Holidays.—*We have tried earnestly to make the holidays as interesting as possible to the youth and children.... Our object has been to keep them away from scenes of amusement among unbelievers....

I have thought that while we restrain our children from worldly pleasures, that have a tendency to corrupt and mislead, we ought to provide them innocent recreation, to lead them in pleasant paths where there is no danger. No child of God need have a sad or mournful experience. Divine commands, divine promises, show that this is so. Wisdom's ways "are ways of pleasantness, and all her paths are peace." Worldly pleasures are infatuating; and for their momentary enjoyment, many sacrifice the friendship of Heaven, with the peace, love, and joy that it affords. But these chosen objects of delight soon become disgusting, unsatisfying.

The Attractions of the Christian Life.—We want to do all in our power to win souls by presenting the attractions of the Christian life. Our God is a lover of the beautiful. He might have clothed the earth with brown and gray, and the trees with vestments of mourning instead of their foliage of living green; but He would have His children happy. Every leaf, every opening bud and blooming flower, is a token of His tender love; and we should aim to represent to others this wonderful love expressed in His created works.

God would have every household and every church exert a winning power to draw the children away from the seducing pleasures of the world, and from association with those whose influence would have a corrupting tendency. Study to win the youth to Jesus. Impress their minds with the mercy and goodness of God in permitting them, sinful though they are, to enjoy the advantages, the glory and honor, of being sons and daughters of the Most High. What a stupendous thought, what unheard-of condescension, what amazing love, that finite men may be allied to the Omnipotent! "To them gave He power to become the sons of God, even to them that believe on His name." "Beloved, now are we the sons of God." Can any worldly honor equal this?

Let us represent the Christian life as it really is; let us make the way cheerful, inviting, interesting. We can do this if we will. We may fill our own minds with vivid pictures of spiritual and eternal things, and in so doing help to make them a reality to other minds. Faith sees Jesus standing as our Mediator at the right hand of God. Faith beholds the mansions He has gone to prepare for those who love Him. Faith sees the robe and crown all prepared for the overcomer. Faith hears the songs of the redeemed, and brings eternal glories near. We must come close to Jesus in loving obedience, if we would see the King in His beauty.—*Review and Herald,* Jan. 29, 1884.

5. The Sense of Moral Obligation

Guided by Moral and Religious Principle.—We are to act from a moral and religious standpoint. We are to be temperate in all things, because an incorruptible crown, a heavenly treasure, is before us.—*Testimonies,* vol. 2, p. 374.

As Christ's followers, we should, in eating and drinking, act from principle.—*Redemption; or the Temptation of Christ,* page 60.

The case of Daniel shows us, that, through religious principle, young men may triumph over the lust of the flesh and remain true to God's requirements, even though it cost them a great sacrifice.—*Testimonies,* vol. 4, p. 570.

No Moral Right to Do as You Please.—Have I not a right to do as I please with my own body?—No, you have no moral right, because you are violating the laws of life and health which God has given you. You are the Lord's property, His by creation and His by redemption. "Thou shalt love thy neighbor as thyself." The law of self-respect and for the property of the Lord is here brought to view. And this will lead to respect for the obligations which every human being is under to preserve the living machinery that is so fearfully and wonderfully made.—Manuscript 49, 1897.

To Sense the Sacredness of Natural Law.—Every law governing the human system is to be strictly regarded; for it is as truly a law of God as is the word of Holy Writ; and every willful deviation from obedience to this law is as certainly sin as a violation of the moral law. All nature expresses the law of God, but in our physical structure Jehovah has written His law with His own finger upon every thrilling nerve, upon every living fiber, and upon every organ of the body. We shall suffer loss and defeat, if we step out of nature's path, which God Himself has marked out, into one of our own devising.

We must strive lawfully, if we would win the boon of eternal life. The path is wide enough, and all who run the race may win the prize. If we create unnatural appetites, and indulge them in any degree, we violate nature's laws, and enfeebled physical, mental, and moral conditions will result. We are hence unfitted for that persevering, energetic, and hopeful effort which we might have made had we been true to nature's laws. If we injure a single organ of the body, we rob God of the service we might render to Him. "Know ye not that your body is the temple of the Holy Ghost which is in you, which ye have of God, and ye are not your own? For ye are bought with a price: therefore glorify God in your body, and in your spirit, which are God's."—*Review and Herald,* Oct. 18, 1881.

A Constant Sense of Responsibility.—Those who have a constant realization that they stand in this relation to God will not place in the stomach food which pleases the appetite, but which injures the digestive organs. They will not spoil the property of God by indulging improper habits of eating, drinking, or dressing. They will take great care of the human machinery, realizing that they must do this in order to work in copartnership with God. He wills that they be healthy, happy, and useful. But in order for them to be this, they must place their wills on the side of His will.—Letter 166, 1903.

Guarded by the Bulwark of Moral Independence.—Parents may, by earnest, persevering effort, unbiased by the customs of fashionable life, build a moral bulwark about their children that will defend them from the miseries and crimes caused by intemperance. Children should not be left to come up as they will, unduly developing traits that should be nipped in the bud; but they should be disciplined carefully, and educated to take their position upon the side of right, of reform and abstinence. In every crisis they will then have moral independence to breast the storm of opposition sure to assail those who take their stand in favor of true reform.—*Pacific Health Journal,* May, 1890.

Bring your children to God in faith, and seek to impress their susceptible minds with a sense of their obligations to their heavenly Father. It will require lesson upon lesson, line upon line, precept upon precept, here a little and there a little. —*Review and Herald,* Nov. 6, 1883.

Teach It as a Privilege and Blessing.—Let pupils be impressed with the thought that the body is a temple in which God desires to dwell; that it must be kept pure, the abiding place of high and noble thoughts. As in the study of physiology they see that they are indeed "fearfully and wonderfully made," they will be inspired with reverence. Instead of marring God's handiwork, they will have an ambition to make all that is possible of themselves, in order to fulfill the Creator's glorious plan. Thus they will come to regard obedience to the laws of health, not as a matter of sacrifice or self-denial, but as it really is, an inestimable privilege and blessing.—*Education,* page 201.

A Great Victory if Seen From the Moral Standpoint.—If we can arouse the moral sensibilities of our people on the subject of temperance, a great victory will be gained. Temperance in all things of this life is to be taught and practiced.— *Signs of the Times,* Oct. 2, 1907.

Each to Answer to God Personally.—Obedience to the laws of life must be made a matter of personal duty. We must answer to God for our habits and practices. The question for us to answer is not, What will the world say? but, How shall I, claiming to be a Christian, treat the habitation God has given me? Shall I work for my highest temporal and spiritual good by keeping my body as a temple for the indwelling of the Holy Spirit, or shall I sacrifice myself to the world's ideas and practices?—Manuscript 86, 1897.

More Than Conquerors.—If Christians will keep the body in subjection and bring all their appetites and passions under the control of enlightened conscience, feeling it a duty that they owe to God and to their neighbor to obey the laws which govern health and life, they will have the blessing of physical and mental vigor. They will have moral power to engage in the warfare against Satan; and in the name of Him who conquered appetite in their behalf, they may be more than conquerors on their own account.—*Review and Herald,* Nov. 21, 1882.

Section XI

OUR RELATIONSHIP TO OTHER TEMPERANCE GROUPS

1. Working Together

Stand Shoulder to Shoulder.—In other churches there are Christians who are standing in defense of the principles of temperance. We should seek to come near to these workers and make a way for them to stand shoulder to shoulder with us. We should call upon great and good men to second our efforts to save that which is lost.—*Testimonies,* vol. 6, pp. 110, 111.

Unite When We Can.—Whenever you can get an opportunity to unite with the temperance people, do so.—*Review and Herald,* Feb. 14, 1888.

In his labors, my husband, whenever he had opportunity, invited the workers in the temperance cause to his meetings, and gave them an opportunity to speak. And when invitations were given us to attend their gatherings, we always responded.—Letter 274, 1907.

Linking Only With Those Loyal to God.—We are not to take our stand with temperance clubs composed of all classes of men, with all kinds of selfish indulgences and call them reformers. There is a higher standard for our people to rally under. We must as a people make a distinction between those who are loyal to the law of God, and those who are disloyal. —Letter 1, 1882.

A Sensible Attitude Toward Other Organizations.—The

temperance question is to be respected by every true Christian, and especially should it receive the sanction of all who profess to be reformers. But there will be those in the church that will not show wisdom in the treatment of this subject. Some will show marked disrespect to any reforms arising from any other people besides those of their own faith; in this they err by being too exclusive.

Others will grasp eagerly every new thing which makes a pretense of temperance, having every other interest swallowed up in this one point; the prosperity and peculiar, holy character of our faith is ignored, the parties upon temperance are embraced, and an alliance formed between God's commandment-keeping people and all classes of persons. Dangers beset the faith of every soul who is not closely connected with God.—Letter 1, 1882.

Lessons From a Detrimental Union With a Superficial Group.—Temperance societies, and clubs have been formed among those who make no profession of the truth.* . . . I was shown that the condition of the church at —— was peculiar. Many who, had they given as much zeal, and manifested as much missionary spirit in the work of reform among us as a people as they have given to the Red-Ribbon Club, their course would have been sanctioned by God. But the different organizations upon temperance are very limited in their ideas of reform.

Those who give so great influence to the agitation of this question and at the same time are devotees of tobacco, drink tea and coffee, and indulge in health-destroying food at their tables, are not temperance people. They make weak and spasmodic movements, full of zeal and excitement, but they do not go to the bottom of true reform, and in a short time

---

*Note: In the latter half of the nineteenth century a number of popular temperance organizations were formed with large memberships. These were relatively short-lived and are not known today by the general public.—Compilers.

Our Relationship to Other Temperance Groups

will show flagging interest, and a returning of many to their old wicked indulgences, because they merely picked off the leaves of the tree instead of laying the ax at its root. This matter of temperance must go to the root of the evil or it will be of but little avail.

Our Influence Must Be With Loyal and True.—While our people mingle with the class who are enemies of Christ and the truth, they neither gain nor give strength. . . . We must not be exclusive as a people; our light is diffusive, constantly seeking to save the perishing. But while we are doing this our strength of influence must ever be found with the loyal and true. . . .

God's House Desecrated.—The house dedicated to the worship of God is not the place to bring in the class that come into the house of God, and defile the temple of God with their intemperance in the use of tobacco while they profess to be temperance advocates. The coarse speeches, the noisy talk and actions, are not a credit to these brethren. . . .

It is impossible for our people to harmonize with any party or temperance club, when our faith is so dissimilar. . . .

Our unbelieving friends have stood exulting while they see the dissension in the church that has grown out of our people uniting with the Red-Ribbon Club. They have had no sympathy for us as a people upon the subject of temperance. They are far behind, and have ridiculed our people as fanatics upon health. They are willing now to be favored, and receive the strength of our influence while they come no nearer in sympathy to our faith; when if the matter had been managed discreetly it might have had that influence upon some to change their opinion of our faith.

If the temperance club had been left to stand on its own ground, we, as a people, standing upon our advanced ground, keeping respectively the high standard God has given us to meet as necessary to our position and faith, there would have been a much more healthy influence existing upon the temperance question in the church than now is revealed.—Letter 1, 1882.

Not to Sacrifice Principle.—From the light God has given me, every member among us should sign the pledge and be connected with the temperance association. . . .

We should unite with other people just as far as we can and not sacrifice principle. This does not mean that we should join their lodges and societies,* but that we should let them know that we are most heartily in sympathy with the temperance question.

We should not work solely for our own people, but should bestow labor also upon noble minds outside of our ranks. We should be at the head in the temperance reform.—*Review and Herald,* Oct. 21, 1884.

An Effective Work in Uniting With Christian Temperance Workers.—Soon after my husband and I returned from California to Michigan in the spring of 1877, we were earnestly solicited to take part in a temperance mass meeting, a very praiseworthy effort in progress among the better portion of the citizens of Battle Creek. This movement embraced the Battle Creek Reform Club, six hundred strong, and the Woman's Christian Temperance Union, two hundred and sixty strong. God, Christ, and Holy Spirit, and the Bible were familiar words with these earnest workers. Much good had

---

* NOTE: These remarks were made by Mrs. White at the annual meeting of the Michigan Health and Temperance Association. Her statement touched on a number of resolutions just presented, among which were the following:

"*Resolved,* That we encourage the organization of a local club in the church to which we belong or with which we are associated. . . .

"*Resolved,* That we urge our young people to take an active part in our local clubs and at the same time endeavor to guard them from the influence of *other societies that do not adopt the high moral and physical standard* that we advocate."—*Review and Herald,* Oct. 21, 1884, p. 669. (Italics supplied by compilers.)

Our Relationship to Other Temperance Groups 221

already been accomplished, and the activity of the workers, the system by which they labored, and the spirit of their meetings, promised greater good in time to come. . . .

By invitation of the Committee of Arrangements, Mayor Austin, W. H. Skinner, cashier of the First National Bank, and C. C. Peavey, I spoke in the mammoth tent, Sunday evening, July 1, upon the subject of Christian temperance. God helped me that evening; and although I spoke ninety minutes, the crowd of fully five thousand persons listened in almost breathless silence.—Manuscript 79, 1902. (Part quoted in *Testimonies,* vol. 4, pp. 274, 275.)

Give Temperance Talks in Other Churches.—Let the talks upon temperance reform which are given to Seventh-day Adventists be given to the other churches. . . . There is to be no raid made by Seventh-day Adventists by pen or voice against any temperance movement.—Letter 107, 1900.

Doctrinal Differences Not to Alienate Us.—Although its friends do not believe with us in many points of doctrine,* yet we will unite with them when by so doing we can aid our fellow men. God would have us individually learn to work with tact and skill in the cause of temperance and other reforms, and employ our talents wisely in benefiting and elevating humanity.

If we would enter into the joy of our Lord, we must be colaborers with Him. With the love of Jesus warm in our hearts, we shall always see some way to reach the minds and hearts of others. It will make us unselfish, thoughtful, and kind; and kindness opens the door of hearts; gentleness is mightier far than a Jehu spirit.—*Review and Herald,* Feb. 10, 1885.

To Sense Our Responsibility.—Those who have labored in

---

*Note: Reference is here made to the Martha Washington Home in Chicago, where, upon invitation, Mrs. White gave a temperance address.—Compilers.

the temperance cause, and who in their work have had the Lord behind them, should have had far more labor put forth in their behalf. We need to feel our responsibility in this work.—*Review and Herald,* May 8, 1900.

Relieved of Establishing Buildings.—It is the plan and constant effort of Satan to entangle the work of God in a supposed beneficent and excellent work, so that doors cannot be opened to enter new fields and work with people who have an advanced acquaintance with temperance principles. To unite with them in their work would be to do a special work for this time, without taking on the responsibilities of a work which will enforce an expenditure of means in establishing buildings that will embarrass the conferences, a work which will absorb and consume but not produce.—Manuscript 46, 1900.

God Will Open the Way.—Seek every opportunity to enlighten and benefit the temperance workers. The temperance organization is one that I have ever respected. If you will be guided by the Holy Spirit, ways will open for you to work.—Letter 316, 1907.

2. Co-operating With the W. C. T. U.

An Organization With Which We Can Unite.—The Woman's Christian Temperance Union is an organization with whose efforts for the spread of temperance principles we can heartily unite. The light has been given me that we are not to stand aloof from them, but, while there is to be no sacrifice of principle on our part, as far as possible we are to unite with them in laboring for temperance reforms. . . . We are to work with them when we can, and we can assuredly do this on the question of utterly closing the saloon.

As the human agent submits his will to the will of God, the Holy Spirit will make the impression upon the hearts of those to whom he ministers. I have been shown that we are not to shun the W.C.T.U. workers. By uniting with them in behalf of total abstinence, we do not change our position regarding the observance of the seventh day, and we can show our appreciation of their position regarding the subject of temperance. By opening the door, and inviting them to unite with us on the temperance question, we secure their help along temperance lines; and they, by uniting with us, will hear new truths which the Holy Spirit is waiting to impress upon hearts.—*Review and Herald,* June 18, 1908.

Surprised at Our Indifference.—I have had some opportunity to see the great advantage to be gained by connecting with the W.C.T.U. workers, and I have been much surprised as I have seen the indifference of many of our leaders to this organization. I call on my brethren to awake.— Letter 274, 1907.

How We May Work Together.—We need at this time to show a decided interest in the work of the Woman's Christian Temperance Union. None who claim to have a part in the work of God, should lose interest in the grand object of this organization in temperance lines.

It would be a good thing if at our camp meetings we should invite the members of the W.C.T.U. to take part in our exercises. This would help them to become acquainted with the reasons of our faith, and open the way for us to unite with them in the temperance work. If we do this, we shall come to see that the temperance question means more than many of us have supposed.

In some matters, the workers of the W.C.T.U. are far in advance of our leaders. The Lord has in that organization precious souls, who can be a great help to us in our efforts to advance the temperance movement. And the education our people have had in Bible truth and in a knowledge of the requirements of the law of Jehovah, will enable our sisters to impart to these noble temperance advocates that which will be for their spiritual welfare. Thus a union and sympathy will be created where in the past there has sometimes existed prejudice and misunderstanding. . . .

We cannot do a better work than to unite, so far as we can do so without compromise, with the W. C. T. U. workers.

Concerning this matter I wrote to one of our sisters in 1898:

"The Lord, I fully believe, is leading you that you may keep the principles of temperance clear and distinct, in all their purity, in connection with the truth for these last days. They that do His will shall know of the doctrine. . . . The Lord does not bid you separate from the Woman's Christian Temperance Union. They need all the light you can give them. Flash all the light possible into their pathway. You can agree with them on the ground of the pure, elevating principles that first brought into existence the Woman's Christian Temperance Union. The Lord has given you capabilities and talents to be preserved uncorrupted in their simplicity. Through Jesus Christ you may do a good work.—*Review and Herald,* Oct. 15, 1914. (Part used in *Gospel Workers,* pages 384, 385.)

They to Teach Our Women How to Work.—Much good would be done if some of the W.T.C.U. women were invited to our camp meetings to take part in the meetings by teaching our sisters how to work. While at the meeting they would be hearing and receiving as well as imparting. There is a great work to be done, and instead of presenting the features of our faith which are objectionable to unbelievers, let us say to them as Philip said to Nathanael, "Come and see."

We Cannot Unite With Them in Exalting Sunday.—I want to unite with the W.C.T.U. workers, but we cannot unite with them in a work of exalting a false Sabbath. We cannot work in lines that would mean the transgression of the law of God, but we say to them, Come on to the right platform.—Manuscript 93, 1908.

Never Refuse Invitations to Speak.—The question has been

asked me, When asked by the W.C.T.U. to speak in their meetings, shall we accept the invitation?

In answer, I reply, When asked to speak in such meetings, never refuse. This is the rule that I have always followed. When asked to speak on temperance, I have never hesitated. Among those who are working for the spread of temperance, the Lord has souls to whom the truth for this time is to be presented. We are to bear a message to the W.C.T.U.

Christ's one purpose when upon this earth was to reflect the light of His righteousness to those in darkness. The W.C.T.U. workers have not the whole truth on all points, but they are doing a good work.—Manuscript 31, 1911.

Free to Act in Concert With Them.—I am deeply interested in the W.C.T.U. It is the Lord's pleasure that you should feel free to act in concert with them. . . . I am not afraid that you will lose your interest, or backslide from the truth because you interest yourself in this people who have taken such a noble stand for the temperance question, and I shall urge our people, and those not of our faith, to help us in carrying forward the work of Christian temperance. . . .

In our labors together, my husband and I always felt that it was our duty to demonstrate in every place where we held meetings that we were fully in harmony with the workers in the temperance cause. We always laid this question before the people in plain lines. Invitations would come to us to speak in different places on the temperance question, and I always accepted these invitations if it was possible. This has been my experience not only in this country, but in Europe and Australia, and other places where I have labored.

Lose Not One Opportunity to Unite With Temperance Work.—I am sorry that there has not been a more lively interest among our people of late years to magnify this branch of the Lord's work. We cannot afford to lose one opportunity to unite with the temperance work in any place. Although the cause of temperance in foreign countries does not always advance as rapidly as we could wish, yet in some places decided success has attended the efforts of those who engaged in it. In Europe we found the people sound on this question. On one occasion, when I accepted an invitation to speak to a large audience on the subject of temperance, the people did me the honor of draping above the pulpit the American flag. My words were received with the deepest attention, and at the close of my talk a hearty vote of thanks was accorded me. I have never, in all my work on this question, had to accept one word of disrespect.—Letter 278, 1907.

Section XII

THE CHALLENGE OF THE HOUR

The advocates of temperance fail to do their whole duty unless they exert their influence by precept and example—by voice and pen and vote—in favor of prohibition and total abstinence.—Gospel Workers, pages 387, 388.

1. The Present Situation

A Repetition of the Same Sins.—The same sins that brought judgments upon the world in the days of Noah, exist in our day. Men and women now carry their eating and drinking so far that it ends in gluttony and drunkenness. This prevailing sin, the indulgence of perverted appetite, inflamed the passions of men in the days of Noah, and led to widespread corruption. Violence and sin reached to heaven. This moral pollution was finally swept from the earth by means of the Flood. . . .

Eating, drinking, and dressing are carried to such excess that they become crimes. They are among the marked sins of the last days, and constitute a sign of Christ's soon coming. Time, money, and strength, which belong to the Lord, but which He has entrusted to us, are wasted in superfluities of dress and luxuries for the perverted appetite, which lessen vitality, and bring suffering and decay.—*Christian Temperance and Bible Hygiene, pages* 11, 12.

A Succession of Falls.—From Adam's day to ours there has been a succession of falls, each greater than the last, in every species of crime. God did not create a race of beings so devoid of health, beauty, and moral power as now exists in the world. Disease of every kind has been fearfully increasing upon the race. This has not been by God's especial providence, but directly contrary to His will. It has come by man's disregard of the very means which God has ordained to shield him from the terrible evils existing. Obedience to God's law in every respect would save men from intemperance, licentiousness, and disease of every type. No one can violate natural law without suffering the penalty.—*Review and Herald,* March 4, 1875.

Thousands Selling Their Mental Capabilities.—What man would, for any sum of money, deliberately sell his mental capabilities? Should one offer him money if he would part with his intellect, he would turn with disgust from the insane suggestion. Yet thousands are parting with health of body, vigor of intellect, and elevation of soul, for the sake of gratifying appetite. Instead of gain, they experience only loss. This they do not realize because of their benumbed sensibilities. They have bartered away their God-given faculties. And for what? Answer. Groveling sensualities and degrading vices. The gratification of taste is indulged at the cost of health and intellect.—*Review and Herald,* March 4, 1875.

The Insidious Gradual Change.—The use of intoxicating liquor dethrones reason, and hardens the heart against every pure and holy influence. The inanimate rock will sooner listen to the appeals of truth and justice than will that man whose sensibilities are paralyzed by intemperance. The finer feelings of the heart are not blunted all at once. A gradual change is wrought. Those who venture to enter the forbidden path are gradually demoralized and corrupted. And though in the cities liquor saloons abound, making indulgence easy, and though youth are surrounded by allurements to tempt the appetite, the evil does not often begin with the use of intoxicating liquors. Tea, coffee, and tobacco are artificial stimulants, and their use creates the demand for the stronger stimulus found in alcoholic beverages. And while Christians are asleep, this giant evil of intemperance is gaining strength and making fresh victims.—*Signs of the Times,* Dec. 6, 1910.

Temptations on Every Hand.—In private lunchrooms and fashionable resorts, ladies are supplied with popular drinks, under some pleasing name, that are really intoxicants. For the sick and the exhausted, there are the widely advertised "bitters," consisting largely of alcohol.

To create the liquor appetite in little children, alcohol is introduced into confectionery. Such confectionery is sold in the shops. And by the gift of these candies the liquor seller entices children into his resorts.

Day by day, month by month, year by year, the work goes on. Fathers and husbands and brothers, the stay and hope and pride of the nation, are steadily passing into the liquor dealer's haunts, to be sent back wrecked and ruined.—*The Ministry of Healing,* pages 338, 339.

On the "March to Death."—That men may not take time to meditate, Satan leads them into a round of gaiety and pleasure seeking, of eating and drinking. He fills them with ambition to make an exhibition that will exalt self. Step by step, the world is reaching the conditions that existed in the days of Noah. Every conceivable crime is committed. The lust of the flesh, the pride of the eyes, the display of selfishness, the misuse of power, the cruelty, . . . all these are the working of satanic agencies. This round of crime and folly men call "life." . . .

The world, who act as though there were no God, absorbed in selfish pursuits, will soon experience sudden destruction, and shall not escape. Many continue in the careless gratification of self until they become so disgusted with life that they kill themselves. Dancing and carousing, drinking and smoking, indulging their animal passions, they go as an ox to the slaughter. Satan is working with all his art and enchantments to keep men marching blindly onward until the Lord arises out of His place to punish the inhabitants of earth for their iniquities, when the earth shall disclose her blood and no more cover her slain. The whole world appears to be in the march to death.—*Evangelism,* page 26.

The Curse Carried to Heathen Nations.—From so-called Christian lands the curse is carried to the regions of idolatry. The poor, ignorant savages are taught the use of liquor. Even among the heathen, men of intelligence recognize and protest against it as a deadly poison; but in vain have they sought to protect their lands from its ravages. By civilized peoples, tobacco, liquor, and opium are forced upon the heathen nations. The ungoverned passions of the savage, stimulated by drink, drag him down to degradation before unknown, and it becomes an almost hopeless undertaking to send missionaries to these lands.

Through their contact with peoples who should have given them a knowledge of God, the heathen are led into vices which are proving the destruction of whole tribes and races. And in the dark places of the earth the men of civilized nations are hated because of this.—*The Ministry of Healing,* page 339.

Even the Christian Churches Paralyzed.—The liquor interest is a power in the world. It has on its side the combined strength of money, habit, appetite. Its power is felt even in the church. Men whose money has been made, directly or indirectly, in the liquor traffic, are members of churches, "in good and regular standing." Many of them give liberally to popular charities. Their contributions help to support the enterprises of the church and to sustain its ministers. They command the consideration shown to the money power. Churches that accept such members are virtually sustaining the liquor traffic. Too often the minister has not the courage to stand for the right. He does not declare to his people what God has said concerning the work of the liquor seller. To speak plainly would mean the offending of his congregation, the sacrifice of his popularity, the loss of his salary.—*The Ministry of Healing,* page 340.

Ministers Have Dropped the Banner.—The Lord has a controversy with the inhabitants of the earth who are living in this time of peril and corruption. Ministers of the gospel have departed from the Lord, and those who profess the name of Christ are guilty of not holding aloft the banner of truth. Ministers are afraid to be open prohibitionists, and they hold their peace concerning the curse of drink, fearing lest their salaries should be diminished or their congregations offended. They fear lest, if they should speak forth Bible truth with power and clearness, showing the line of distinction between the sacred and the common, they would lose their popularity; for there are large numbers who are enrolled as church members who are receiving a revenue, either directly or indirectly, from the drink traffic.

These people are not ignorant of the sin that they are committing. No one needs to be informed that the drink traffic is one that entails upon its victims, misery, shame, degradation, and death, with the eternal ruin of their souls. Those who reap a revenue, either directly or indirectly, from this traffic, are putting into the till the money which has come through the loss of souls of men.

The churches that retain members who are connected with this liquor business, make themselves responsible for the transactions that occur through the drink traffic. . . .

Money Stained With the Blood of Souls.—The world and the church may unite in eulogizing the man who has tempted the appetite, and answered the craving of the appetite he has helped to create; they may look with a smile upon him who has helped to debase a man who was formed in the image of

God, until that image is virtually effaced; but God looks with a frown upon him, and writes his condemnation in the ledger of death. . . .

This very man may make large donations to the church; but will God accept of the money that is wrung from the family of the drunkard? It is stained with the blood of souls, and the curse of God is upon it. God says, "For I the Lord love judgment, I hate robbery for burnt offering." The church may praise the liberality of one who gives such an offering; but were the eyes of the church members anointed with heavenly eyesalve, they would not call good evil and iniquity righteousness. The Lord says, "To what purpose is the multitude of your sacrifices unto Me? . . . When ye come to appear before Me, who hath required this at your hand, to tread My courts? Bring no more vain oblations; incense is an abomination unto Me." "Ye have wearied the Lord with your words. Yet ye say, Wherein have we wearied Him? When ye say, Everyone that doeth evil is good in the sight of the Lord, and He delighteth in them; or, Where is the God of judgment?"—*Review and Herald,* May 15, 1894.

Conditions Which Call for God's Judgments.—Because of the wickedness that follows largely as the result of the use of liquor, the judgments of God are falling upon our earth today. Have we not a solemn responsibility to put forth earnest efforts in opposition to this great evil?—*Counsels on Health,* page 432.

A Reformation Due.—There needs to be a great reformation on the subject of temperance. The world is filled with self-indulgence of every kind. Because of the benumbing influence of stimulants and narcotics the minds of many are unable to discern between the sacred and the common.—*Counsels on Health,* page 432.

God's Call to Help the Inebriate.—Your neighbor may be yielding to the temptation to destroy himself by liquor drinking and tobacco using. He may be burning up his vital organs by fiery stimulant. He is pursuing this course to the ruination of himself and his wife and children, who have no success in trying to stay the feet that are traveling the road to perdition. God calls upon you to work in His vineyard, to do all in your power to save your fellow creatures.—Manuscript 87, 1898.

As we face these things, and see the terrible consequences of liquor drinking, shall we not do all in our power to rally to the help of God in fighting against this great evil?—*Evangelism*, page 265.

2. Called to the Battle

Our Place in the Forefront.—Of all who claim to be numbered among the friends of temperance, Seventh-day Adventists should stand in the front ranks.—*Gospel Workers*, page 384.

On the subject of temperance they should be in advance of all other people.—*Medical Ministry*, page 273.

While intemperance has its open, avowed supporters, shall not we who claim to honor temperance come to the front and show ourselves firm on the side of temperance, striving for a crown of immortal life, and not giving the least influence to this terrible evil, intemperance? —*Review and Herald*, April 19, 1887.

I feel distressed as I look upon our people and know that they are holding very loosely the temperance question. . . . We should be at the head in the temperance reform.—*Review and Herald*, Oct. 21, 1884.

Not a Matter of Jest.—Many make the subject of temperance a matter of jest. They claim that the Lord does not concern Himself with such minor matters as our eating and drinking. But if the Lord had no care for these things, He would not have revealed Himself to the wife of Manoah, giving her definite instructions, and twice enjoining upon her to beware lest she disregard them. Is not this sufficient evidence that He does care for these things?—*Signs of the Times,* Sept. 13, 1910.

A Part of the Third Angel's Message.—Every true reform has its place in the work of the third angel's message. Especially does the temperance reform demand our attention and support.—*Testimonies,* vol. 6, p. 110.

Shall there not be among us as a people a revival of the temperance work? Why are we not putting forth much more decided efforts to oppose the liquor traffic, which is ruining the souls of men, and is causing violence and crime of every description? With the great light that God has entrusted to us, we should be in the forefront of every true reform.—*Counsels on Health,* page 432.

Earnest Continual Efforts.—Intemperance still continues its ravages. Iniquity in every form stands like a mighty barrier to prevent the progress of truth and righteousness. Social wrongs, born of ignorance and vice, are still causing untold misery, and casting their baleful shadow upon both the church and the world. Depravity among the youth is increasing instead of decreasing. Nothing but earnest, continual effort will avail to remove this desolating curse. The conflict with interest and appetite, with evil habits and unholy passions, will be fierce and deadly; only those who shall move from principle can gain the victory in this warfare.—*Review and Herald,* Nov. 6, 1883.

God Works Through His Church.—If men, and women as well, are to be thus beguiled, will not the Lord work through His church, impressing His people to do their duty to these deceived victims? By many, liquor has been regarded as the only solace in trouble. This need not be if God's people seized the opportunities offered them. If their eyes were not blinded by selfishness, they would see the work waiting to be done. They would be sent by God to do the work He would have had them do in the beginning of their experience, when their souls were filled with joy and gladness because their sins had been pardoned.—Manuscript 87, 1898.

A Weapon More Effective Than the Ax.—God wants us to stand where we can warn the people. He desires us to take up the temperance question. By wrong habits of eating and drinking, men are destroying what power they have for thought and intelligence. We do not need to take an ax and break into their saloons. We have a stronger weapon than this,—the word of the living God. That will cleave its way through the hellish shadow which Satan seeks to cast athwart their pathway. God is mighty and powerful. He will speak to their hearts. We have seen Him doing this.—*General Conference Bulletin,* April 23, 1901.

Youth to Join in Staying the Evil.—There is no class of persons capable of accomplishing more in the warfare against intemperance than are God-fearing youth. In this age the young men in our cities should unite as an army, firmly and decidedly to set themselves against every form of selfish, health-destroying indulgence. What a power they might be for good! How many they might save from becoming demoralized in the halls and gardens fitted up with music and other attractions to allure the youth! . . .

The young men and young women who claim to believe the truth for this time can please Jesus only by uniting in an effort to meet the evils that have, with seductive influence, crept in upon society. They should do all they can to stay the tide of intemperance now spreading with demoralizing power over the land. Realizing that intemperance has open, avowed supporters, those who honor God take their position firmly against this tide of evil by which both men and women are being swiftly carried to perdition.—*The Youth's Instructor,* July 16, 1903.

Called to the Holy War Against Appetite and Lust.—Are our young men prepared to lift their voices in the cause of temperance and show its bearing upon Christianity? Will they engage in the holy war against appetite and lust? Our artificial civilization encourages evils which are destroying sound principles. And the Lord is at the door. Where are the men who will go forth to the work, fully trusting in God, ready to do and to dare? God calls, "Son, go work today in My vineyard."—Manuscript 134, 1898.

To Follow God's Instruction.—We must begin to labor on the subject of temperance. We must take this matter up in the way that the Lord has often presented to me should be done.—Letter 334, 1905.

Called to Join Our Temperance Society.—Temperance societies, and clubs have been formed among those who make no profession of the truth, while our people although far ahead of every other denomination in the land in principle and practical temperance have been slow to organize into temperance societies, and thus have failed to exert the influence they otherwise might.—Letter 1, 1882.

From the light God has given me, every member among us should sign the pledge and be connected with the temperance association.—*Review and Herald,* Oct. 21, 1884.

Every Church Member to Work.—Let those who have their Bibles and who believe the word of God become active temperance workers. Who will now seek to advance the work of our Redeemer? Let every church member work in right lines.—Letter 18a, 1906.

We want everyone to be a temperance worker.—Manuscript 18, 1894.

Power of Example.—By our example and personal effort we may be the means of saving many souls from the degradation of intemperance, crime, and death.—*Testimonies,* vol. 3, p. 489.

Need of Men Like Daniel.—There is need now of men like Daniel,—men who have the self-denial and the courage to be radical temperance reformers. Let every Christian see that his example and his influence are on the side of reform. Let ministers of the gospel be faithful in instructing and warning the people. And let all remember that our happiness in two worlds depends upon the right improvement of one.—*Signs of the Times,* Dec. 6, 1910.

3. By Voice—a Part of Our Evangelistic Message

Present Temperance With Spiritual Truths.—In connection with the presentation of spiritual truths, we should also present what the word of God says upon the questions of health and temperance. In every way possible, we must seek to bring souls under the convicting and converting power of God.—Letter 148, 1909.

I have heard some, when speaking in reference to temperance, say, "I have not time. I have so much to do in preaching here and there upon the third angel's message and the reasons of our faith, that I cannot take time to engage in the health and temperance work." If these men would cut their sermons short about one third, the people would receive more benefit from them, and they would then have time to speak upon this question.—*Review and Herald,* Feb. 14, 1888.

Temperance and Salvation.—As a people we have been given the work of making known the principles of health reform. There are some who think that the question of diet is not of sufficient importance to be included in their evangelistic work. But such make a great mistake. God's word declares: "Whether therefore ye eat, or drink, or whatsoever ye do, do all to the glory of God." 1 Corinthians 10:31. The subject of temperance, in all its bearings, has an important place in the work of salvation.—*Testimonies,* vol. 9, p. 112.

A Part of the Third Angel's Message.—Brethren and sisters, we want you to see the importance of this temperance question, and we want our workers to interest themselves in it, and to know that it is just as much connected with the third angel's message as the right arm is with the body. We ought to make advancement in this work.—*Review and Herald,* Feb. 14, 1888.

To make plain natural law, and urge the obedience of it, is the work that accompanies the third angel's message to prepare a people for the coming of the Lord.—*Testimonies,* vol. 3, p. 161.

Stir the Public Mind.—Those who are to prepare the way for the second coming of Christ are represented by faithful Elijah, as John came in the spirit of Elijah to prepare the way for Christ's first advent. The great subject of reform is to be agitated, and the public mind is to be stirred. Temperance in all things is to be connected with the message, to turn the people of God from their idolatry, their gluttony, and their extravagance in dress and other things.—*Testimonies,* vol. 3, p. 62.

Let us raise our voices against the curse of drunkenness. Let us strive to warn the world against its seductive influences. Let us portray before young and old the terrible results of indulgence of appetite.—Manuscript 80, 1903.

When temperance is presented as a part of the gospel, many will see their need of reform. They will see the evil of intoxicating liquors and that total abstinence is the only platform on which God's people can conscientiously stand.—*Testimonies,* vol. 7, p. 75.

No Tame Message Now.—The conflict against this evil, which is destroying the image of God in man, must be vigorously maintained. The warfare is before us. No tame message will have influence now. God looks upon our world as revolted and corrupted, but He will send His holy angels to aid those who will engage to destroy the worship of these idols.—Letter 102a, 1897.

The evil [of intemperance] must be more boldly met in the future than it has been in the past.—*The Youth's Instructor,* March 9, 1909.

Temperance Sermons in Every City Effort.—In the advocacy of the cause of temperance, our efforts are to be multiplied. The subject of Christian temperance should find a place in our sermons in every city where we labor. Health reform in all its bearings is to be presented before the people, and special efforts made to instruct the youth, the middle-aged, and the aged in the principles of Christian living. Let this phase of the message be revived, and let the truth go forth as a lamp that burneth.—Manuscript 61, 1909.

With Convincing Arguments and Strong Appeals.—In all our large gatherings we must bring the temperance question before our hearers in the strongest appeals and by the most convincing arguments. The Lord has given us the work of teaching Christian temperance from a Bible standpoint.—Manuscript 82, 1900.

Schools of Health to Follow Public Meetings.—There is a great work to be done in bringing the principles of health reform to the notice of the people. Public meetings should be held to introduce the subject, and schools should be held in which those who are interested can be told more particularly about our health foods and of how a wholesome, nourishing, appetizing diet can be provided without the use of meat, tea, or coffee. . . .

Press home the temperance question with all the force of the Holy Spirit's unction. Show the need of total abstinence from all intoxicating liquor. Show the terrible harm that is wrought in the human system by the use of tobacco and alcohol.—*Evangelism,* page 534.

Show Why We Have Changed Our Dietetic Habits.—Lectures should be given explaining why reforms in diet are essential, and showing that the use of highly seasoned food causes inflammation of the delicate lining of the digestive organs. Let it be shown why we as a people have changed our habits of eating and drinking. Show why we discard tobacco and all intoxicating liquor. Lay down the principles of health reform clearly and plainly, and with this, let there be placed on the table an abundance of wholesome food, tastefully prepared; and the Lord will help you to make impressive the urgency of reform, and will lead them to see that this reform is for their highest good.—*Medical Ministry,* page 286.

Drive It to the Hilt.—When we have shown the people that we have right principles regarding health reform, we should then take up the temperance question in all its bearings, and drive it home to the hilt.—*Letter 63, 1905.*

Present It Attractively.—Present the principles of temperance in their most attractive form. Circulate the books that give instruction in regard to healthful living.—*Testimonies,* vol. 7, p. 136.

The High Standard for Temperance Meetings.—Great care should be taken to make the temperance meetings as elevated and ennobling as possible. Avoid a surface work and everything of a theatrical character. Those who realize the solemn character of this work will keep the standard high. But there is a class who have no real respect for the cause of temperance; their only concern is to show off their smartness upon the stage. The pure, the thoughtful, and those who understand the object of the work, should be encouraged to labor in these great branches of reform. They may not be intellectually great, but if pure and humble, God-fearing and true, the Lord will accept their labors.—*Testimonies,* vol. 5, p. 127.

Not to Work Alone.—One man should not try to do this work alone. Let several unite in such an effort. Let them come to the front with a message from heaven, imbued with the power of the Holy Spirit. . . . Let men and women be shown the evil of spending money in indulgences that destroy the health of mind and soul and body.—*Evangelism,* page 531.

Present God's Appointed Way.—The self-denial, humility, and temperance required of the righteous, whom God especially leads and blesses, is to be presented to the people in contrast to the extravagant, health-destroying habits of those who live in this degenerate age. God has shown that health reform is as closely connected with the third angel's message as the hand is with the body. There is nowhere to be found so great a cause of physical and moral degeneracy as a neglect of this important subject. Those who indulge appetite and passion, and close their eyes to the light for fear they will see sinful indulgences which they are unwilling to forsake, are guilty before God.

The Hazard of Turning From the Light.—Whoever turns from the light in one instance hardens his heart to disregard the light upon other matters. Whoever violates moral obligations in the matter of eating and dressing prepares the way to violate the claims of God in regard to eternal interests. . . .

The people whom God is leading will be peculiar. They will not be like the world. But if they follow the leadings of God they will accomplish His purposes, and will yield their will to His will. Christ will dwell in the heart. The temple of God will be holy. Your body, says the apostle, is the temple of the Holy Ghost.

Called to Obedience of Natural Laws.—God does not require His children to deny themselves to the injury of physical strength. He requires them to obey natural law, to preserve physical health. Nature's path is the road He marks out, and it is broad enough for any Christian. God has, with a lavish hand, provided us with rich and varied bounties for our sustenance and enjoyment. But in order for us to enjoy the natural appetite, which will preserve health and prolong life, He restricts the appetite. He says: Beware; restrain, deny, unnatural appetite. If we create a perverted appetite, we violate the laws of our being and assume the responsibility of abusing our bodies and of bringing disease upon ourselves.—*Testimonies,* vol. 3, pp. 62, 63.

An Effective Entering Wedge.—I have been informed by my guide that not only should those who believe the truth practice health reform but they should also teach it diligently to others; for it will be an agency through which the truth can be presented to the attention of unbelievers. They will reason that if we have such sound ideas in regard to health and temperance, there must be something in our religious belief that is worth investigation. If we backslide in health reform we shall lose much of our influence with the outside world.—*Evangelism,* page 514.

Temperance Sermons Will Reach Many.—Careful attention is to be given to helping those who are enslaved by evil habits. They are to hear discourses from the word of God concerning Christian temperance. We must lead them to the cross of Christ. Persons who have not entered a church for nearly a score of years have come to such gatherings and have been converted. The result was, they discarded tea and coffee, tobacco, beer, and liquor. Most marvelous changes in character have taken place. While many thus receive the light, others reject it, to their own eternal loss. This work costs time and wearing effort, and it causes much anguish of soul to see so many hear and understand, but, because of the cross, refuse to accept of Jesus Christ.—Manuscript 52, 1900.

Personal Work for the Intemperate.—Work for the intemperate man and the tobacco user, telling them that no drunkard shall inherit the kingdom of God, and that "there shall in nowise enter into it anything that defileth." Show them the good they could do with the money they now spend for that which does them only harm.—*Medical Ministry,* page 268.

Work, Pray, Uplift.—The wretched victim of intemperance may refuse to seize the opportunity of regaining his manliness by breaking with Satan. Is it any less your duty to strive to awaken the soul dead in trespasses and sins by doing all that human effort can do? Jesus will work wonderful miracles if men will but do their God-given part. In his own strength man can never recover souls from Satan's grasp. A union with Christ only can accomplish this restoration. Man must work, he must pray, he must uplift the discouraged and hopeless by his human endeavor, while he grasps the arm of the Mighty One, and wrestles as did Jacob for the victory. His cry must be, I cannot, I will not, let Thee go unless Thou bless me.—Manuscript 87, 1898.

Why the Temperance Message Is Vital.—The Christian will be temperate in all things,—in eating, in drinking, in dress, and in every phase of life. "Every man that striveth for the mastery is temperate in all things. Now they do it to obtain a corruptible crown; but we an incorruptible." We have no right to indulge in anything that will result in a condition of mind that hinders the Spirit of God from impressing us with the sense of our duty. It is a masterpiece of satanic skill to place men where they can with difficulty be reached with the gospel.—*Review and Herald,* Aug. 29, 1907.

Laymen Called to Public Temperance Work.—A working church is a living church. Church members, let the light shine forth. Let your voices be heard in humble prayer, in witness against the intemperance, the folly, and the amusements of this world, and in the proclamation of the truth for this time. Your voice, your influence, your time,—all these are gifts from God, and are to be used in winning souls to Christ. Visit your neighbors, and show an interest in the salvation of their souls.—*Medical Ministry,* page 332.

Sunday a Day to Work for Temperance.—Sunday can be used for carrying forward various lines of work that will accomplish much for the Lord. . . . Speak on temperance and on true religious experience. You will thus learn much about how to work, and will reach many souls.—*Testimonies,* vol. 9, p. 233.

At Camp Meetings.—In our labors at the camp meetings more attention should be given to the work of teaching the principles of health and temperance reform; these questions are to take an important place in our efforts at this time. My message is, Educate, educate on the question of temperance. —Manuscript 65, 1908.

In Our Churches.—Every church needs a clear, sharp testimony, giving the trumpet a certain sound. If we can arouse the moral sensibilities upon the subject of practicing temperance in all things, a very great victory will be gained.—Manuscript 59, 1900.

Prepare to Teach Others.—I will inquire why some of our ministerial brethren are so far behind in proclaiming the exalted theme of temperance. Why is it that greater interest is not shown in health reform?—Letter 42, 1898.

We should educate ourselves, not only to live in harmony with the laws of health, but to teach others the better way. Many, even of those who profess to believe the special truths for this time, are lamentably ignorant with regard to health and temperance. They need to be educated, line upon line, precept upon precept. The subject must be kept fresh before them. This matter must not be passed over as nonessential; for nearly every family needs to be stirred up on the question. The conscience must be aroused to the duty of practicing the principles of true reform. God requires that His people shall be temperate in all things. . . .

Not to Be Deterred by Ridicule.—Our ministers should become intelligent upon this question. They should not ignore it, nor be turned aside by those who call them extremists. Let them find out what constitutes true health reform, and teach its principles, both by precept and by a quiet, consistent example. At our large gatherings, instruction should be given upon health and temperance. Seek to arouse the intellect and the conscience. Bring into service all the talent at command, and follow up the work with publications upon the subject. "Educate, educate, educate," is the message that has been impressed upon me.—*Christian Temperance and Bible Hygiene,* page 117.

4. Temperance Education an Objective of Our Medical Work

Established to Preach True Temperance.—Our Sanitariums are established, to preach the truth of true temperance.—*Counsels on Diet and Foods,* page 162.

Presented From Moral Standpoint.—In our sanitariums our ministers, who labor in word and doctrine, should give short talks upon the principles of temperance, showing that the body is the temple of the Holy Spirit, and bringing to the minds of the people the responsibility resting upon them as God's purchased possession to make the body a holy temple, fit for the indwelling of the Holy Spirit. As this instruction is given, the people will become interested in Bible doctrine.

There must also be presented the moral pestilence that is

making the inhabitants of the world today like the inhabitants of the world before the Flood—bold, blasphemous, intemperate, corrupted. The sins that are practiced are making this earth a lazar house of corruption. These sins must be sternly rebuked. Those who preach must uplift the standard of temperance from a Christian standpoint. As temperance is presented as a part of the gospel, many will see their need of reform.—Manuscript 14, 1901.

Doctors to Instruct in Temperance Lines.—They should give instruction to the people in regard to the dangers of intemperance. This evil must be more boldly met in the future than it has been in the past. Ministers and doctors should set forth the evils of intemperance. Both should work in the gospel with power to condemn sin and exalt righteousness. Those ministers or doctors who do not make personal appeals to the people are remiss in their duty. They fail of doing the work which God has appointed them.—*Testimonies,* vol. 6, p. 110.

To Teach Strict Temperance.—When a physician sees a patient suffering from disease caused by improper eating and drinking or other wrong habits, yet neglects to tell him of this, he is doing his fellow being an injury. Drunkards, maniacs, those who are given over to licentiousness, all appeal to the physician to declare clearly and distinctly that suffering results from sin. Those who understand the principles of life should be in earnest in striving to counteract the causes of disease. Seeing the continual conflict with pain, laboring constantly to alleviate suffering, how can the physician hold his peace? Is he benevolent and merciful if he does not teach strict temperance as a remedy for disease?—*The Ministry of Healing,* page 114.

A Guardian of Physical and Moral Health.—The true physician is an educator. He recognizes his responsibility, not only to the sick who are under his direct care, but also to the community in which he lives. He stands as a guardian of both physical and moral health. It is his endeavor not only to teach right methods for the treatment of the sick, but to encourage right habits of living, and to spread a knowledge of right principles.

Education in health principles was never more needed than now. Notwithstanding the wonderful progress in so many lines relating to the comforts and conveniences of life, even to sanitary matters and to the treatment of disease, the decline in physical vigor and power of endurance is alarming. It demands the attention of all who have at heart the well-being of their fellow men.

Our artificial civilization is encouraging evils destructive of sound principles. Custom and fashion are at war with nature. The practices they enjoin, and the indulgences they foster, are steadily lessening both physical and mental strength, and bringing upon the race an intolerable burden. Intemperance and crime, disease and wretchedness, are everywhere.

Many transgress the laws of health through ignorance, and they need instruction. But the greater number know better than they do. They need to be impressed with the importance of making their knowledge a guide of life. The physician has many opportunities both of imparting a knowledge of health principles, and of showing the importance of putting them in practice. By right instruction he can do much to correct evils that are working untold harm.—*The Ministry of Healing,* pages 125, 126.

The Sanitarium an Educating Force.—In all our sanitarium and school work, let matters pertaining to health reform take a leading part. The Lord desires to make our sanitariums an educating force in every place. Whether they are large or small institutions, their responsibility remains the same. The Saviour's commission to us is, "Let your light so shine before men, that they may see your good works, and glorify your Father which is in heaven."—Manuscript 65, 1908.

Patients Will Lose Feeling of Need for Stimulants and Narcotics.—In our medical institutions clear instruction should be given in regard to temperance. The patients should be shown the evil of intoxicating liquor, and the blessing of total abstinence. They should be asked to discard the things that have ruined their health, and the place of these things should be supplied with an abundance of fruit. . . .

And as the sick are led to put forth physical effort, the wearied brain and nerves will find relief, and pure water and wholesome, palatable food will build them up and strengthen them. They will feel no need for health-destroying drugs or intoxicating drink.—Letter 145, 1904.

In Connection With Hygienic Restaurants.—Hygienic restaurants are to be established in the cities, and by them the message of temperance is to be proclaimed. Arrangements should be made to hold meetings in connection with our restaurants. Whenever possible, let a room be provided where the patrons can be invited to lectures on the science of health and Christian temperance, where they can receive instruction on the preparation of wholesome food and on other important subjects. In these meetings there should be prayer and singing and talks, not only on health and temperance topics, but also on other appropriate Bible subjects. As the people are taught how to preserve physical health, many opportunities will be found to sow the seeds of the gospel of the kingdom.—*Testimonies,* vol. 7, p. 115.

5. The Influence of the Pen

Temperance Literature.—We have a work to do along temperance lines besides that of speaking in public. We must present our principles in pamphlets and in our papers.—*Gospel Workers,* page 385.

Every Adventist to Circulate It.—The temperance question is to receive decided support from God's people. Intemperance is striving for the mastery; self-indulgence is increasing, and the publications treating on health reform are greatly needed. Literature bearing on this point is the helping hand of the gospel, leading souls to search the Bible for a better understanding of the truth. The note of warning against the great evil of intemperance should be sounded; and that this may be done, every Sabbathkeeper should study and practice the instruction contained in our health periodicals and our health books. And they should do more than this: they should make earnest efforts to circulate these publications among their neighbors.—*Counsels on Health,* page 462.

Reach the People Where They Are.—The circulation of our health publications is a most important work. It is a work in which all who believe the special truths for this time should have a living interest. God desires that now, as never before, the minds of the people shall be deeply stirred to investigate the great temperance question and principles underlying true health reform. The physical life is to be carefully educated, cultivated, and developed, that through men and women, the divine nature may be revealed in its fullness. Both the physical and the mental powers, with the affections, are to be so trained that they can reach the highest efficiency. Reform, continual reform, must be kept before the people. . . .

The light God has given on health reform is for our salvation and the salvation of the world. Men and women should be informed in regard to the human habitation fitted up by our Creator as His dwelling place, and over which He desires us to be faithful stewards. These grand truths must be given to the world. We must reach the people where they are, and by example and precept lead them to see the beauties of the better way. . . .

Let none think that the circulation of the health journals is a minor matter. All should take hold of this work with more interest, and make greater efforts in this direction. God will greatly bless those who take hold of it in earnest; for it is a work that should receive attention at this time.

Ministers can and should do much to urge the circulation of the health journals. Every member of the church should work as earnestly for these journals as for our other periodicals. . . .

The circulation of the health journals will be a powerful agency in preparing the people to accept those special truths that are to fit them for the soon coming of the Son of man.—*Counsels on Health,* pages 445-447.

Our People Everywhere to Take Hold.—Wherever you are, let your light shine forth. Hand our papers and pamphlets to those with whom you associate, when you are riding on the cars, visiting, conversing with your neighbors; and improve every opportunity to speak a word in season. The Holy Spirit will make the seed productive in some hearts. . . .

I have words of encouragement to speak in regard to the special [temperance] number of the *Watchman* [*Our Times*], which the Southern Publishing House is soon to bring out. I shall rejoice to see our conferences help in this work by taking a large number of this issue for circulation. Let there be no forbiddings placed upon the effort, but let all take hold to give this temperance number a wide circulation.

There could be no better time than now for a movement of this kind, when the temperance question is creating such widespread interest. Let our people everywhere take hold decidedly to let it be seen where we stand on the temperance question. Let everything possible be done to circulate strong, stirring appeals for the closing of the saloon. Let this paper be made a power for good. Our work for temperance is to be more spirited, more decided.—*Review and Herald,* June 18, 1908.

Our Responsibility in This Solemn Hour.—Upon us, to whom God has given great light, rests the solemn responsibility of calling the attention of thinking men and women to the significance of the prevalence of drunkenness and crime with which they are so familiar. We should bring before their minds the scriptures that plainly portray the conditions which shall exist just prior to the second coming of Christ. . . .

In these times, when the daily newspapers are filled with many horrible details of revolting drunkenness and terrible crime, there is a tendency to become so familiar with existing conditions that we lose sight of the significance of these conditions. Violence is in the land. More intoxicating liquor is used than has ever been used heretofore. The story of the resultant crime is given fully in the newspapers. And yet, notwithstanding the many evidences of increasing lawlessness, men seldom stop to consider seriously the meaning of these things. Almost without exception, men boast of the enlightenment and progress of the present age. . . .

How important it is that God's messengers shall call the attention of statesmen, of editors, of thinking men everywhere, to the deep significance of the drunkenness and the violence now filling the land with desolation and death! As faithful colaborers with God, we must bear a clear, decided testimony on the temperance question. . . .

Now is our golden opportunity to co-operate with heavenly intelligences in enlightening the understanding of those who are studying the meaning of the rapid increase of crime and disaster. As we do our part faithfully, the Lord will bless our efforts to the saving of many precious souls.—*Review and Herald,* Oct. 25, 1906.

Go With Hands Full of Reading Matter.—Publications upon health reform will reach many who will not see or read anything upon important Bible subjects. The gratification of every perverted appetite is doing its work of death. Intemperance must be met. With united, intelligent effort make known the evils of beclouding the powers that God has given, with wine and strong drinks. The truth must come to the people upon health reform. This is essential in order to arrest the attention in regard to Bible truth.

God requires that His people shall be temperate in all things. Unless they practice temperance, they will not, cannot, be sanctified through the truth. Their very thoughts and minds become depraved. Many of those looked upon as hopelessly depraved, will, if properly instructed in regard to their unhealthful practices, be arrested with the truth. Then they may be elevated, ennobled, sanctified, fit vessels for the Master's use. Go with your hands full of proper reading matter, and your heart full of the love of Christ for their souls, reaching them where they are.—Manuscript 1, 1875.

Organize and Prepare for Effective Work.—We need to work in the interests of temperance reform, and to make this question one of living interest. This is one way in which we may become fishers of men. A good work is being done in the circulation of our literature. Form yourselves into companies for the prosecution of a vigilant work. Learn to speak in such a way that you will not give offense. Cultivate gentleness of speech. Let the grace of Christ dwell in you richly, speaking to one another encouraging words. I make an earnest appeal to all our people, Come into line, come into line.—Manuscript 99, 1908.

Sound the Warning.—God's people are to be of a ready mind, quick to see and to avail themselves of every opportunity to advance the Lord's cause. They have a message to bear. By pen and voice they are to sound the note of warning. Only a few will listen; only a few will have ears to hear. Satan has artfully devised many ways of keeping men and women under his influence. He leads them to weaken their organs by the gratification of perverted appetite and by indulgence in worldly pleasure. Intoxicating liquor, tobacco, the theater and the racecourse,—these and many other evils are benumbing man's sensibilities, and causing multitudes to turn a deaf ear to God's merciful entreaties.—*Review and Herald,* June 23, 1903.

6. The Power of the Vote

Our Responsibility as Citizens.—While we are in no wise to become involved in political questions, yet it is our privilege to take our stand decidedly on all questions relating to temperance reform. Concerning this I have often borne a plain testimony. In an article published in the *Review* of November 8, 1881, I wrote: . . .

"There is a cause for the moral paralysis upon society. Our laws sustain an evil which is sapping their very foundations. Many deplore the wrongs which they know exist, but consider themselves free from all responsibility in the matter. This cannot be. Every individual exerts an influence in society.

Every Voter Has a Voice.—"In our favored land, every voter has some voice in determining what laws shall control the nation. Should not that influence and that vote be cast on the side of temperance and virtue? . . .

"We may call upon the friends of the temperance cause to rally to the conflict and seek to press back the tide of evil that is demoralizing the world; but of what avail are all our efforts while liquor selling is sustained by law? Must the curse of intemperance forever rest like a blight upon our land? Must it every year sweep like a devouring fire over thousands of happy homes?

By Voice, Pen, and Vote.—"We talk of the results, tremble at the results, and wonder what we can do with the terrible results, while too often we tolerate and even sanction the cause. The advocates of temperance fail to do their whole duty unless they exert their influence by precept and example—by voice and pen and vote—in favor of prohibition and total abstinence. We need not expect that God will work a miracle to bring about this reform, and thus remove the necessity for our exertion. We ourselves must grapple with this giant foe, our motto, No compromise and no cessation of our efforts till the victory is gained."—*Review and Herald,* Oct. 15, 1914. (Quoted in *Gospel Workers,* pages 387, 388.)

The Choice of Right Men.—Intemperate men should not by vote of the people be placed in positions of trust.—*Signs of the Times,* July 8, 1880.

At the Mercy of Intemperate Men.—Many men are voted into office whose minds are deprived of their full vigor by indulgence in spirituous liquors, or constantly beclouded by the use of the narcotic tobacco. . . . The peace of happy families, reputation, property, liberty, and even life itself, are at the mercy of intemperate men in our legislative halls and our courts of justice.

By giving themselves up to the indulgence of appetite, many who were once upright, once beneficent, lose their integrity and their love for their fellow men, and unite with the dishonest and profligate, espouse their cause, and share their guilt.

Sacred Prerogative as Citizen Forfeited.—How many forfeit their prerogative as citizens of a republic,—bribed with a glass of whisky to cast their vote for some villainous candidate. As a class, the intemperate will not hesitate to employ deception, bribery, and even violence against those who refuse unbounded license to perverted appetite.—*Review and Herald,* Nov. 8, 1881.

Responsibility of Passive Citizens.—Many give their influence to the great destroyer, aiding him by voice and vote to destroy the moral image of God in man, not thinking of the families that are degraded by a perverted appetite for liquor.—Manuscript 87, 1898.

And those who by their votes sanction the liquor traffic will be held accountable for the wickedness that is done by those who are under the influence of strong drink.—Letter 243a, 1905.

Our Pioneers Reach an Important Decision.—[A page from Ellen G. White's 1859 diary.] "Attended meeting in the eve. Had quite a free, interesting meeting. After it was time to close, the subject of voting was considered and dwelt upon. James first talked, then Brother Andrews talked, and it was thought by them best to give their influence in favor of right and against wrong. They think it right to vote in favor of temperance men being in office in our city instead of by their silence running the risk of having intemperance men put in office. Brother Hewett tells his experience of a few days [since] and is settled that [it] is right to cast his vote. Brother Hart talks well. Brother Lyon opposes. No others object to voting, but Brother Kellogg begins to feel that it is right. Pleasant feelings exist among all the brethren. O that they may all act in the fear of God.

NOTE: In the early summer of 1881 at the Des Moines, Iowa, camp meeting, a resolution was placed before the delegates which read:

"*Resolved,* That we express our deep interest in the temperance movement now going forward in this state; and that we instruct all our ministers to use their influence among our churches and with the people at large to induce them to put forth every consistent effort, by personal labor, and at the ballot box, in favor of the prohibitory amendment of the Constitution, which the friends of temperance are seeking to secure."—*Review and Herald,* July 5, 1881.

But some objected to the clause which called for action at "the ballot box," and urged its deletion. Mrs. White, who was attending this camp meeting, had retired, but she was summoned to give her counsel.

Writing of it at the time she says: "I dressed and found I was to speak to the point of whether our people should vote for prohibition. I told them 'Yes,' and spoke twenty minutes."—Letter 6, 1881.

"Men of intemperance have been in the office today in a flattering manner expressing their approbation of the course of the Sabbathkeepers not voting and expressed hopes that they will stick to their course and like the Quakers, not cast their vote. Satan and his evil angels are busy at this time, and he has workers upon the earth. May Satan be disappointed, is my prayer."—*E. G. White diary, Sunday, Mar. 6, 1859.*

The Lesson of Ancient Kingdoms.—The prosperity of a nation is dependent upon the virtue and intelligence of its citizens. To secure these blessings, habits of strict temperance are indispensable. The history of ancient kingdoms is replete with lessons of warning for us. Luxury, self-indulgence, and dissipation prepare the way for their downfall. It remains to be seen whether our own republic will be admonished by their example, and avoid their fate.—*Gospel Workers, page 388.*

7. The Call to the Harvest

It Is Time for Us to Work.—Now, brethren and sisters, is it not time for us to work? Is it not time for us to arouse our God-given capabilities, to catch holy zeal that we have not had as yet? And is it not time that we should stand as Calebs, come to the front, raise our voices, and cry out against the reports that are going all around us? Are we not able to possess the land? We are able in God to do a mighty work upon the point of temperance.—*Manuscript 3, 1888.*

Who Will Help?—All around us are the victims of depraved appetite, and what are you going to do for them? Can you not, by your example, help them to place their feet in the path of temperance? Can you have a sense of the temptations that are coming upon the youth who are growing up around us, and not seek to warn and save them? Who will stand on the Lord's side? Who will help to press back this tide of immorality, of woe and wretchedness, that is filling the world? —*Christian Temperance and Bible Hygiene, page 40.*

Our Day of Opportunity.—Intemperance of every kind is taking the world captive, and those who are true educators at this time, those who instruct along the lines of self-denial and self-sacrifice, will have their reward. Now is our time, now is our opportunity, to do a blessed work.—*Medical Ministry,* page 25.

We Are Accountable.—We are just as accountable for evils that we might have checked in others, by reproof, by warning, by exercise of parental or pastoral authority, as if we were guilty of the acts ourselves.—*Testimonies,* vol. 4, p. 516.

Revive the Temperance Work.—The temperance cause needs to be revived as it has not yet been.—*Review and Herald,* Jan. 14, 1909.

Years ago we regarded the spread of temperance principles as one of our most important duties. It should be so today.—*Gospel Workers,* page 384.

If the work of temperance were carried forward by us as it was begun thirty years ago;* if at our camp meetings we presented before the people the evils of intemperance in eating and drinking, and especially the evil of liquor drinking; if these things were presented in connection with the evidences of Christ's soon coming, there would be a shaking among the people. If we showed a zeal in proportion to the importance of the truths we are handling, we might be instrumental in rescuing hundreds, yea thousands, from ruin.—*Testimonies,* vol. 6, p. 111.

If our people can be made to realize how much is at stake, and will seek to redeem the time that has been lost, by now putting heart and soul and strength into the temperance cause, great good will be seen as the result.—Letter 78, 1911.

With God We Are a Majority.—You say, We are in the

---

* First published in 1900.

minority. Is not God a majority? If we are on the side of the God who made the heaven and the earth, are we not on the side of the majority? We have the angels that excel in strength on our side.—Manuscript 27, 1893.

With our feeble human hands we can do but little, but we have an unfailing Helper. We must not forget that the arm of Christ can reach to the very depths of human woe and degradation. He can give us help to conquer even this terrible demon of intemperance.—*Christian Temperance and Bible Hygiene,* page 21.

Fields Ready to Harvest.—In every place the temperance question is to be made more prominent. Drunkenness, and the crime that always follows drunkenness, call for the voice to be raised to combat this evil. Christ sees a plentiful harvest waiting to be gathered in. Souls are hungering for the truth, thirsting for the water of life. Many are on the very verge of the kingdom, waiting only to be gathered in. Cannot the people who know the truth see? Will they not hear the voice of Christ saying, "Say not ye, There are yet four months, and then cometh harvest? Behold, I say unto you, Lift up your eyes and look on the fields; for they are white already to harvest."—Letter 10, 1899.

Appendix A

ELLEN G. WHITE A TEMPERANCE WORKER

Commissioned to Speak on Temperance.—I was also to speak on the subject of temperance, as the Lord's appointed messenger. I have been called to many places to speak on temperance before large assemblies. For many years I was known as a speaker on temperance.—Manuscript 140, 1905.

I rejoice that it has been my privilege to bear my testimony on this subject before crowded assemblies in many countries. Many times I have spoken on this subject to large congregations at our camp meetings.—Letter 78, 1911.

The Plan of Presentation.—We left the beaten track of the popular lecturer, and traced the origin of the prevailing intemperance to the home, the family board, and the indulgence of appetite in the child. Stimulating food creates a desire for still stronger stimulants. The boy whose taste is thus vitiated, and who is not taught self-control, is the drunkard, or tobacco slave of later years. The subject was taken up upon this wide basis; and the duty of parents was pointed out in training their children to right views of life and its responsibilities, and in laying the foundation for their upright Christian characters. The great work of temperance reform, to be thoroughly successful, must begin in the home.—*Review and Herald,* Aug. 23, 1877.

A Large Temperance Meeting at Kokomo, Indiana.—The editor of the *Kokomo Dispatch* was on the ground upon the Sabbath. He afterward issued notices to the effect that we were to address the people on the subject of Christian temperance, at the camp ground on Sunday afternoon. . . . Three excursion trains poured their living freight upon the grounds. The people here are very enthusiastic on the temperance question. At 2:30 p.m. we spoke to about eight thousand people on the subject of temperance, taken from a moral and Christian standpoint. We were blessed with remarkable clearness and liberty, and were heard with the best attention from the large audience present.—*Review and Herald,* Aug. 23, 1877.

Presenting Temperance at Salem, Oregon.—On Sunday, June 23 [1873], I spoke in the Methodist church of Salem [Oregon], on the subject of temperance. The attendance was unusually good, and I had freedom in treating this, my favorite subject. I was requested to speak again in the same place on the Sunday following the camp meeting, but was prevented by hoarseness. On the next Tuesday evening, however, I again spoke in this church. Many invitations were tendered me to speak on temperance in various cities and towns of Oregon, but the state of my health forbade my complying with these requests.

[Early in August, 1878,] we stopped in Boulder City [Colorado], and beheld with joy our canvas meetinghouse, where Elder Cornell was holding a series of meetings. . . . The tent had been lent to hold temperance meetings in, and, by special invitation, I spoke to a tent full of attentive hearers. Though wearied by my journey, the Lord helped me to successfully present before the people the necessity of practicing strict temperance in all things.—*Testimonies,* vol. 4, pp. 290-297.

Only eternity will reveal what has been accomplished by this kind of ministry—how many souls, sick with doubt, and tired of worldliness and unrest, have been brought to the Great Physician, who longs to save to the uttermost all who come unto Him. Christ is a risen Saviour, and there is healing in His wings.—*Testimonies,* vol. 6, p. 111.

Uniting With Others to Aid Fellow Men.—The evening after the Sabbath I spoke in Washingtonian Hall.* . . . Sunday afternoon I spoke in the same hall on the subject of temperance to a good congregation, who listened with deepest interest. I had freedom and power in presenting Jesus, who took upon Himself the infirmities and bore the griefs and sorrows of humanity, and conquered in our behalf. . . .

At the close of the meeting, I was favored with an introduction to the president of the Washingtonian Home. He thanked me in behalf of the family and friends for the pleasure of listening to the remarks made. I was cordially invited to visit them when I should again pass through Chicago, and I assured them I should consider it a privilege to do so. I was gratified that I had this opportunity of presenting temperance from the Christian standpoint before the inmates of this home for inebriates, where they are assisted in overcoming the strong habit which is binding so many in almost hopeless slavery. I was informed that among those who are obliged to seek its friendly aid are lawyers, doctors, and even ministers. —*Review and Herald,* Feb. 10, 1885.

Encouraging Responses.—I speak most decidedly on this subject [temperance], and it has a telling influence upon other minds. Often the testimony is borne, "I have not used any tobacco, wine, or any stimulant or narcotic since that discourse you gave upon temperance." Now, they say, "I must furnish myself with enlightened principles for action; for I want others to know the benefits I have received. This reformation involves great consequences to me and all with whom I come in contact. I will choose the better part, to work with Christ

---

*Note: A hall controlled by the ladies of the Martha Washington Home in Chicago, a society devoted to the reformation of intemperate women.

with settled principles and aims, to win a crown of life as an overcomer."—Letter 96, 1899.

In our public meetings in Australia we took special pains to present clearly the fundamental principles of temperance reform. Generally, when I spoke to the people on Sunday, my theme was health and temperance. During some of the camp meetings, daily instruction was given on this subject. In several places the interest aroused over our position on the use of stimulants and narcotics led the friends of temperance to attend our meetings and learn more of the various doctrines of our faith.—Manuscript 79, 1907.

Contacts With W.C.T.U. Workers at Melbourne.—Dr. M. G. Kellogg came to my tent to see if I would have an interview with the president and secretary of the W.C.T.U. We invited them to our tent, and we had a very pleasant visit. The president is a strict vegetarian, not having tasted meat for four years. She bears a clear countenance, which does credit to her abstemious habits. The secretary is a young woman. Both are ladies of intelligence. They manifest deep interest in all they have heard. They have made a request that I speak in the beautiful hall in which they hold their meetings, and they asked Brother Starr to write for their temperance paper.

The president expressed an earnest desire that we should harmonize in the temperance work. "Be assured," they said, "we shall enter every door open to us that we may let our light shine to others." They seemed highly gratified in seeing and hearing and being convinced that the fruits of the Spirit are possessed and revealed by this people. I gave each of them a copy of *Christian Temperance,* to one *The Great Controversy,* to the other *Patriarchs and Prophets.*—Manuscript 2, 1894.

Following Up With Health Education.—Captain Press and his wife, the president of the W.C.T.U. of Victoria, were present. Mrs. Press had visited me at my tent on the campground, and she was urgent that I should speak to their society. After the discourse on Sunday she came to me and, grasping my hand, said, "I thank you for that discourse. I see many new points which have made a lasting impression upon my mind. I shall never lose their force."

I was introduced to her husband, a most noble-looking man. He is a pilot, and fills a very important position. Brother and Sister Starr took dinner with them, and formed a very pleasant acquaintance. Mrs. Press, in behalf of the W.C.T.U., has made a very earnest request for instruction in hygienic cooking. We have arranged to have a cooking school, to be held in Melbourne in the room adjoining the hall of the W.C.T.U. Four lessons are to be given, one each week, beginning next Thursday. The cooking of eight different dishes is to be taught at each lesson. Great enthusiasm has been created on the subject. Mrs. Press is a vegetarian, not having tasted meat for four years.

Well, the very first class of people attend our meetings in Williamstown. Mr. Press and his wife attended some of the meetings on the campground, and they say that the Bible is now a new book to them. They see that it is full of precious truth, which is a feast to the soul.—Manuscript 6, 1894.

Maintaining the Acquaintance.—Mrs. Press, president of the Victorian W.C.T.U., and Mrs. Kirk the secretary, her sister and two elder ladies, with the niece of Mrs. Press, have taken dinner with us. We became acquainted with Mrs. Press and Mrs. Kirk in Melbourne; they have just now been attending a temperance convention in Sydney. We have had a pleasant interview, and now they have gone out in our carriage to see the country, while I resume my writing. I hope that these sisters will be brought to a knowledge of the truth. We long to see those who are intelligent converted, and standing in vindication of the truth.—Manuscript 30, 1893.

Open-Air Temperance Meetings in New Zealand.—Some of the hearers were very enthusiastic over the matter. The mayor, the policeman, and several others, said it was by far the best gospel temperance discourse that they had ever heard. We pronounced it a success and decided that we would have a similar meeting the next Sunday afternoon. Although the sky was cloudy and threatened rain, we were favored, and I had more listeners than the Sunday previous. There were a large number of young men who listened as if spellbound. Some of them were as solemn as the grave. This was a special time. There had been a two days' horse race and a cattle show. This had excited the people to such an intensity that I feared we would not have so good a hearing. The agricultural and cattle show had been talked of for weeks, and preparations made for the same. Well, this was my opportunity to speak to those whom I would not have had a chance to speak to had it not been a special occasion.

One youth, about seventeen years of age, wept like a child as I read an article of how a youth of seventeen was enticed into a liquor saloon, and drank his first glass of liquor, and it did what it always will do, maddened the brain. After taking this liquor the youth remembered nothing about what had transpired. A quarrel had taken place in this saloon, and in the youth's hand was found a knife that had taken the life or a human being, and he was charged with the murder, and five years' imprisonment was his sentence. It was a touching article and brought tears to many eyes of both old and young.
—Letter 68, 1893.

Attention Held by Unique Approach.—My subject was temperance, treated from the Christian standpoint, the fall of Adam, the promise of Eden, the coming of Christ to our world, His baptism, His temptation in the wilderness, and His victory. And all this to give man another trial, making it possible for man to overcome in his own behalf, on his own account, through the merits of Jesus Christ. Christ came to bring to man moral power that he may be victorious in overcoming temptations on the point of appetite, and break the chain of the slavery of habit and indulgence of perverted appetite and stand forth in moral power as a man, and the record of heaven accredits him in its books as a man in the sight of God.

It was so different from anything that they had ever heard on temperance, they were held as if spellbound.—Manuscript 55, 1893.

Effective Use of Scripture and Song.—I spoke in the afternoon on the subject of temperance, taking the first chapter of Daniel as my text. All listened attentively, seeming surprised to hear temperance presented from the Bible. After dwelling on the integrity and firmness of the Hebrew captives, I asked the choir to sing, "Dare to be a Daniel, dare to stand alone! Dare to have a purpose firm! Dare to make it known!" The inspiring notes of this song rang out from the singers on the stand, who were joined by the congregation. I then resumed my talk, and I know that before I had finished, many present had a better understanding of the meaning of Christian temperance. The Lord gave me freedom and His blessing, and a most solemn impression was left upon many minds.—Letter 42, 1900.

Filling a W.C.T.U. Appointment.—During a series of meetings held late in the year 1899, at Maitland, New South Wales, I was requested by the president of the Maitland branch of the W.C.T.U. to speak to them one evening. She said that they would be very glad to hear me, even if I should speak for only ten minutes. I asked her if the ten minutes that she proposed for me to speak was all the time that was allowed, because sometimes the Spirit of the Lord came upon me, and I had more than a ten minutes' talk to give. "Oh," she said, "your people told me that you did not speak in the evening, and I specified ten minutes as the time, thinking that I would not get you at all if I made it longer. The longer you can speak to us, the more thankful we shall be."

I asked Mrs. Winter, the president, if it was her custom to read a portion of Scripture at the opening of the meeting. She said that it was. I then asked for the privilege of praying, which was gladly granted. I spoke with freedom to them for an hour. Some of the women present that night afterward attended the meetings in the tent.—Manuscript 79, 1907.

Appendix B

TYPICAL TEMPERANCE ADDRESSES BY ELLEN G. WHITE

1. At Christiania, Norway—1886

On Sunday, by request of the president of the temperance society, I spoke upon the subject of temperance. The meeting was held in the soldiers' military gymnasium, the largest hall in the city. An American flag was placed as a canopy above the pulpit; this was an attention which I highly appreciated. There were about sixteen hundred assembled. Among them was a bishop of the state church, with a number of the clergy; a large proportion were of the better class of society.

The Approach.—I took up the subject from a religious standpoint, showing that the Bible is full of history bearing upon temperance, and that Christ was connected with the work of temperance, even from the beginning. It was by the indulgence of appetite that our first parents sinned and fell. Christ redeemed man's failure. In the wilderness of temptation He endured the test which man had failed to bear. While He was suffering the keenest pangs of hunger, weak and emaciated from fasting, Satan was at hand with his manifold temptations to assail the Son of God, to take advantage of His weakness and overcome Him, and thus thwart the plan of salvation. But Christ was steadfast. He overcame in behalf of the race, that He might rescue them from the degradation of the Fall. He showed that in His strength it is possible for us to overcome. Jesus sympathizes with the weakness of men; He came to earth that He might bring to us moral power. However strong the passion or appetite, we can gain the victory, because we may have divine strength to unite with our feeble efforts. Those who flee to Christ will have a stronghold in the day of temptation.

The Warning of Bible History.—I showed the importance of temperate habits by citing warnings and examples from Bible history. Nadab and Abihu were men in holy office; but by the use of wine their minds became so beclouded that they could not distinguish between sacred and common things. By the offering of "strange fire," they disregarded God's command, and they were slain by His judgments. The Lord, through Moses, expressly prohibited the use of wine and strong drink by those who were to minister in holy things, that they might "put difference between holy and unholy," and might teach "the statutes which the Lord hath spoken." The effect of intoxicating liquors is to weaken the body, confuse the mind, and debase the morals. All who occupied positions of responsibility were to be men of strict temperance, that their minds might be clear to discriminate between right and wrong, that they might possess firmness of principle, and wisdom to administer justice and to show mercy.

This direct and solemn command was to extend from generation to generation, to the close of time. In our legislative halls and courts of justice, no less than in our schools and churches, men of principle are needed; men of self-control, of keen perceptions and sound judgment. If the mind is beclouded or the principles debased by intemperance, how can the judge render a just decision? He has rendered himself incapable of weighing evidence or entering into critical investigation; he has not moral power to rise above motives of self-interest or the influence of partiality or prejudice. And because of this a human life may be sacrificed, or an innocent man robbed of his liberty or of the fair fame which is dearer than life itself. God has forbidden that those to whom He has committed sacred trusts as teachers or rulers of the people should thus unfit themselves for the duties of their high position.

Instruction to Manoah and Zacharias.—There is a lesson for parents in the instruction given to the wife of Manoah, and to Zacharias, the father of John the Baptist. The angel of the Lord brought the tidings that Manoah should become the father of a son who was to deliver Israel; and in reply to the anxious inquiry, "How shall we order the child, and how shall we do unto him?" the angel gave special directions for the mother: "Neither let her drink wine or strong drink, nor eat any unclean thing: all that I commanded her let her observe." The child will be affected, for good or evil, by the habits of the mother. She must herself be controlled by principle, and must practice temperance and self-denial, if she would seek the welfare of her child.

And fathers as well as mothers are included in this responsibility. Both parents transmit their own characteristics, mental and physical, their dispositions and appetites, to their children. As the result of parental intemperance, the children often lack physical strength and mental and moral power. Liquor drinkers and tobacco lovers hand down their own insatiable craving, their inflamed blood and irritated nerves, as a legacy to their offspring. And as the children have less power to resist temptation than had the parents, each generation falls lower than the preceding.

The inquiry of every father and mother should be, "What shall we do unto the child that shall be born unto us?" Many are inclined to treat this subject lightly; but the fact that an angel of heaven was sent to those Hebrew parents, with instruction twice given in the most explicit and solemn manner, shows that God regards it as one of great importance.

When the angel Gabriel appeared to Zacharias, foretelling the birth of John the Baptist, this was the message which he brought: "He shall be great in the sight of the Lord, and shall drink neither wine nor strong drink; and he shall be filled with the Holy Ghost." God had an important work for the promised child of Zacharias to do; a work that required active thought and vigorous action. He must have a sound physical constitution, and mental and moral strength; and it was to secure for him these necessary qualifications that his habits were to be carefully regulated, even from infancy. The first steps in intemperance are often taken in childhood and early youth; therefore most earnest efforts should be directed toward enlightening parents as to their responsibility. Those who place wine and beer upon their tables are cultivating in their children an appetite for strong drink. We urge that the principles of temperance be carried into all the details of home life; that the example of parents be a lesson of temperance; that self-denial and self-control be taught to the children and enforced upon them, so far as possible, even from babyhood.

The Youth an Index to Future Society.—The future of society is indexed by the youth of today. In them we see the future teachers and lawmakers and judges, the leaders and the people, that determine the character and destiny of the nation. How important, then, the mission of those who are to form the habits and influence the lives of the rising generation. To deal with minds is the greatest work ever committed to men. The time of parents is too valuable to be spent in the gratification of appetite or the pursuit of wealth or fashion. God has placed in their hands the precious youth, not only to be fitted for a place of usefulness in this life, but to be prepared for the heavenly courts. We should ever keep the future life in view, and so labor that when we come to the gates of paradise we may be able to say, "Here, Lord, am I, and the children whom Thou hast given me."

But in the work of temperance there are duties devolving upon the young which no other can do for them. While parents are responsible for the stamp of character as well as for the education and training which they give their sons and daughters, it is still true that our position and usefulness in the world depend, to a great degree, upon our own course of action.

Daniel a Noble Example.—Nowhere shall we find a more comprehensive and forcible illustration of true temperance and its attendant blessings than in the history of the youthful Daniel and his associates in the court of Babylon. When they were selected to be taught the learning and tongue of the Chaldeans, that they might "stand in the king's palace," "the king appointed them a daily provision of the king's meat, and of the wine which he drank." "But Daniel purposed in his heart that he would not defile himself with the portion of the king's meat, nor with the wine which he drank." Not only did these young men decline to drink the king's wine, but they refrained from the luxuries of his table. They obeyed the divine law, both natural and moral. With their habits of self-denial were coupled earnestness of purpose, diligence, and steadfastness. And the result shows the wisdom of their course.

God always honors the right. The most promising youth of every land subdued by the great conqueror, had been gathered at Babylon; yet amid them all, the Hebrew captives were without a rival. The erect form, the firm, elastic step, the fair countenance showing that the blood was uncorrupted, the undimmed senses, the untainted breath,—all were so many certificates of good habits, insignia of the nobility with which nature honors those who are obedient to her laws. And when their ability and acquirements were tested by the king at the close of the three years of training, none were found "like Daniel, Hananiah, Mishael, and Azariah." Their keen apprehension, their choice and exact language, their extensive and varied knowledge, testified to the unimpaired strength and vigor of their mental powers.

The history of Daniel and his companions has been recorded on the pages of the Inspired Word for the benefit of the youth of all succeeding ages. Those who would preserve their powers unimpaired for the service of God must observe strict temperance in the use of all His bounties, as well as total abstinence from every injurious or debasing indulgence. What men have done, men may do. Did those faithful Hebrews stand firm amid great temptation, and bear a noble testimony in favor of true temperance? The youth of today may bear a similar testimony, even under circumstances as unfavorable. Would that they would emulate the example of those Hebrew youth; for all who will, may, like them, enjoy the favor and blessing of God.

Money That Might Have Done Good.—There is still another aspect of the temperance question which should be carefully considered. Not only is the use of unnatural stimulants needless and pernicious, but it is also extravagant and wasteful. An immense sum is thus squandered every year. The money that is spent for tobacco would support all the missions in the world; the means worse than wasted upon strong drink would educate the youth now drifting into a life of ignorance and crime, and prepare them to do a noble work for God. There are thousands upon thousands of parents who spend their earnings in self-indulgence, robbing their children of food and clothing and the benefits of education. And multitudes of professed Christians encourage these practices by their example. What account will be rendered to God for this waste of His bounties?

Money is one of the gifts entrusted to us with which to feed the hungry, to clothe the naked, to minister to the afflicted, and to send the gospel to the poor. But how is this work neglected! When the Master shall come to reckon with His servants, will He not say to many, "Inasmuch as ye did it not to one of the least of these, ye did it not to Me"? All around us there is work to do for God. Our means, our time, our strength, and our influence are needed. Shall we take hold of this work, and live to glorify God and bless our fellow men? Shall we build up the Lord's kingdom in the earth?

There is need now of men like Daniel,—men who have the self-denial and the courage to be radical temperance reformers. Let every Christian see that his example and influence are on the side of reform. Let ministers of the gospel be faithful in sounding the warnings to the people. And let all remember that our happiness in two worlds depends upon the right improvement of one.—*Historical Sketches of S.D.A. Foreign Missions,* pages 207-211.

2. A Talk on Temperance—1891

Satan was the first rebel in the universe, and ever since his expulsion from heaven he has been seeking to make every member of the human family an apostate from God, even as he is himself. He laid his plans to ruin man, and through the unlawful indulgence of appetite, led him to transgress the commandments of God. He tempted Adam and Eve to partake of the forbidden fruit, and so accomplished their fall, and their expulsion from Eden. How many say, "If I had been in Adam's place, I would never have transgressed on so simple a test." But you who make this boast have a grand opportunity of showing your strength of purpose, your fidelity to principle under trial. Do you render obedience to every command of God? Does God see no sin in your life?

Would that the Fall of Adam and Eve had been the only fall; but from the loss of Eden to the present time, there has been a succession of falls. Satan has planned to ruin man, by leading him away from loyalty to the commandments of God, and one of his most successful methods is that of tempting him to the gratification of perverted appetite. We see on all sides the marks of man's intemperance. In our cities and villages the saloon is on every corner, and in the countenances of its patrons we see the dreadful work of ruin and destruction. On every side, Satan seeks to entice the youth into the path of perdition; and if he can once get their feet set in the way, he hurries them on in their downward course, leading them from one dissipation to another, until his victims lose their tenderness of conscience, and have no more the fear of God before their eyes. They exercise less and less self-restraint. They become addicted to the use of wine and alcohol, tobacco and opium, and go from one stage of debasement to another. They are slaves to appetite. Counsel which they once respected, they learn to despise. They put on swaggering airs, and boast of liberty when they are the servants of corruption. They mean by liberty that they are slaves to selfishness, debased appetite, and licentiousness.

The Controversy Is On.—A great controversy is going on in the world. Satan is determined to have the human race as his subjects, but Christ has paid an infinite price that man may be redeemed from the enemy, and that the moral image of God may be restored to the fallen race. In instituting the plan of salvation, God has made it manifest that He values man at an infinite price; but Satan is seeking to make this plan of no effect, by keeping man from meeting the conditions upon which salvation is provided.

When Christ began His ministry, He bowed on the banks of Jordan, and offered a petition to Heaven in behalf of the human race. He had received baptism at the hands of John, and the heavens opened, the Spirit of God in the form of a dove encircled His form, and a voice was heard from heaven saying, "This is My beloved Son, in whom I am well pleased." The prayer of Christ for a lost world was heard, and all who believe in Him are accepted in the Beloved. Fallen men may through Christ find access to the Father, may have grace to enable them to be overcomers through the merits of a crucified and risen Saviour.

Significance of Christ's Victory.—After His baptism, Christ was led of the Spirit into the wilderness. He had taken humanity upon Himself, and Satan boasted that he would overcome Him, as he had overcome the strong men of the past ages, and he assailed Him with the temptations that had caused man's downfall. It was in this world that the great conflict between Christ and Satan was to be decided. If the tempter could succeed in overcoming Christ in even one point, the world must be left to perish. Satan would have power to bruise the heel of the Son of God; but the seed of the woman was to bruise the serpent's head: Christ was to baffle the prince of the powers of darkness. For forty days Christ fasted in the wilderness. What was this for? Was there anything in the character of the Son of God that required such great humiliation and suffering? No, He was sinless. All this humiliation and keen anguish were endured for the sake of fallen man, and never can we comprehend the grievous character of the sin of indulging perverted appetite except as we comprehend the spiritual meaning of the long fast of the Son of God. Never can we understand the strength and bondage of appetite until we discern the character of the Saviour's conflict in overcoming Satan, and thus placing man on vantage ground, where, through the merit of the blood of Christ, he may be able to resist the powers of darkness, and overcome in his own behalf.

After this long fast, Christ was in a famishing condition, and in His weakness Satan assailed Him with the fiercest temptations. "The devil said unto Him, If Thou be the Son of God, command this stone that it be made bread." Satan represented himself as the messenger of God, claiming that God had seen the willingness of the Saviour to place His feet in the path of self-denial, and that He was not required to suffer further humiliation and pain, but might be released from the terrible conflict that was before Him as the Redeemer of the world. He tried to persuade Him that God designed only to test His fidelity, that now His loyalty was fully manifest, and He was at liberty to use His divine power to relieve His necessities. But Christ discerned the temptation, and declared, "It is written, That man shall not live by bread alone, but by every word of God."

When tempted to the unlawful gratification of appetite, you should remember the example of Christ, and stand firm, overcoming as Christ overcame. You should answer, saying, "Thus saith the Lord," and in this way settle the question forever with the prince of darkness. If you parley with temptation, and use your own words, feeling self-sufficient, full of self-importance, you will be overcome. The weapons which Christ used were the words of God, "It is written;" and if you wield the sword of the Spirit, you also may come off victorious through the merit of your Redeemer.

Satan More Successful With Man.—The three leading temptations by which man is beset were endured by the Son of God. He refused to yield to the enemy on the point of appetite, ambition, and the love of the world. But Satan is more successful when assailing the human heart. Through inducing men to yield to his temptations, he can get control of them. And through no class of temptations does he achieve greater success than through those addressed to the appetite. If he can control the appetite, he can control the whole man.

There are but two powers that control the minds of men— the power of God and the power of Satan. Christ is man's Creator and Redeemer; Satan is man's enemy and destroyer. He who has given himself to God will build himself up for the glory of God, in body, soul, and spirit. He who has given himself to the control of Satan tears himself down. Many a man sells reason for a glass of liquor, and becomes a menace to his family, his neighborhood, and his country. His children hide when he comes home, and his discouraged wife fears to meet him, for he greets her with cruel blows. He spends his money for strong drink, while his wife and children suffer for the necessities of life.

Satan leads the victims of appetite to deeds of violence. The liquor drinker is a man of fierce and easily excited passions, and any trivial excuse is made a cause for quarrel; and when under the influence of passion, the drunkard will not spare his best friend. How often do we hear of murder and deeds of violence, and find that their chief source is the liquor habit.

Moderate Drinking.—There are those who call themselves advocates of temperance who will yet indulge in the use of wine and cider, claiming that these stimulants are harmless, and even healthful. It is thus that many take the first step in the downward path. Intoxication is just as really produced by wine and cider as by stronger drinks, and it is the worst kind of inebriation. The passions are more perverse; the transformation of character is greater, more determined and obstinate. A few quarts of cider or wine may awaken a taste for stronger drinks, and in many cases those who have become confirmed drunkards have thus laid the foundation of the drinking habit.

For persons who have inherited an appetite for stimulants, it is by no means safe to have wine and cider in the house; for Satan is continually soliciting them to indulge. If they yield to his temptations, they do not know where to stop; appetite clamors for indulgence, and is gratified to their ruin. The brain is clouded; reason no longer holds the reins, but lays them on the neck of lust. Liscentiousness abounds, and vices of almost every type are practiced as the result of indulging the appetite for wine and cider. It is impossible for one who loves these stimulants and accustoms himself to their use, to grow in grace. He becomes gross and sensual; the animal passions control the higher powers of the mind, and virtue is not cherished.

Moderate drinking is the school in which men are receiving an education for the drunkard's career. So gradually does Satan lead away from the strongholds of temperance, so insidiously do wine and cider exert their influence upon the taste, that the highway to drunkenness is entered upon all unsuspectingly. The taste for stimulants is cultivated; the nervous system is disordered; Satan keeps the mind in a fever of unrest; and the poor victim, imagining himself perfectly secure, goes on and on, until every barrier is broken down, every principle sacrificed. The strongest resolutions are undermined, and eternal interests are too weak to keep the debased appetite under the control of reason. Some are never really drunk, but are always under the influence of mild intoxicants. They are feverish, unstable in mind, not really delirious, but as truly unbalanced; for the nobler powers of the mind are perverted.

Tobacco Also.—Those also who use tobacco are weakening their physical and mental power. The use of tobacco has no foundation in nature. Nature rebels against the narcotic, and when the tobacco user first tries to force this unnatural habit upon the system, a hard battle is fought. The stomach, and, indeed, the whole system, revolts against the abominable practice, but the evildoer perseveres until nature gives up the struggle, and the man becomes a slave of tobacco.

If salvation were offered to man on terms as hard to endure, God would be looked upon as a hard master. Satan is a hard master, and requires his subjects to undergo severe tests, and to make themselves the slaves of passion and appetite; but God is consistent in all His requirements, and asks of His children that only which will work for their present and eternal happiness.

"Thou shalt worship the Lord thy God, and Him only shalt thou serve." This is the command of God, and yet how many, even of those who profess to be the servants of God, are the devotees of tobacco, and make it their idol. When men should be out in the pure air, with sweet breath, praising God for His benefits, they are polluting the atmosphere with the fumes of pipe or cigar. They must go through the ordeal of smoking, in order to stimulate the poor relaxed nerves as a preparation for the duties of the day; for if they did not have their smoke, they would be irritable and unable to control their thoughts.

He Had Not Had His Tobacco.—As an illustration of the inability of tobacco users to command their senses when without the stimulant, I will relate an occurrence that came to my notice. An aged man who was at one time my next-door neighbor was a great user of tobacco; but one morning he had not taken his usual smoke when I went in to get a book I had lent him. Instead of getting the book I had asked for, he handed me a bridle. In vain I strove to make him understand what I wanted; I had to go away without the book. Next day I went again and made the same request, and he immediately handed me the book. Then I asked him why he had not given it to me the day before. He said: "Why, were you in yesterday? I do not remember it. Oh, I know what was the trouble, I had not had my tobacco!" This was the effect upon his mind when he was without the stimulant. His physician told him that he must cease its use or he could not live. He did give it up, but all his life after he suffered from the constant longing for the accustomed stimulant; he had to fight a continual battle.

When ninety years old, he was one day seen searching for something. When asked what he wanted, he replied, "I was looking for my tobacco." He suffered without it, and yet it would have been death to him to continue its use.

A Way of Deliverance.—God requires that His children shall keep themselves free from such unnatural and disastrous habits. But when men are bound in these chains, is there no way of deliverance? Yes, the Lord Jesus has died that through the merits of His life and death men may be overcomers. He is able also to save them to the uttermost that come unto God by Him. He came to earth that He might combine divine power with human effort, and by co-operation with Christ, by placing the will on the side of God, the slave may become free, an heir of God and joint heir with Christ.

Moral Sensibilities Benumbed With Wine.—In the days of Israel, when the sanctuary service was instituted, the Lord directed that only sacred fire should be used in the burning of incense. The holy fire was of God's own kindling, and the fragrant smoke represented the prayers of the people as they ascended before God. Nadab and Abihu were priests of the sanctuary, and although it was not lawful to use common fire, these priests, when they went in before God, presumed to kindle their incense with unconsecrated fire. The priests had been indulging in the use of wine, and their moral sensibilities were benumbed; they did not discern the character of their actions, or realize what would be the fearful consequences of their sin. A fire blazed out from the holy of holies and consumed them.

After the destruction of Nadab and Abihu, the Lord spoke to Aaron, saying: "Do not drink wine nor strong drink, thou, nor thy sons with thee, when ye go into the tabernacle of the congregation, lest ye die: it shall be a statute forever throughout your generations: and that ye may put difference between holy and unholy, and between unclean and clean; and that ye may teach the children of Israel all the statutes which the Lord hath spoken unto them by the hand of Moses." The priests and judges of Israel were to be men of strict temperance, that their minds might be clear to discriminate between right and wrong, that they might possess firmness of principle, and wisdom to administer justice and to show mercy.

If Men Were Strictly Temperate.—What an improvement

would there be in our own land if these injunctions were carried out, if men in sacred and judicial positions should live by every word that proceedeth out of the mouth of God. Does not God, who made man, know what is best for him, what is most conducive to his spiritual and eternal interests? God is working for the highest good of His creatures. If men were strictly temperate, we should not have a tithe of the deaths we now have, and physical and mental suffering would be greatly diminished. There would be far fewer accidents by land and sea. It is because man will do as he pleases, instead of submitting to God's requirement, that so much evil is in the world.

God has given us laws whereby to live, but now, as in the Noachic age, the imagination of men's hearts is evil and only evil continually; men walk after the desire and devices of their own hearts, and so accomplish their own ruin. God would have men stand in their God-given manhood, free from the slavery of appetite.

How can men trust the decisions of jurors who are addicted to the use of liquor and tobacco? If they are called to decide on an important case when deprived of their accustomed stimulants, they cannot exercise their minds in a healthful way; they are in no condition to render an intelligent judgment; and what would their decision be worth?

Men in responsible positions should be men of temperance and integrity, and especially should those who are entrusted with judicial functions be men of sober habits, that they may render justice, and be unbiased by bribe or prejudice. But how widely different is the condition of our judicial and governmental affairs from that made possible through obedience to the commands of God. Liquor, tobacco, low morals, lead men to *deal* treacherously with their fellow men.

Temptation on Every Hand.—On every hand there is temptation for our young men, as well as for those of mature years. In both America and Europe the places of vice and destruction are made attractive by exhibitions and music, that unwary feet may be led into the snare. Everything possible is done to lure the young into the saloon. What shall be done to save our youth? Christ made an infinite sacrifice, He became poor that we through His poverty might become rich and have a life that measures with the life of God, and shall we make no sacrifice to save those who are going to ruin about us? What are we doing for the cause of temperance, to save our youth today? Who is standing by the side of Christ, as a laborer together with God?

Parents, are you teaching your children to overcome? Are you seeking to check the tide of evil that threatens to overwhelm our land? Mothers, are you doing your work as educators? Are you teaching your children in their childhood habits of self-control and temperance? Do not wait till passion holds them in its iron bands, but now take them to God, teach them that Jesus loves them, that Heaven has claims upon them. In their youth put their hands into the hands of Christ, that He may lead them up. Mothers, rouse to your moral responsibility, and work for your children as those who must give an account. We must do something to stop the tide of evil, that the children and youth may not be swept down to perdition. We must be overcomers, and must teach our children to overcome.

Christ Overcame in Our Behalf.—In the wilderness of temptation, Christ passed over the ground where Adam fell. He began the work where the ruin began, and on the point of appetite He overcame the power of the evil one in our behalf. Satan left the field a vanquished foe, and no one is excused from entering the battle on the Lord's side, for there is no reason why man may not be an overcomer if he trusts in Christ. "To him that overcometh will I grant to sit with Me in My throne, even as I also overcame, and am set down with My Father in His throne."

Through the merits of Christ we are to be purified, refined, redeemed, and given a place with Christ on His throne. Could any greater honor be conferred upon man than this? Could we aspire to anything greater? If we are overcomers, Christ declares, "I will not blot out his name out of the book of life, but I will confess his name before My Father, and before His angels."—*Signs of the Times,* June 22, 29, and July 6, 1891.

3. At Sydney, Australia—1893

"And as it was in the days of Noah, so shall it be also in the days of the Son of man. They did eat, they drank, they married wives, they were given in marriage, until the day that Noah entered into the ark, and the Flood came, and destroyed them all. Likewise also as it was in the days of Lot; they did eat, they drank, they bought, they sold, they planted, they builded; but the same day that Lot went out of Sodom it rained fire and brimstone from heaven, and destroyed them all. Even thus shall it be in the day when the Son of man is revealed." Luke 17:26-30. Now, we know that intemperance is in our world everywhere. There is no sin in eating and drinking to sustain us physically, and in doing that which is for our spiritual good. But when we lose eternity out of our reckoning, and carry these necessary things to excess, that is when the sin comes in. We see on every side such crime, such iniquity. Is it not time that we shall begin to study for ourselves? We have souls to save or souls to lose. God created our first parents and placed them in Paradise. God made only one restriction. "The fruit of the tree which is in the midst of the garden, God hath said, Ye shall not eat of it, neither shall ye touch it, lest ye die." They would forfeit their life, if they did not obey the restriction.

Satan is represented by the serpent. The tempter is everywhere, on every side, and when God says ye shall not, what is the result? In many instances in the place of obeying the voice of warning they listen to the tempter. And in the place of all the attractions that Satan presents they have woe and misery. Adam and Eve had everything given that their wants required, but they listened to the tempter and disobeyed God.

When God came to inquire of Adam, he laid all the blame upon Eve. God said, "And I will put enmity between thee and the woman, and between thy seed and her seed; it shall bruise thy head, and thou shalt bruise his heel." The enemy cannot touch you unless you let him. But here is the enmity which God puts against the serpent. There is no enmity between evil men and the angels, but there is enmity between those that serve the Lord and the hosts of darkness.

A Tremendously Important Question.—The temperance question is of tremendous importance to each one of us. It is far-reaching. I have spoken twenty-one times in succession on this subject, and then only touched on it. But here we must take up just a few ideas. When this first gospel sermon was spoken in Eden by God Himself, it was as a star of hope to illuminate the dark and dismal future. The pair in Eden should not be left to hopeless ruin.

When Christ came into our world as a babe in Bethlehem, the angels sang out, "Glory to God in the highest, and on earth peace, good will toward men." "And the angel said unto them, Fear not: for, behold, I bring you good tidings of great joy, which shall be to all people. For unto you is born this day in the city of David a Saviour, which is Christ the Lord."

Satan with all his synagogue—for Satan claims to be religious—determined that Christ should not carry out the counsels of heaven. After Christ was baptized, He bowed on the banks of Jordan; and never before had heaven listened to such a prayer as came from His divine lips. Christ took our nature upon Himself. The glory of God, in the form of a dove of burnished gold, rested upon Him, and from the infinite glory was heard these words, "This is My beloved Son, in whom I am well pleased." The human race is encircled by the human arm of Christ, while with His divine arm He grasps the throne of the Infinite One. The prayer of Christ cleaved right through the darkness and entered where God is. To each of us it means that heaven is open before us. It means that the gates are ajar, that the glory is imparted to the Son of God and all who believe in His name. Our petition will be heard in heaven, as God answered the petition of our Surety, our Substitute, the Son of the infinite God.

Christ Tested on the Three Leading Temptations.—Christ entered into the wilderness with the Spirit of God upon Him, to be tempted of the devil. The enemy was to tempt the Son of God. Christ was tempted with the three leading temptations wherewith man is beset.

"And Jesus being full of the Holy Ghost returned from Jordan, and was led by the Spirit into the wilderness, being forty days tempted of the devil. And in those days He did eat nothing: and when they were ended, He afterward hungered. And the devil said unto Him, If Thou be the Son of God, command this stone that it be made bread. And Jesus answered him, saying, It is written, That man shall not live by bread alone, but by every word of God." Here was the Son of the infinite God, and Satan came as an angel of light to Him. Here he tempted Him on the point of appetite. Christ was hungry and in need of food. Why did He not work this miracle? It was not in God's plan, for Christ was to work no miracle on His own account. What was His position? He was passing over the ground where Adam fell. Adam had everything that his wants required. But fierce hunger was upon Christ, and what He wanted was food. The devil was foiled in this temptation.

"Then the devil taketh Him up into the Holy City, and setteth Him on a pinnacle of the temple, and saith unto Him, If Thou be the Son of God, cast Thyself down: for it is written,

He shall give His angels charge concerning Thee: and in their hands they shall bear Thee up, lest at any time Thou dash Thy foot against a stone." What did he leave out the other part for, which says, "to keep thee in all thy ways"? While Christ was in the ways of God, no harm could come to Him. Jesus said of Satan, He found "nothing in Me." This temptation of Satan to Christ was a dare. Satan said, "If" Thou be the Son of God. What would have been gained if Christ did as Satan asked Him to do? Nothing. Christ meets him with "It is written." Satan saw he could do nothing there.

Now he tempts Him on another point. He has all the world pass before Him in its grandeur, and Satan wants Christ to bow down before him. Satan had power over the human family. "Again, the devil taketh Him up into an exceeding high mountain, and showeth Him all the kingdoms of the world, and the glory of them; and saith unto Him, All these things will I give Thee, if Thou wilt fall down and worship me." Divinity flashed through humanity, and Christ said, "Get thee hence, Satan: for it is written, Thou shalt worship the Lord thy God, and Him only shalt thou serve."

Satan left the field as a conquered foe. Our Saviour passed over the ground and was victor. He was fainting on the field of battle. There was no bosom to cradle His head, and no hand to pass over His brow. Angels came and ministered unto Him. Just such help we may claim. Christ saw it was impossible for man to overcome in his own behalf. He came to bring moral power to man. This is our only hope.

Victory Through Christ.—We see the importance of overcoming appetite. Christ overcame, and we may obtain the victory as Christ did. He passed over the ground, and there is victory for man. What has He done for the human family? He has elevated man in the scale of moral value. We may become conquerors through our Sufficiency. There is hope for the most hopeless, in Christ. "Can the Ethiopian change his skin, or the leopard his spots? then may ye also do good, that are accustomed to do evil." "Come now, and let us reason together, saith the Lord: though your sins be as scarlet, they shall be as white as snow; though they be red like crimson, they shall be as wool." There we have the rich promises of God. What did Christ come here for? To represent the Father. What a heart of love and sympathy! He came to bring eternal life, to break every band. When God gave His Son, He gave all heaven. He could give no more.

The Value of a Soul.—"The Spirit of the Lord God is upon me; because the Lord hath anointed me to preach good tidings unto the meek, He hath sent me to bind up the brokenhearted, to proclaim liberty to the captives, and the opening of the prison to them that are bound." He is the only One that had power to do it. Here the great price has been paid for souls sunk in sin. Man must be of value. Christ weighs him. Christ's taking human nature upon Himself shows that He places a value upon every soul. "What? know ye not that your body is the temple of the Holy Ghost which is in you, which ye have of God, and ye are not your own? For ye are bought with a price: therefore glorify God in your body, and in your spirit, which are God's." This is the value God places upon man, and again He says, "I will make a man more precious than fine gold; even a man than the golden wedge of Ophir." But God will do nothing without the co-operation of the human agent.

Beclouded by Intemperance.—"And Nadab and Abihu, the sons of Aaron, took either of them his censer, and put fire therein, and put incense thereon, and offered strange fire before the Lord, which He commanded them not. And there went out fire from the Lord, and devoured them, and they died before the Lord. Then Moses said unto Aaron, This is it that the Lord spake, saying, I will be sanctified in them that come nigh Me, and before all the people I will be glorified. And Aaron held his peace. . . . And the Lord spake unto Aaron, saying, Do not drink wine nor strong drink, thou, nor thy sons with thee, when ye go into the tabernacle of the congregation, lest ye die: it shall be a statute forever throughout your generations: and that ye may put difference between holy and unholy, and between unclean and clean." The minds of Nadab and Abihu were beclouded because of intemperance, and in the place of taking the fire God had commanded them they took the common fire, and God destroyed them. If they had kept themselves free from wine they would have distinguished the difference between the sacred and the common. But they went directly contrary to God's requirements.

A Cause of Accidents.—We read of steamboat disasters, and railroad accidents, and what is the matter? Somebody in many, many cases has beclouded the mind with intoxicating drink. He did not feel the weight of responsibility resting upon him. Many, many lives have been lost because somebody got drunk. Thus lives will be charged to the man that put the bottle to his neighbor's lips.

In olden times when a man had a vicious animal he paid for it. It says in Exodus 21:28, 29: "If an ox gore a man or a woman, that they die: then the ox shall be surely stoned, and his flesh shall not be eaten; but the owner of the ox shall be quit. But if the ox were wont to push with his horn in time past, and it hath been testified to his owner, and he hath not kept him in, but that he hath killed a man or woman; the ox shall be stoned, and his owner also shall be put to death."

Now we wish to carry this principle right out to those that brew the deadly poison. Here is the law that the God of heaven gave to regulate what to do with vicious animals. Christ is seeking to save, and Satan to destroy. I ask you that have reasoning powers to think on these things. The man that is intoxicated is robbed of his reason. Satan comes in

Appendices

and takes possession of him and imbues him with his spirit; and his first desire is to bruise or kill some of his loved ones. Yet men will allow this accursed thing to go on, that makes man lower than the beast. What has the drunkard obtained? Nothing but a madman's brain. And here the laws are such that the temptations are continually before them.

That liquor seller will have to answer for all the sins of the drunkard, and the drunkard will have to give account of his deeds. Their only hope is to lay their souls upon the crucified and risen Saviour. "For God so loved the world, that He gave His only-begotten Son, that whosoever believeth in Him should not perish, but have everlasting life." What does Christ say? Ye "are laborers together with God." Christ came to bring back to man moral power. Here we see human passions destroying human beings. Here are our youth being tempted. The minds of many are being taken up with gambling and horse racing. May God help us to arouse.

Those that are in legislative councils should not drink wine or strong drink. They need clear brains that they may have sharp and clean-cut reason. The destiny of human life is in their power, whether this or that man shall meet with death as his penalty, or be punished otherwise. We have known of a drunken carousal in the courts of justice. Have they had a clear brain and an eye single to the glory of God? Nature is defaced in man. Christ came to elevate. "Touch not, taste not," should be your motto. You should be temperate in eating. But, liquor—let it alone. Touch it not. There can be no temperance in its use. Satan would sweep in the human family. Christ came to redeem, to elevate man, for He took human nature upon Him.

Begin With the Children.—Parents, you must arouse to your God-given duty. Teach your children obedience. Many have lost respect for father and mother. They will have just as much respect for their heavenly Father as for their own parents. Teach your children. Give them lessons when babies in your arms. Angels will be around you when you do this. When those weary mothers knew not what to do with their children, they thought that they would bring them to Jesus. And as one mother started, and would say to another, "I want Jesus to bless my children," then another would join the company, and still another, and so on until quite a little group came to Jesus with their children. As they came to where Jesus was, He caught the sound. He knew when they had first left. Jesus Christ sympathized with these mothers. As they brought their little ones to Jesus, He said, "Suffer little children to come unto Me, and forbid them not: for of such is the kingdom of God." Parents, take hold; the gates are ajar.

The tone of voice that you use is a means of educating your children. No one ever knows all the troubles that the little hands give. Mothers, there is One who knows all—that is, the God of heaven. Every day that you fulfill your duties, mothers, the words "Conqueror through Christ Jesus" are written opposite your names. What barriers are you going to build up against their souls? Do not threaten them with the wrath of God if they do wrong, but bring them in your prayers to Christ. Have your home as attractive as you can have it. Put back the drapery and let heaven's doctor in, which is sunlight. You want peace and quiet in your homes. You want your children to have beautiful characters. Make home so attractive that they will not want to go to the saloon. Show them the flowers and leaves of the tree. Tell them that God made every spire of grass, and gave the beautiful tints to every flower. Tell them that here is the expression of God's love to you, that this is the voice of God speaking to you that He loves you.

Homes Like Abraham's—You want your homes to be like Abraham's. He commanded his household after him. He taught them to obey the commands of God. These are the lessons, mothers, that you are to patiently teach your children. You cannot afford to spend time in studying the fashions of the day. Teach them that they are Christ's property. We are making characters today. Young men, young women, you are determining your lot in the future today. Let Christ come in. He will preserve you from temptation.

Tobacco is undermining the constitutions of many. It is entering into the fluids and solids of the body. We have known tobacco devotees cured of this vile habit. My husband and I founded a health institution in America. The testimony from those that treated the tobacco patients was alarming. They told of the alarming effluvia in the baths and on the treatment sheets. But they were brought on solid rock. We have seen many who said they could not overcome, brought safely out.

A Majority With God.—No one can be written in the books of heaven who is a drunkard. Resist temptation as a man. In the name of Jesus Christ of Nazareth you can lay hold upon divine power. Christ will work in behalf of every one of you. The tobacco appetite is created which hath no foundation in nature. Nevertheless you can have the victory. The curse of God is upon them who pass the bottle to their neighbors' lips. You say we are in the minority. Is not God a majority? If we are on the side of the God who made the heaven and the earth, are we not on the side of the majority? We have the angels that excel in strength, on our side. Away with the fashions of this degenerate age. Sisters and mothers, you are abusing the bodies which God has given you. What does it mean, young women, this girdling of the waist which does not give your lungs, liver, and vital organs their proper capacity? Your future posterity will testify against you. How could I have spoken as I have, if I would girdle myself as some of you do? You see, nothing is pressing against these vital organs. We sometimes see women who have some records to read, and they cannot speak loudly. They seem to have no voice. They are girdled until they have tiny waists, as though God did not know how to make them.

The Lord would have the wife of Manoah adhere to strict habits of temperance. "And the angel of the Lord appeared unto the woman, and said unto her, Behold now, thou art barren, and bearest not: but thou shalt conceive, and bear a son. Now therefore beware, I pray thee, and drink not wine nor strong drink, and eat not any unclean thing." The angel who appeared to Zacharias and Elisabeth said, "Thy prayer is heard; and thy wife Elisabeth shall bear thee a son, and thou shalt call his name John. And thou shalt have joy and gladness; and many shall rejoice at his birth. For he shall be great in the sight of the Lord, and shall drink neither wine nor strong drink; and he shall be filled with the Holy Ghost." Here we have the child taken before his birth and after. You mothers should place value on these things. The appetites of the mother are transmitted to the children. Many of you who indulge in things to satisfy appetite are taking the underpinning out of your house. There are men who might have had as clear a record as Daniel. Satan is playing his cards for your soul. We want to stand free and pure from the degradations of this world. "He that overcometh, the same shall be clothed in white raiment; and I will not blot out his name out of the book of life, but I will confess his name before My Father, and before His angels." Christ overcame in our behalf. We may overcome through the name of Jesus Christ of Nazareth.

As the redeemed enter in through the gates into the city, Jesus Christ welcomes all, and they will have harps of gold and will sing to the glory of Jesus Christ, and will wear robes woven in the loom of heaven with not one thread of humanity in them.

We want heaven, and Jesus Christ means that we shall have it, if we co-operate with Him.—Manuscript 27, 1893.

SUBJECT INDEX

ABRAHAM, home of 290, 291
Abstinence, *see* Total abstinence.
Accidents, relation of, to intemperance 34-36, 46-49, 208, 281
Account, God keeps, of every work 143
Accountability, for evils we might have checked 257
   for wasted money 66
Action and reaction of tea and coffee 75, 76
Activity to be directed, not repressed 193
Adam, and Eve, diet of, in beginning 160, 161
   tempted through appetite 14, 15, 20, 273, 284
   perfection of, at creation 11
   with his advantages might have overcome, but we cannot 121
Age, advanced, of persons is no argument in favor of stimulants 74
Alliances with other temperance groups 217-226
Angels, as helpers to temperance workers 129
   often protect vessels 35
Antediluvians, carried lawful habits to extremes 141
   corruption of 95
Appetite, and passion to be brought under control of enlightened conscience 150, 216
   Christ's victory over, defeated Satan's object 20
   clamors of, prevail over natural affection 67
   conquest of, gives victory over every temptation 16
   controlling power of, ruins thousands 21
   for liquor, removal of, most effective 194
   God demands that, be cleansed 81
   gratification of, antediluvians overcome through 14
   indulgence of, fearful results of, caused Christ's anguish 20
      is Satan's strongest temptation 20
      is sin 104
      See also Indulgence.
   is an unsafe guide 159, 160
   man's idol 20
   many prefer death to reform in 16, 17
   only victims of intemperance can know power of 128
   overcoming, enables victory over every temptation 21
   persistent perversion of, enfeebles every function 16
   perverted, if indulged, injures health and intellect 80
   world corrupted through 12
   Satan controls the mind through 94
   Satan pleased when men are governed by 16
   Satan's strongest means to control race 13
   slavery to, results in debasing passions 17
   to be controlled by reason and conscience 12, 146
   unnatural, beware, restrain, deny 242
   victory over established, difficult 177
Appetites and inclinations, natural, God appointed 12

Apples and grapes, God's gifts, may be used excellently or wrongly 100
Army, let, be formed to stop liquor sales 209
Atmosphere, of Christ's presence makes evil abhorrent 136
   of heaven, keep soul in 192
Atonement, we live in antitypical day of 99
Australasia, temperance labors of Ellen G. White in 262-266
Ax, we have stronger weapon than 235

BACKSLIDING, of intemperate, worker not to be discouraged at 128, 129
   prevented only by prayer and vigilance 19
Battle Creek, 1877 temperance rally in 220, 221
Battle may be hard, but God will help 103
Beast, vicious, responsibility of owner of 206, 207, 288, 289
Belshazzar, feast of 48
Body, as temple of Holy Spirit 142, 216
   diseased, affects the mind 14
   God's pledge to keep, in health 11
   only medium for mind and soul to operate 102
Books, of record and the liquor dealer 40
   on health to be circulated 240
Borrowed capital, many living on 139
Boulder, Colorado, temperance meeting in tent at 260
Brain, bone, and muscle need harmonious action 74
   nerves of, Heaven's only means of communication 13

Brandy, effect of moderate use of 159
Breath, every, a prayer 135
Bribery of citizens to vote for evil 254
Burdens cast upon Burden Bearer 121
Butler, Elder G. I., convinced of duty to sign pledge 202

CAFFEINE DRINKS, effects of 77
Calebs, we to stand as 256
Camp meeting, pledge signing at, in 1879 202, 203
Camp meetings, call for signers to pledge at 199
   temperance work at 244
   W.C.T.U. speakers at 223, 224
Candies with alcohol, children enticed by 229
Character, largely formed in early years 176
   reshaped by grace of Christ 102
Cheerfulness and clear conscience better than drugs 111
Chicago, temperance meeting at 261
Childhood, suffering of, considered necessary evil 205
Child training in first three years 177
Children, and, their eating 158
   youth, tobacco works untold harm among 56
   discipline and education of 215
   enticed by alcoholic confectionary 229
   of drunkard, perils and tragedies of 34
   point to example of tobacco-using fathers 68, 71
   prepare, to meet temptation 185

Subject Index

temperance instruction to begin with 289, 290
unborn, sinned against by indulgent parents 84, 85
Choice, a God-given power 112, 123
Christ, *see* Jesus Christ.
Christian, churches, intemperate members of 231, 232
life to be attractive 211-213
Christians, duty of, to raise warning signal 39
professed, pray with defiled mouths 65
sin of, greater than avowed unbeliever 68
to support temperance reform 126
to take lead in self-denial and in temperance 67
Christiania [Oslo] Norway, address of Ellen G. White at 267-273
Church, God works through His 235
members all to take hold 236, 249, 250
should disfellowship manufacturer of wine for market 99
temperance a condition of membership in 165, 166
to be a school for temperance 165
Cider, sweet, preparation of, often unwholesome 94
Circumstances, look not to, but to power of word 107
Cities, special allurements in 101, 155, 187, 211
City, effort, temperance to find a place in every 239
of God may be entered only as a conqueror 114
place for rehabilitation needed in every 127
Citizens, our responsibilities as 253-255

Clergymen, *see* Ministers.
Coffee more harmful than tea 76, 77
See also Tea and coffee.
Colporteur-evangelists witness to temperance 82
Communion table, wine for, to be unfermented 97, 98
Companies for work to be organized 252
Compassion for depraved should be strongest bond of union with Christ 133, 134
Condiments, and spices, effects of 57, 157
tobacco, and liquor are steps in intemperance 183
Conscience, enlightened, appetites and passions to be under control of 21, 145, 216
to be given supreme place 143
Consecration impossible with lustful appetite 148
Contestants in foot races, care of, in diet 144
Conversion the secret of victory 104
Cooking, deplorable ignorance of, among mothers 158
Country versus city homes 210, 211
Courage, moral, needed to resist temptation 199
Craving, unnatural, overbears the will 78
Crime, increase of 23
relation of, to intemperance 23, 277
resulting from liquor and tobacco 38, 39, 59
Criminal, guilt of, not lessened because of intoxication 25
Crisis, times of, in important work 148

Crown, victor's, obtained through Christ's warfare with evil 20, 21
Crowns for the overcomer 114
Crusades, against intemperance by parents 175-179
    temperance, not needed if parents were faithful 185
Customs of world versus laws of God 157

DANIEL, and companions, 213, 271-273
    experience of 150-155, 188-191
    temperance principles of 101
    an example of what God's grace can do 152
    men like, needed today 237
    not bigoted 152
Day of judgment, decisions of 152
Death, premature, through indulgence of appetite 14
Decision of a moment may fix destiny 135
Degeneracy of race through intemperance 174
Degeneration of humanity, causes of 17
Demoniac of Capernaum saved by Christ 122-124
Demons, Christ's power over 122
Diary of Ellen G. White, 1859, citations from 255, 256
Diet, an important element in religion 162, 163
    Christian will guard his 19
    Daniel's, example of benefits of abstemious 191
    few realize influence of, on destiny 138
    relation of, to temptation and sin 15
    simplicity of, for foot racers 144
    See also Appetite; Indulgence.
Digestion helped by sun and air 159
Discouraged too easily in rescue work 130, 131
Disease, fearful increase of 227
    hinders man's service to God 14
    most of, caused by ignorance 84
    producers, many are, because of ignorance 196
Dissipation, last hours of probation spent in 18
Doctrine, differences in, not to alienate us 221, 222
Dressing, temperance in 138, 139
Drug medication induces twofold greater evil than it relieves 86
Drugs, educate away from 85
    inconsistent to use, while continuing evil habits 84
    only change form and location of disease 86
    poisonous, free use of 82, 83
    substituted for natural remedies 85
Drugstore, simple living versus 84
Drunkard, capable of better things 28
    degradation of, step by step 204
    responsibility of, for own misdeeds 33, 34
    sells himself for cup of poison 142
Drunkards made by home tables 158
    two thirds of, developed appetite from tobacco 72
Drunkenness, *see* Intemperance.

EATING, and drinking, habits of, determine our allegiance 141
    is somebody's business 183

Subject Index

between meals 182
drinking, and dressing, excess in, becomes crime 227
too frequently or too much 138
Eat to live not live to eat 181-186
Eden, first gospel sermon in 283
lost and regained by indulgence or denial of appetite 150
Educate, educate, educate 169, 244, 245
Education, in health never more needed 247
in prevention of disease 86
in temperance 194-197
more effective than rescuing fallen 194
of people the only hope 85
to be given at institutes and conventions 169
Employment necessary for would-be reformers 115
Endurance, greater if temperate 167
of meat eater lessened 159
Evangelistic message, temperance a part of 237-240
Example, Christian, will exert powerful influence 131
of, intemperate ministers 69
professed Christians in intemperance 71
temperance, we must manifest 119
Excess of food, rather than scarcity, our danger 101

FACULTIES, harmonious action of, sold for indulgence of appetite 59
Faculty, cultivate every, to highest degree 137, 143
Faith, brings eternal glories near 213
in God, power of 195

Fallen, workers for, often disappointed 115
Falls, a succession of, since Adam 227, 273
Families suffering for conveniences of life 67
Fashion, demands of 147
Fast, Christ's, of six weeks, assures man's victory 20
of three days recommended for particular children 158
Fathers, example of, before children 68
tobacco-using, disqualified to bring up children 70
Final reckoning, parents and children to meet in day of 179
Fisherman, how an Australian, overcame 118, 119
Flesh meat, a mild stimulant 158, 159
craving for, not natural 160.
effects of 161
Flesh meats, effects of, on Israelites 160
highly seasoned, cause craving for stronger stimulants 57
Food, life-giving, converted into poisons 12
Foot races, contestants in, had simple diet 144
Fruits, vegetables, and grains an adequate diet 160

GAME OF LIFE, playing, with Satan 38
Games in Corinth and the Christian race 144, 145
Garments may be kept unstained 136
God, as particular as in time of Moses 45
personal relationship with, as Father 104
God's temple defiled by tobacco 65

Good Samaritan, Christians to act part of 127
Gossip following the drinking of coffee and tea 79
Government, God at head of good and just 48
Grace, divine, powerless to enliven users of stimulants 74
Grains and fruits converted into intoxicants 31

HABITS, daily weaving a web of 188
  early, difficult to overcome 176, 179
  hurtful, the earlier formed the greater the hold 73
  loose, overcome only by prayer and vigilance 19
  wrong, Satan's scheme for self-destruction 14
Harvest, Christ sees a plentiful 258
Healing, natural methods of 83
Health, God's pledge to keep body in 11
  publications, circulation of 248-252
  reform, all being tested regarding 163
    an effective entering wedge 242
    light on, sent by heavenly Father 141
    light on, to be cherished 19
    not agitated as it must be 89
    sustained only by obedience to nature's laws 11, 12
Healthful living, necessity for instruction in 115
Heart, reformation must be from 102
Heathen nations, curse carried to 230
Heaven, all, watching fight against temptations 191

Help, feeblest prayer for, is heard 114
Heredity, drug poisons transmitted through 56, 84, 85
  power of 130, 170-175, 269, 270
Herod, dissolute life of 49-52
Herodias plots to take John's life 49-52
Highway to drunkenness 93, 97
Holidays, evils of intemperance increased by 30
  make, interesting to children 211, 212
Holy Spirit, a helper in reform 105
  influence of, deadened by stimulants 80
  losing sensibility to influence of 80
Home, of drunkard, sufferings and misery in 31, 33, 34
  to be made attractive 209, 210, 290
Hope in Christ for most hopeless 286, 287
Hops, raising of, lends influence against temperance 98, 100
House of God desecrated by tobacco users 219
Hunter, Colonel, testimony of, at camp meeting 202, 203
Hygienic restaurants in cities 248

IDOLATRY practiced by liquor drinker 38
Ignorance regarding God's laws is deplorable 146
Imbecility, prevalence of 146
Incense to satanic majesty, tobacco burned as 62
Indulgence of appetite, continued, causes craving for stimulants 157
  greatest cause of physical and mental debility 15

inflames passions 183
Inebriates would give money to be free from habit 60
Infants die martyrs to lust for tobacco 59
Influence for good of one consecrated youth 188
Ingratitude, act of, to weaken vital forces 164
Inhumanity of man to man is greatest sin 134
Institutes and conventions, health education at 169
Intellect benumbed by use of stimulants 73, 74
Intemperance, beclouds the brain and senses 35, 36, 50
  begun at family tables 182, 183
  benumbs the finer sensibilities 17
  brings one under Satan's control 24, 25
  causes, crime and violence 23, 24
    misery in the home 31-34
    nine tenths of children's wickedness 150
    poverty, disease, degradation, death 28
    uncontrollable appetite 37
    unnatural exhilaration 50
  destroys reasoning faculties 25
  enfeebles digestive organs 16
  foundation of most ills 137
  gives loose rein to debasing passions 17
  horrors of, indescribable 205
  inception of, devised by Satan 12
  injures brain 37
  meaning of, is broad 137-141, 162
  perverts reasoning powers 36
  prevalence of 196, 203, 227-233, 251
  puts millions in devil's treasury 30
  relation of, to crime, 23
  results, in failure to perfect Christian character 21
    of 206-208
  roots of, deeper than liquor drinking 196, 209
  ruins youth in soul and body 33, 38
  traced to food on tables 156-163
  transmits corrupt tendencies to posterity 38
  usually begun in childhood 178
  victims of, among all classes 36, 37
    under power of demon 127
  weakens, power to appreciate spiritual things 148
  will power 37
  See also Drunkenness; Liquor.
Intemperate, men should not be voted to positions of trust 47, 254
  not regarded by God as hopeless 126
  personal work for 243
Intoxicants, milder 90-101
Intoxication does not lessen guilt of criminal 25
Israelites, reasons why God withheld flesh meat from 160
  wine a cause of captivity of 52, 53

JESUS CHRIST, example of 167
  fearful results of indulged appetite caused anguish of 20
  help in, for the fallen 121, 122
  love of, for the contrite 124
  mission of, to uplift humanity 40

Jesus Christ—*continued*
  point sinners to His ideal of character 107
  social habits of 193
  taught total abstinence consistently 97
  temptation and victory of, in wilderness, 19, 20, 82, 97, 109, 110, 161, 267, 275, 276, 285, 286
  total dependence on, is only hope 116
John the Baptist, a representative of God's people in last days 91
  instruction on habits of 90, 91
  temperance of, an example 173
  the victim of a death inspired by intemperance 50-52
Judgments of God for wickedness due to liquor 26, 232
Jurors addicted to tobacco and alcohol 281
Justice of God combined with tenderness and love 134

KINGDOMS, ancient, lessons from, a warning 256
Kisses of children not to be on lips of tobacco-using father 60
Kokomo, Indiana, temperance meetings at 259, 260

LABOR, temperance in 138, 139
Lawmakers, need of, for unclouded faculties 46
  responsibility of, for evils of liquor traffic 28
Law of God, intemperance a violation of 164, 165
  obedience to, would save from intemperance 228
  versus customs of world 157
Laws, legalizing liquor traffic 37, 39, 43
  of being, all should understand 159
  of health, obedience to, a privilege and blessing 215
  violation of, brings suffering 139, 140
  of life, parents to study 184
  transgression of, is transgression of God's law 143
  of nature, disobedience to, cause of degeneracy 17
  obedience to, necessary, 11, 12
  Satan controls will through transgression of 16
Laymen called to public work 243, 244
Leading men not to forget law and pervert judgment 53
  See also Legislators; Ministers; Responsible men.
Ledger of heaven, record in 33
Legislative councils, men in, need clear brains 289
Legislators, responsibility of, for laws 38
License laws, ineffectiveness of 203, 204
Life, one lease of, granted 137
Light, peril of turning from single ray of 241
Liquor, and tobacco, desire for, no foundation in nature 12
  users of, are as wood, hay, stubble 142
  users of, should not be taken into church 166
  drinking, benumbs intellect, excites passions 23, 24
  debases man below level of brute 23
  dethrones reason 228
  impoverishes thousands 31
  promotes dishonesty and violence 27
  interests, power of 231
  sellers and lawmakers, joint responsibility of 28

business of, means robbery 28
cruelty and avarice of 33
evil work of 24
houses of, built with wages of unrighteousness 27
protection of, by law 32, 33
responsibilities of 37, 38, 39-42
selling a work of robbery 204
traffic, God's people to raise voices against 27
imperils interests of everyone 208
leads to perdition 43
protection of, by law 204-209
tragic results of legalized 204, 205
use of, increasing 23
user condemned by some who gratify other hurtful indulgences 74
warnings in Bible against 52, 53
See also Intemperance.
Literature, worthless, some would substitute better class of fiction for 101
Little attentions, powerful influence of 132
Liver and lungs affected by vegetable and mineral poisons 87
Lives sacrificed to alcohol and tobacco 57
Lost coin sought for its value 133
Lost sheep, parable of 134
Lustful indulgence wars against health and peace 149
Lusts, fleshly, include use of stimulants and narcotics 73

MAJORITY, with God we are a 257, 258, 291
Man, perfection of, at creation 11
Manoah, instruction to wife of, by angel 233, 234, 269, 292
Marriage vows melted in fiery liquid 31
McEnterfer, Sara, encourages Australian tea addict 119
Means, *see* Money.
Meat eating, excessive, before Flood 95
See also Flesh meats.
Medicine, impatient call for 83
preventive, importance of 86, 87
Mental, powers, disqualification of, a sin 45
superiority promoted by right physical habits 156
Mind, acquires new vigor with taxation 168
affected by intemperance 13
and body, necessity of maintaining soundness of 15
controlled by two powers 276
God does not control, without our consent 123
Ministers, accountable for willing ignorance 169
efficiency of, increased if temperate 166, 167
example of, to children 68
fear loss of popularity 231
intemperate, example of 164, 165
tobacco-using 65, 69
to control appetites 166, 167
to urge circulation of health journals 250
with polluted lips, offering strange fire 45
Misery, why so much, in world today 91, 92
Moderate drinking 278
Money, bloodstained, donated to church 232
waste of, for tobacco and liquor 29, 66, 67, 272

Moral, independence, educate children for 184
obligations, sense of 213-216
Mother, work of, more elevated than of king 180
Mothers, accountable for future generations 172
bring children to Jesus 290
deplorable ignorance of cookery among 158
reform to begin with 170
rouse to moral responsibility 282

NADAB AND ABIHU, lessons from 43, 44, 65, 92, 149, 187, 268, 280, 287, 288
Natural law is of God as truly as is Holy Writ 214
Nature, assist, to expel impurities 86
needs time to recover from abuse 81
unabused, will furnish all needed stimulus 159
will do her work efficiently if false props are expelled 77
Nature's remedies, pure air, water, clear conscience 85
Neighbor, your, may need rescuing 232, 233
Nervous system affected more by tobacco than by liquor 55
Noah's day and ours 25, 95, 100, 227, 281, 283
Nostrums, many, lay foundation of liquor habit 83

OBEDIENCE, path of, only path that leads to heaven 60
perfect, required 106, 107
Occupation, useful, value of 210
Opportunity, now is our time of 257
Organ of body, injury to single, is robbery of God 214

Outcasts, many rescued will enter heaven 130, 131
Overcoming, man must be co-worker with Christ in 111
Overeating is a common fault 162
Ox, vicious, owner of, responsible for 206, 207, 288, 289

PARENTS, build moral bulwark about children 215
duty of, to counteract evil heritage of children 175
enlightenment of, most effective temperance efforts 178
God supplements faithful efforts of 180
of Daniel had trained him in temperance 189
radical change needed in, before temperance can succeed 72
responsible for, child's character 156, 180
intemperate children 182
sin against unborn children 84, 85
tobacco-using, cannot teach children temperance principles 71
to be mild but firm 181
to teach children from infancy 175-179
train children to obey laws of God 157
Passions, debased by indulgence of appetite 17, 183
stimulated by meat, tobacco, and liquor 161
to be controlled by the will 103
Patent nostrums, many use, unwisely 83
Patience needed in working for intemperate 127, 128

Subject Index

Patients, proper diet and treatment for, in sanitariums 88
Peculiar people, opportunity to manifest that we are 199
Penalty, fixed, for every transgression 83, 84
Perseverance, determined, will bring victory 81
Personal labor for intemperate 131-133
Peter warns against fleshly lusts 73
Physical, and moral powers, sympathy between 148, 149
   health improved by connection with Christ 108
Physician, imperils reputation by giving plain facts 86
   prescribed use of tobacco 63
Physicians, and nurses to understand health principles 169
   inconsistency of tobacco using 69, 70
   responsible for making many drunkards 42
   to set forth evils of intemperance 246
Physiology, education in, essential to youth 183-185
   study of, inspires reverence 215
Pipe or heaven, woman's choice between 63, 64
Plagues, time of, reveals value of temperance 201, 202
Planet, this fallen, Satan confident of his control of 20
Pleasure lovers, record of, a beacon of warning 18
Pleasures, innocent, to be substituted for sinful 211, 212
Pledge, every member to sign 220
   everywhere the call for signers to temperance 126
   signing at Missouri camp meeting 202, 203
   tea and coffee should be included in 81, 82
Pledges, excuses of some for not signing 199-202
   to be circulated and signed 197-202
Powers, physical and moral, relationship between 12, 13
Prayer, and faith to be combined with treatment 88
   and vigilance necessary to overcome loose habits 19
   for sick, not answered when indulgence is continued 84
   useless if use of drugs is continued 142
   links with Christ 107, 108
   temptations make, a necessity 135
Prenatal influence 170-175
Priests, tobacco-using, would suffer fate of Nadab and Abihu 64, 65
Principle, acting from, in eating, drinking 213
Probation, last hours of, spent in dissipation 18
Prodigals, many, brought to Father by saved sinners 117
Prohibition, and total abstinence, vote for 254
   laws, rigidly enforced 194
Prohibitions, of God, reasons for 53, 54
   consequences of disregarding 15, 16
Promises, as leaves of tree of life 128
   of God, exceeding great, look to 107
   grasping, for forgiveness 105
   precious 125
Public sentiment to be aroused against liquor traffic 28, 29

RACE, Christian, runners in, should practice self-denial 144, 145, 214
Reason, and conscience to control appetite 146
is out when drink is in 30
kingly power of, to rule in the life 103
Reasoning faculties, perverted through drink 36
the criminal is responsible for destroying his 25
Recreation, substitute innocent, for harmful 211, 212
Redemption, Christ began, where ruin began 19, 20
Red-Ribbon Club 218, 219
Reform, advancement in, step by step 82
in habits of diet, dressing, sleeping 196
none genuine apart from Christ 109, 110
Reformers to be most unselfish, kind, courteous 132, 133
Reformation cannot be effected by degrees 103
work of, to begin at tables 196, 201
Rehabilitation of intemperate 126-136
Remedies, so-called, create evil habits and appetites 83
Rescued to help others 116, 117
Resolutions avail nothing in own strength 106, 112
Responsible men, and drink 34
qualifications of 168, 169
should be strictly temperate 48
See also Leading men.
Revenue of liquor traffic less than evils of 207
Revival of temperance work called for 234
Rich foods not for children 158
Rulers, *see* Lawmakers.

SALEM, OREGON, temperance meeting at 260
Saloons, results of opening, after San Francisco earthquake 26, 27
Satan's death traps 39
to be closed on all days of the week 208, 209
Salt, avoid undue amount of 157
Salvation, plan of, began where ruin began 19, 20
wrecked by indulgence of appetite 14
Samson, instruction to mother regarding 90, 171
Sanctification, impossible when violating God's laws 148
true, health reform necessary to 19
Sanctified, the truly, will overcome every hurtful lust 67
San Francisco, earthquake in, saloons closed after, with decreasing crime 26, 27
Sanitariums, to give temperance education 245, 247, 248
why established 87-89
Satan, a hard master 278
caused Israel to lust for flesh meat 160
devised inception of intemperance 12
enfeebles and degrades physical powers 102
first rebel in universe 273
gains easy access to slaves of appetite 146
leads, gradually from temperance stronghold 93
march of death 229, 230
minds engrossed in eating and dressing 148
perverts senses by artificial stimulants 71
places men where with difficulty they can be reached with the gospel 243

Subject Index

purpose of, to palsy brain, confuse judgment 60
success of, in ruination of world 12
   in temptations to indulge appetite 20
temptations of 34
tempts through appetite 161
weakens bodies by indulgence 252, 253
when power of, to tempt is small 147

Savages, tobacco and alcohol carried to 230
Saved, gratitude of, to human instruments 135
Schools, might be established with wasted money 29
   of health to follow public efforts 239
Second advent, signs of, drunkenness and crime are 25, 227
   to be brought before others 27
Self-control, loss of, most deplorable 102
   need of, to regain Eden 20
   of present generations weakened 163, 164, 175
   teach and enforce, from infancy 181
Self-denial lacking in others than drunkards 74
Self-development our first duty to God and man 137
Self-gratification, supremacy of, since Fall 15
Self-indulgence a moral sin and physical disease 37, 127
Self-indulgent must see necessity for moral renovation 111
Self-support, encourage every effort toward 115
Seventh-day Adventist, every, to sign pledge 197-200
Seventh-day Adventists, in forefront of battle 233, 234
   temperance revival called for among 234
Sickness, ascertain cause of 85, 86
Sin, made attractive through covering of light 16, 146
   man's inhumanity to man our greatest 134
   the heaviest burden we have to bear 120
   to destroy health 111
Society, work to be done for all classes of 29
Sodom, our world becoming a second 186
Soul, infinite value of every 287
Spices and condiments cause craving for stronger stimulants 182, 183
Spiritual life, tea and coffee inimical to 80
Starvation in home resulting from drunkenness 33
Stimulants, and narcotics 73-89
   are habit-forming 78
   avoid creating desire for 42
   cause, lessening of susceptibility to Holy Spirit 80
     loss of time on account of sickness 77
   create craving for something stronger 78, 80
   discontinuance of, followed by distress 81
   effects of 159
   excitement of, followed by reaction 73, 75, 76, 78
   lessen physical strength, benumb intellect 73, 74
   loosen the tongue for scandal 79
   strength from, is short-lived 75
   whole system suffers from 78
   will power is overborne by use of 78
Students to be careful of diet 191, 192

Study, temperance in 140
Sun and air help digestion 159
Sunday, closing of saloons insufficient 208, 209
    temperance work on 244

TABLES, family, lead to intemperance 182, 183
Taste, mental and moral vigor sold for pleasure of 59
Tea, and coffee, are narcotics 75, 79
    cause craving for stronger stimulants 72
    do not nourish 75, 76
    effects of 75-82
    habit as difficult as liquor to overcome 81
    habit-forming 78
    Australian gained victory over 119
    coffee, and flesh meat, create desire for stimulants 158
    produce immediate effects 157
    coffee, and tobacco, are artificial stimulants 228
    are degrees in scale of stimulants 72
    cause craving for liquor 202
    drinking helps to destroy God's temple 142
    primary and secondary effects of 76
Temperance, an aid to rapid clear thinking 168
    and sanctification 154, 155
    clubs, are they loyal to God's law? 217
    crusade, why victories of, are not permanent 196
    effort, purpose of all true 102
    efforts for, are most effective when they enlighten parents 178
    must go to root of evil 219
    groups, our relation to other 217-226
    in, daily life and sanctification 141
    variety of dishes 161, 162
    instruction to begin with children 289, 290
    lectures, points to stress in 197, 239-241
    literature to be circulated 248
    pass not over as nonessential 245
    pledges to be signed by all classes 198-203
    principles, carry, in details of home 180
    of, are far-reaching 149
    reform demands the support of Christians 126
    relation of, to spirituality 146-150
    sermons, effectiveness of 242, 243
    societies, slowness to organize among us 236
Temple of God is the body 18, 142, 143
Temptation, a way of escape from every 105
    better discerned and resisted by temperate 188
    divine strength provided for overcoming 21
    drunkard has no strength to resist 38
    entering into, and being tempted 192
    first, one refusing, is worthy of honor 188
    indulgence of appetite is Satan's strongest 13
    prepare children to meet 185
    victory over every, gained by control of appetite 16
Temptations, not alike to all 74
    three: appetite, ambition, love of world 276
Third angel's message, every reform a part of 234, 237-240

Subject Index

Three years, importance of first 177
Time, loss of, because of sickness 77
  of trouble, why many will fall in 150
Tithes and offerings, robbing of God in, through wasting 66, 67
Tobacco, a poison 55, 57
  and alcohol as twin evils 72
  benumbs sensibilities 55, 59, 64
  burned as incense to Satanic majesty 62
  causes, loss of promptness and force in will power 62
    trembling nerves, giddy head, irritability 60, 61
  condemned by James, Peter, Paul, Jesus 64
  corrupts morals 56
  deprivation of, effects from 279
  devotees, Australian, gain victory 118
    in bondage to narcotic 60, 61
  disqualifies parents for child care 71
  dulls appreciation of atonement and eternal things 63
  dwarfs body and corrupts morals of youth 56
  effects of 55-72, 278, 279
    on nervous system 55, 63, 64
  encourages appetite for liquor 56, 58, 72
  excites, then paralyzes 57
  factor in increase of crime 59
  families suffer for conveniences of life because of 67
  fouls the atmosphere 58, 59
  God's money squandered on 66
  habit, cannot be overcome in own strength 105, 106
  inconvenient, unclean, expensive 62
  popularity of 68
  infants poisoned by 58, 59
  lessens vital force 64
  lowers resistance, weakens restorative powers 56
  mental inability, physical weakness, because of 56, 62, 68, 69
  palsies brain, confuses judgment 60
  pollutes the blood 57
  robs God's treasury 64, 67
  slow suicide from use of 57
  stupefies senses, enchains the will 56, 58, 62
  use of, by ministers 45, 46
  users guilty before God 55
  using, origin of, in perverted knowledge 75
  weakens healing power of nature 56
Tongue loosened at social entertainments 79
Touch not, taste not, handle not 42, 94, 103, 163, 289
Total abstinence only safety 36, 101, 103, 163-165, 186-188, 196
Transformations, marvelous, through faith 124
Treasury, devil's, filled with money spent on drink 30
  robbed by indulging unnatural appetite 64
Tree of life, Satan's counterfeit of 75

VERGE OF KINGDOM, many on, waiting 258
Vice, grace of Christ only remedy for 106
Victory, assured through Christ's sinless life 107
  impossible without temperance 144, 145

Victory—*continued*
  must be through changed life 102-125
  of Christ is for us 286, 287
  over appetite, difficulty of 177
  over health-destroying habits through faith in Christ 89
  power for, in Christ alone 108
  won through determined perseverance 81
Victories, precious, lost to slaves of appetite 167
  to gain 150
Violence, land filled with 23
Vision, spiritual, impaired 167
Voice, of nation to be heard 209
  tone of, important 290
Vote, not to be cast for intemperate men 47
  power of 253, 254
Voter, every, has responsibility 253, 254

WARFARE between, higher and lower attributes 149
  virtue and vice constant 189
Watchman, temperance number of 250
Water, is adequate to quench thirst 101
  use of, considered too laborious 85
Weakness of humanity all known by Christ 120
Wealth, temperance in 140
White, Elder and Mrs. James, temperance activities of 217, 220, 225
White, Ellen G., as a temperance worker 259-266
  refused to sell grapes to winery 99
  temperance activities of 226
Wickedness, nine tenths of among children is caused by intemperance 150
Will, everything depends on right action of 112, 113
  God cannot save man against his 111
  power of, lost through youthful indulgence 36
    strengthened by God's grace 163
  Satan's scheme to control, through intemperance 16
  to be placed on side of God's 214
  under control of God to control passions 103
Wine, and cider, effects of 277, 278
  intoxicating effects of 94-96
  manufacture of, Christians should not engage in 98, 99
  and strong drink forbidden by Bible 42
  at Cana was not fermented 97
  for communion service to be unfermented 97, 98
  or cider arouses inherited tendencies 92
  or liquor, like tobacco, degrades whole being 65
  Scriptural reasons for nonuse of 44
  unfermented, a wholesome drink 93
  use of, a cause for Israel's captivity 52, 53
Woman's Christian Temperance Union, address of Ellen G. White to, in Australia 265, 266
  co-operation with 222-226
Women, and children suffer from inhaling tobacco fumes 58, 59
  increasing number of, drinking 34
  revolting picture of tobacco using 60
Words of kindness as welcome as smiles of angels 132

Subject Index

YOKE OF CHRIST for weary, heavy-laden 120
Youth cannot be as sedate and grave as the aged 211
  depravity among, increasing 234
  effects of intemperance on 36, 37
  influence of one upright 188
  making drunkards of, continues 206
  not told of injurious effects of tobacco 68
  the impressible age 186
  today's, an index of future 186
  to unite in warfare 235, 236

ZACHARIAS, Gabriel's instruction to, regarding John 173, 269, 292
Zeal proportionate to importance of truth, results of 257